Dilemmas of Educational Ethics

Cases and Commentaries

Edited by

MEIRA LEVINSON
JACOB FAY

HARVARD EDUCATION PRESS
Cambridge, Massachusetts

Library of Congress Control Number 2015955161

Paperback ISBN 978-1-61250-932-7
Library Edition ISBN 978-1-61250-933-4

Published by Harvard Education Press,
an imprint of the Harvard Education Publishing Group

Harvard Education Press
8 Story Street
Cambridge, MA 02138

Cover Design: Wilcox Design

The typefaces used in this book are Sabon and Myriad Pro.

Dilemmas of Educational Ethics

Contents

Introduction

MEIRA LEVINSON AND JACOB FAY

E ducators, including teachers and school leaders, face challenging ethical decisions on a regular basis. For example: How should teachers proceed with a student who has not met numerous criteria for passing eighth grade, but who will predictably drop out if she is held back? What should be done about a student with diagnosed impulse control issues who benefits from being mainstreamed with her peers, but who also frequently disrupts class and increases everyone's stress level even when she is under control? How stringent should teachers and department heads be in calculating grades if they know that grade inflation helps students secure admission to selective colleges and universities, but fear that students will never learn what they're truly capable of if held to lower expectations? Should a high school teacher report a student who steals her cell phone if she knows that the likely consequence of turning him in is his conviction and incarceration on adult felony charges?

Education policy makers also frequently confront questions especially of justice and equity. For example: In designing a new school assignment plan, is it ethical to pander to middle class families' preferences so as to draw them—and their social and economic capital—into the state system? Should a high-achieving, "no excuses" charter school be required to reduce its well-above-average attrition rates as a condition of expanding its charter if its academic success rests in part on students' and families' compliance with its expectations? Is it appropriate for school, district, or state policy makers to constrain some families' choices in the name of increasing or equalizing opportunities across the board?

These questions are both utterly ordinary and immensely challenging. These are not exotic problems; they are everyday dilemmas. But educators and policy makers generally receive little support in thinking them through other than as technocratic challenges, especially in the current context of global education reform. The cases are treated as challenges of compliance, leadership, communication, data analysis, student support, or instruction. They are rarely treated as *ethical* challenges of equity, merit, respect, inclusion, fairness, or human rights—that is, as challenges that require educators and policy makers to think carefully about the values and moral principles at stake. We believe this needs to change, since students, educators, and citizens alike deserve school systems that enact ethical practices and policies.

Given the lack of a public conversation about dilemmas of educational ethics, educators and policy makers often wrestle with these issues on their own. Many teachers and school and district leaders, for example, agonize about having perpetrated injustices or failed to treat others ethically in the course of their everyday decisions.[1] But they lack tools for, and practice in, analyzing and making collective decisions about these kinds of practical ethical conundrums. Rather, ethical challenges remain private affairs, embarrassing for educators and policy makers to reveal to others lest they expose themselves as having potentially perpetrated unjust or ethically questionable acts. Ethical uncertainty is treated as an admission of weakness rather than an opportunity for collective learning.

Furthermore, when considerations of educational justice in particular are brought to the fore, they are usually treated as having determinate content: they are used to exhort, not to educate or to explore. After all, there is no shortage of moralistic mantras in contemporary national discourse about education: Former US Secretary of Education Arne Duncan emphasized repeatedly that education is the "civil rights issue of our time"; numerous teacher training programs claim to prepare graduates to promote "education for social justice"; charter networks and districts alike propound that "all children deserve a great education"; and a decade of federal education policy was designed to "leave no child behind."[2] These declarations are often treated as offering self-evident guidance for education practice and policy, as giving clear rather than murky answers about how to serve individual students and foster strong schools while at the same time striving for massive social transformation.

In practice, however, such mantras obscure moral tensions swirling just under the surface. Is justice better realized by pulling a kid up through the cracks, but then leaving others to contend with the yawning chasms in her academic preparation, or by letting her fall through in hopes of creating better systems to serve all kids—but not her? When students' future opportunities are shaped by present-day interpersonal, institutional, and structural racism, will schools better fulfill their "civil rights" missions to provide a "great education" for "social justice" by teaching students what they need to survive within the system, or by preparing them for a more just world that may or may not ever come into being? When more children have needs than teachers have minutes in the day to serve them, what or who should give? When a particular practice harms children or the system as a whole, but collective action is necessary to change the practice and individual defections may in the meantime actually make things worse, what should any one teacher, school leader, or district policy maker do?

These are the kinds of questions that educators, school leaders, and education policy makers are grappling with each day. They (we!) are struggling with them in wealthy and in middle- and low-income schools; in rural, suburban, and urban districts; in magnet, regular district, charter, parochial, and independent schools; along the coasts, in the American heartland, from south to north, and everywhere in between. Our purpose in this book is to initiate a collective conversation about these kinds of questions.

In so doing, we hope to provide support and affirmation to educators and policy makers who are already wrestling with these issues, and to strengthen their capacities to address ethical dilemmas in their own work. We also hope to provoke philosophers—those with professional expertise in ethical reasoning—to attend more carefully to these kinds of challenges. By doing so, they can develop moral, political, and education theory that can provide context-sensitive guidance about complex problems of education policy and practice. Finally, we hope to enable a more open conversation among all stakeholders—education scholars and other empirical researchers, policy makers and practitioners, philosophers, activists, parents, students, business leaders, journalists, and citizens—about what values and principles we should collectively be trying to realize in education policy and practice.

CASES AND COMMENTARIES AS GUIDES FOR PHRONETIC INQUIRY

This is an ambitious set of goals. How do we try to achieve them? At the center of the book are six normative case studies, which we define as *richly described, realistic accounts of complex ethical dilemmas that arise within practice or policy contexts, in which protagonists must decide among courses of action, none of which is self-evident as the right one to take.*[3] The case studies in this book have been developed over the past three years as part of a research project on Justice in Schools at the Harvard Graduate School of Education led by Meira Levinson. The case studies focus on dilemmas of educational ethics that have arisen in classrooms, schools, and school districts in recent years—specifically, the dilemmas with which we opened this introduction. Four of the case studies are works of fiction inspired by true events and two are entirely factual. They cut across private and public, urban and suburban, impoverished to wealthy schools. They also address curricular, pedagogical, and cultural decisions at the classroom and school levels, and raise policy questions at the school, district, and state levels.

Although each case is rooted in a specific context and grade level, similar and/or analogous dilemmas can arise across elementary, secondary, and higher education, which is part of their point. Deep investigation into the particular can offer insights into the general. At the same time, we do not claim that these are *the* six most important dilemmas of educational ethics; frankly, we could have substituted six others that we view as of equal significance. But we do think that, individually, each case addresses one or more paradigmatic challenges of educational ethics, and that taken together, they define a number of central questions in education policy and practice.

Following each case are six short commentaries, written by a mix of philosophers, social scientists, and education policy makers and practitioners. Each commentary offers specific insights into the case at hand, and also provides a model or framework for how to think more generally about complex ethical dilemmas of education policy and practice. By combining commentaries from diverse disciplinary and professional sources, and by encouraging readers both to delve deeply into particular cases and commentaries and to reflect expansively across them, this book attempts to model a *phronetic* approach to practical ethics. We borrow the concept of *phronesis*, or practical wisdom, from Aristotle.[4] He emphasizes phronesis as embodied in a practical understanding of particular cases, not just abstract knowledge of universal principles. Diverging from Aristotle, however, we also conceptualize phronesis as a *method* for conducting ethical inquiry. Specifically, we contend that complex ethical thinking in a particular context requires a marriage of theory and practice, one that crosses disciplinary and professional lines and that iterates repeatedly among field-based, data-oriented, and values-oriented expertise.[5] The commentaries are designed to model this phronetic process of iterating among theory, research, and practice in response to particular cases; they also are intended to promote phronesis itself as readers gain new understandings about the cases. Ultimately, we hope that this book will help readers use phronetic approaches to test, generate, and learn how to seek insights into educational ethics that are rigorous, relevant, and actionable. As we discuss at greater length in chapter 7, we envision that these cases and commentaries can be used by K–12 educators, school and district leaders, policy makers, parents, and even students to guide collective inquiry about ethical policy and practice in their particular setting. They are similarly useful for professional development settings, including preservice and in-service teacher education, as the cases pose concrete dilemmas that can be read quickly, are narratively engaging, and can often provoke a shock of recognition: "I had that kid in my class last year!" The commentaries, likewise, offer both specific insights into the cases at hand and models for how to approach such dilemmas in general. Educators may hence in some instances be able to apply insights from a case and its commentaries in order to resolve ongoing challenges or tensions in their school. More frequently, the cases and commentaries can provide a means to initiate open conversations about the ethical issues at stake. More important than providing *answers* to a limited number of scenarios, they are effective means of surfacing the right kinds of *questions,* and at provoking searching, collaborative inquiry into the principles and values that guide ethical education policy and practice. In this respect, we also anticipate that the cases and commentaries will be useful in undergraduate and graduate-level courses in education, philosophy, sociology, political science, and public policy.

OUR APPROACH

In taking this stance, we first reject an approach, likely to be familiar to many, that identifies a few distinct fundamental moral theories (always utilitarianism and deontological—or rights-oriented—theory, and often virtue ethics as well) and then applies one or more of these abstract theories to a particular problem. As we have just suggested, we believe that good ethical judgment about problems of practice inevitably draws upon a multiplicity of theoretical, empirical, and pragmatic perspectives. This is a *methodological* claim about how we achieve phronetic insight.

Second, we are also skeptical that comparing and contrasting highly idealized and abstract general theories actually impacts individuals' actions. This is a *pedagogical* concern; we doubt that people's actions and choices are likely to change over time thanks to such an exercise. We have never met a school principal, for example, who says, "Wait, let's apply deontological reasoning to this question of what we should do with a child who's throwing a screaming fit in the middle of class." More generally, there is considerable evidence across fields that people find it hard to transfer theoretical knowledge to practical problems. Harvard physics majors are the classic case: they ace the tests, but outside the classroom fall back on naive, pretheoretical intuitions about the distance of the earth from the sun when asked to explain why it's colder in winter.[6] It thus seems self-defeating to attempt to address complex educational dilemmas by reflecting solely on abstract theoretical concepts.

Third, we are skeptical that any meaningfully complex problem of ethical practice can be reliably solved by the application of a very general theory. This is an *epistemological* concern about the limits of our knowledge. Grand moral theories are necessarily abstract. They offer general or even universal rules for action. But how those rules and principles should be enacted with respect to specific problems of policy or practice will almost always be underspecified. This is a version of our point above that knowing one is committed to social justice, equality, or civil rights is not enough to know what to do in a particular complex case. Careful philosophical analyses of ethical principles and moral values might be great starting points for reflecting about an educator's, institution's, or system's obligations, but it is unlikely that in complex cases—the kind that keep educators and policy makers awake at night, and that we find ourselves returning to months or even years later, questioning whether we did the right thing—they can offer determinate ending points with clear answers about the right thing to do.

Hence, we contend that ethical judgment must join *philosophical* insight and expertise with *social scientific* insight into empirical patterns and logics, and *pragmatic* expertise developed by educators and policy makers themselves.

Social scientists can reveal how specific decision points are related to larger systems and practices. They can clarify how a particular case exemplifies or diverges from broader patterns, processes, and relationships. Empirical research may identify logics of interaction that frame the understandings and actions of all who are involved, and show how shifting those logics might open up new avenues for action or problem solving. Findings from related contexts may suggest likely consequences of various actions in particular educational settings, or help educators and policy makers see how decisions about one question (say, whether to exclude a child from the classroom) may reflect or impact decisions in other parts of the system (say, reflect racialized patterns of discipline, or impact academic performance among students with disabilities).

At the same time, judgment about educational ethics also demands the insights of practiced educators and policy makers themselves. Their pedagogical, organizational, instructional, cultural, and leadership repertoire is crucial for making sense of the range of options for action. A nonpractitioner may see only a binary decision between two choices: Keep a disruptive student in the classroom or kick him out? Renew a school's charter or deny it? Experienced educators, administrators, and policy makers, however, often see novel options that cut through what otherwise appear to be intractable normative challenges. Furthermore, every ethical dilemma is enacted—and must be resolved—within a complex web of practices, cultures, personalities, rules, politics, and even legal requirements. Practitioners often intuitively understand these webs better than anyone else.

By combining richly described, realistic accounts of complex ethical dilemmas in education practice and policy (i.e., normative case studies) with focused commentaries by philosophers, empirical researchers, and education policy makers and practitioners, we hope to model phronetic inquiry in practice. We also hope readers can use the cases and commentaries to clarify and test their existing theories, beliefs, values, and modes of action, as well as to generate new ideas and practices as needed to further guide ethical action in context.

A ROADMAP FOR READING

We have organized the normative case studies with two guiding logics in mind. First, the setting of ethical inquiry gradually expands from classrooms and schools to districts and states. Second, the object of inquiry gradually expands from specific students and teachers to larger communities, institutions, and systems. These logics are not rigid; as many of the commentaries make clear, cases situated immediately in classroom practice turn out to raise broader policy questions, and vice versa. Furthermore, we do not assume that the chapters (each containing one case and six commentaries about the case) will necessarily be read in order. Each chapter is thus designed to be self-sufficient. On the other hand, we do think there is a great deal of value in delving into multiple cases and commentaries, and we believe our sequencing provides a useful path through the diverse array of actors, contexts, and dilemmas.

We have organized the commentaries within each chapter to approximate a conversation among highly informed, and also highly diverse, interlocutors.

Indeed, the range of perspectives among the commentaries for each case is remarkable. In some cases the different disciplinary voices raise starkly divergent concerns. In others, similar ideas are explored through different lenses and in different registers, suggesting ways in which practitioners, social scientists, and philosophers share common insights. Taken together, these voices illuminate the profound complexity of decisions made in, about, and for children and schools.

The final chapter of the book provides some summative reflections across the cases as well as resources for using the cases and commentaries to promote shared ethical inquiry in a variety of classroom and professional settings. It includes suggestions for structuring discussion groups, sample questions for discussion, and options for adapting the cases if time is short.

By offering practical, realistic cases and a set of corresponding responses for readers to consider, we believe this book has the potential to strengthen educators' and education policy makers' own capacities to apply normative principles and analytic skills in their work. At the very least, educators and policy makers who already care about the ethical dimensions of their practice will acquire some new ideas and tools to promote justice in schools and to feel reinforced in their convictions that ethical considerations really do matter. More ambitiously, we hope that these projects will help elevate educational ethics to a new level of urgency within US and international education reform movements—on a par with educational leadership, assessment, and instruction as subjects of research, policy, and reform. By providing models of and guidance in reflective analysis of educational ethics, we also hope to enable scholars, policy makers, and practitioners to act on this urgency in productive and nuanced ways. On the scholarly front in particular, we expect that this book will reveal new arenas for research in applied philosophy, political and education theory, and normatively oriented sociology. In this respect, we hope this book will be in the vanguard of a new flowering of grounded scholarship and practice in educational ethics.

CHAPTER ONE

Promotion or Retention?

MEIRA LEVINSON

On a sweltering afternoon in early June, the eighth-grade team at Innovation Academy was gathered in Ms. Castro's room, grade books open on the desks pulled into a rough circle.[1] A fan whirred in the background, bringing a faint hint of a breeze as it slowly rotated. Mrs. Angly cleared her throat, but before she could speak, another announcement blared over the PA. "Teachers, please remember to submit students' final grades and graduation robe measurements to the office by 5 p.m. today. No exceptions. Mr. Thompson is already overdue with the order." Mrs. Angly and Mr. Rodriguez both winced. This is why they were meeting, to make the tough decisions about who would actually graduate the following week.

With a slight cough, Mrs. Angly started again to speak. "I just think there's got to be another way. If we hold Adahuaris back, we know she's just going to drop out. She turns sixteen this October. She's not going to stick around the eighth grade, hanging out with the thirteen-year-old babies. I know she hasn't achieved everything that we hope for her—or that she hopes for herself. But consider the circumstances. Also, what good does it do anybody if she drops out? That's the fastest route to poverty I know."

Ms. Castro and Mr. Rodriguez glanced at each other; then Ms. Castro spoke up. "But, Barbara, what good does it do if we promote her? Adahuaris is reading at a fifth-grade level. There's no way she'll be able to handle the texts they throw at her in high school. We've provided her support almost every day after school, and even so, she's failing social studies. And science. Not to mention her seventeen absences this spring. Other kids have struggles at home, but they pull it together. I know you love Ada. We all do. We all want her to succeed. But wishing can't make it so."

Mr. Rodriguez chimed in, "Don't confuse caring for Ada with making it easy for her. You know I grew up here. Nobody made it easy for me—and if they had, I would have been worse off. You can't survive by being soft."

"I'm being soft by refusing to countenance that we contribute to another teenage dropout and pregnancy statistic? By saying that her absences maybe shouldn't be held against her while she was bounced among three different foster homes this spring, all the time grieving for her brother?! By pointing out that maybe her hard work should stand her in good stead, rather than be used to prove that she can't make it?!!" Mrs. Angly's voice had risen despite herself. She knew she shouldn't take this personally, that they all wanted to do what was right by their kids, that they had to stay united if they were going to survive the challenges of Innovation Academy. She paused, took a deep breath, and started again a half-octave lower. "I don't know how to look Adahuaris in the eye and tell her that we think she needs to hang tough in the eighth grade one more year. That somehow next year is going to be different from this year. That her best just isn't good enough. How do I tell her that?" Mrs. Angly wiped sweat from her face, hoping it wouldn't be mistaken for tears—although she wasn't sure even she could tell the difference any more.

The room fell silent, save for the grinding fan, as each teacher reflected on the challenge that was Adahuaris. Nobody disputed Mrs. Angly's prediction that Ada would drop out if she were retained. She had entered Innovation Academy overage, having been retained in second grade by her elementary school principal. He was known to hold back kids whose poor reading skills would bring down the school's standardized test scores when they began third grade. Not that an extra year had made much of a difference for Adahuaris; she had entered eighth grade reading at a third-grade level. Still, she had made amazing progress in reading that year. Thanks to Ms. Castro's efforts with her during and after school, and Innovation Academy's new extra literacy block for struggling readers, Ada had tested at a solid fifth-grade reading level on the May tests. She had made two years' growth in a single year—a year in which she also watched her brother die from a gunshot wound on their front porch, and found herself shuttled around the foster system through a series of ever more dysfunctional homes. Her progress had inspired everyone, not least Adahuaris herself. No wonder she stayed after school nearly every day she made it to school; it was the most welcoming and stable place she had in her life.

Her grades were admittedly a problem. She had a 55 average in social studies, and was doing even worse in science. Her failing science grade was thanks in part to the science teacher's going on maternity leave; Mr. Beecher, the long-term sub, couldn't help Ada make up work she had missed while moving among foster homes. On the other hand, Ada also hadn't kept up with her science assignments even when she was in school. Her homework average was in the 40s, and even though Mr. Beecher offered to let Ada retake a test she had bombed, she hadn't done so. "What's the point, Mr. B?" she responded when he pressed her. "We both know I ain't gonna do no better the second time round. And, no offense, but it's not like you going to become Mr. Science now, neither." Mr. Beecher couldn't dispute that. Although he had been working twelve-hour days for less than half the pay of regular teachers and no benefits, he still found teaching science challenging—no small surprise for a French and theater major. He had taken the sub job at Innovation Academy to add some teaching experience to his resume, not because he had any aspiration to become "Mr. Science." Mr. Beecher stayed silent, doodling in the margins of his lesson plan book, unsure what he had to offer to the conversation.

Mrs. Angly tore a sheet of paper out of a notebook and drew a T-chart in thick black marker. Scooting her desk further into the middle of the circle so the others could see what she was writing, she labeled the left side of the chart "Actions"; on the right side, she wrote "Outcomes." Grabbing a red pen, she started filling in the chart. "Retain her" on the left was matched by "Ada drops out" on the right. Mrs. Angly looked up, making eye contact with Mr. Rodriguez, Ms. Castro, and Mr. Beecher in turn, as if daring them to contradict her. None did.

Next, she wrote "Send Ada to summer school." Ms. Castro gave a wan smile, reached over, and crossed it out. They all knew that budget troubles had led to district leaders' deciding in April to eliminate summer school for middle schoolers this year. Ada had been hoping to do credit recovery over the summer, which is part of what made it feel unfair to retain her. She could have retaken social studies and science if summer school were still an option. On the other hand, the April decision came early enough that other students at risk of failure had stepped up to the plate, worked their tails off, and earned final-quarter grades that were high enough to give them a passing average for the year. Ada hadn't.

Pencil still in hand, Ms. Castro pulled the paper onto her desk and wrote under Actions, "Give Ada passing grades in science and social studies." She drew two lines pointing to the right side of the T-chart, which she filled in: "Ada learns there aren't consequences for her actions," "Other students learn that standards don't matter." As Mr. Rodriguez gave a "Mmm" of assent, Mrs. Angly drew in her breath as if to speak. The others turned toward her expectantly, but Mrs. Angly simply let out a long sigh and shrugged weakly. She wasn't sure herself what she had to say.

After a pause, Ms. Castro turned back to the chart. She slowly added a third line under the first two and wrote, "A. feels grateful for second chance and gets on track." Resolutely avoiding eye contact with any of her colleagues, Ms. Castro pushed the T-chart back into the middle of the circle and looked down at her desk. Seeing a memo from the principal there, she flipped it over and drew a large question mark covering the back, cross-hatching it carefully in gray pencil.

A whine emanated from the corner of the room, where the fan had gotten stuck. Mr. Rodriguez stood up and strode over to fix it. With his back to the group, he posed a question. "Why are we willing to bend the rules for Ada, when we didn't bend them for Joachim, D'Andre, or Silvania? Why are we willing to forfeit our expectations for this child but not for the others? D'Andre arrived three months ago. We've never met his mom. How do we know he isn't battling as much as Adahuaris is? What's to say D'Andre doesn't have it even worse?"

Giving the fan a practiced thwack to start it rotating again, Mr. Rodriguez turned and faced the group. "We're the Innovation Academy eighth-grade team. We're the ones who agreed we wouldn't play the game of pretending to teach while our students pretended to learn. We decided together that we would stand by our graduates: that we could guarantee when they walked across the stage, they were ready to succeed in high school, then college, and beyond. Are we ready to give that commitment up, to sacrifice our integrity and the values we stand for so soon?" Mr. Rodriguez was pacing back and forth, hyped up, looking each of his colleagues in the eye as he spoke. "Barbara, do you really think that Ada couldn't have earned the five points to lift her social studies grade to a D– if she had wanted to? Chuck, are you ready to start your teaching career by falsifying a student's grade? Maria, do you think any of us will be able to push our kids next year if they know we passed a failing student on this year? It's not just Ada we need to think about. We owe all of our students the guarantee that an Innovation Academy diploma means something real. We owe them all our integrity, and our love. We show them that through our high expectations."

"You're right, David," Mrs. Angly responded, "about our responsibilities to our students as a whole. But we're not talking about the group here, we're talking about Adahuaris. How do we show *Ada* our love? How do we act with integrity toward *her*? I'm not sure I accept that her dropping out of the school is the price of our integrity."

Mr. Beecher shifted uncomfortably in his seat, and finally spoke. "What about the alternative school? Doesn't it serve kids like Adahuaris? Couldn't she go there in the fall and then maybe start high school in the spring?" His voice trailed off as all three teachers stared at him disbelievingly.

"Have you ever visited there?" Mrs. Angly asked. "It's the express bus on the school-to-prison pipeline. Adahuaris would get eaten alive there. We care about her, at least, and we want to show her the right way forward. Those teachers? They're lucky if they keep the stabbings under control. Even if she survives, she wouldn't learn anything there."

Ms. Castro concurred. "I didn't spend every day after school with Ada to watch her get fed to the lions. She has potential. She's a good kid. No way we're sending her to that crazy house."

Mr. Thompson's voice then boomed out over the PA. "Eighth-grade teachers, I'm still waiting on grade sheets and graduation robe measurements. I can't hold off any longer. Respect the deadline, please. I expect you to bring them down to the office in the next ten minutes."

Stricken, the eighth-grade team looked at one another. What should they do?

Square Pegs, Round Holes

The Need for Reform

MELISSA AGUIRRE

As a classroom teacher for five years, I know that this ethical dilemma of promotion or retention is one that is all too familiar. As a secondary school teacher, I find the need for alternatives for high school students who are aging out even more crucial. That there is no safety net beyond high school forces us into an undesirable set of choices: do we graduate the student with a meaningless diploma, or leave the student diploma-less with even fewer job prospects? I must admit that my response at the secondary level for a student who is aging out is to promote and graduate. However, at earlier grades, we have—or should have—other options. Therefore, I argue the teachers in this case should retain Adahuaris at the middle school level. That said, this case illustrates how the current model of schooling does not fit Adahuaris's needs and why changes are needed to offer her a better chance at gaining a meaningful diploma.

RISKS OF RETAINING ADAHUARIS

First, let us acknowledge that, as the teachers at the Innovation Academy thoughtfully point out, retaining Adahuaris has its risks. The spike in dropout rates and pregnancy rates that we witness at this juncture in education represent potential real-life consequences for Adahuaris. To make matters worse, the all too familiar circumstances of this case make a solution appear distant. For example, the well-intentioned Mr. Beecher—who cares deeply, but is not adequately trained in pedagogy or content to be able to deliver thoughtful, standards-based lessons—is a familiar face, especially in poor-performing schools.[2] The lack of summer school as an option for those students who need it most also rings true. Despite well-established research on "summer reading loss,"[3] too many schools and districts fail to provide academic opportunities in the summer. Furthermore, schools divided into discrete grades K–12, where students are moved along based on "seat hours" and aggregated course credits, reflect other archaic features of our education system.

This case resonates with me not only as a fellow educator, but also as a guardian. When I was twenty-two years old, I became the legal guardian for my fourteen-year-old cousin, Juanita (pseudonym), who had recently arrived from the Dominican Republic. Even prior to my teaching career, I knew my cousin needed a bilingual program where she could learn basic Spanish literacy and begin to transfer those skills to a second language. After two years in a bilingual program at a middle school, Juanita also faced a promotion dilemma. She was in the eighth grade, but to say she was reading in English at a third-grade level would be generous. Yet, as a guardian I consented to her promotion and graduation even though I knew that, as with Adahuaris, her academic success would be an uphill battle. And it was. Juanita never completed the ninth grade and dropped out. She is twenty-four years old and has yet to return to pursue any education.

Ten years later, I have encountered many Juanitas. At my last school, I wrestled with a similar dilemma with a student who was facing expulsion because of her behavior. Our team was considering this punitive measure while understanding that the consequences of expulsion would be severe, especially since the school community was the only positive niche she inhabited. In other words, we, too, faced the decision to keep her and perhaps risk the integrity of the expectations we had set for our students, or expel her and, more than likely, visit her in jail.

FROM EQUALITY TO EQUITY

I mention these two additional cases to convey that I recognize the nuances of Adahuaris's situation. But in Juanita's case, I advocated for promotion because the alternative—staying at her school—was not going to produce a different result in one, two, or even three years. Despite her teachers' efforts, the model at her school was broken. And when we think about justice in schools, the biggest injustice is that we insist on fitting square pegs into round holes.

In other words, our education system fails to adapt to the generation of students before us. We have insisted on pursuing the American notion of *equality* in our education system when what we should really be paying attention to is *equity*. We prefer equality because it is neater. It suggests consistency. But consistency can also be conveyed as a commitment to giving each student what he/she needs—equity—instead of giving each student the same dosage of resources.

So what needs to change?

First, we must shift toward competency-based education, which will compel us to welcome mixed-age classrooms as feasible and necessary. We need to integrate wrap-around social support systems. Also, we need to perform educational triage to respond to the many needs students have even as they walk through the doors of the school building.

Consider Adahuaris's case in a true competency-based education model. In such a model, the expectations for promotion rest on a set of skills across content areas that show students' ability to read, write, reason, and think critically. These skills would be tied to college readiness and career success. As such, mastering these skills would activate Adahuaris's and other students' sense of purpose.[4] Adahuaris could see how much progress she has made in reading comprehension, for example, and set clear goals accordingly.

Second, our obsession with "age-appropriate education," anchored in an antiquated K–12 system, must be tempered with competency-based education *regardless* of age. My experiences working at a charter school serving youth ages sixteen to twenty-four in Washington, DC, convinced me that placing students of varying ages in the same educational settings to work through a competency-based curriculum is more effective than the current system we employ at many public schools. We not only recognize that sixteen- and twenty-four-year-olds may face similar challenges and benefit from similar services or curricula, but we also extend the philosophy of equity to the social supports these students receive. For example, we decided to support students who could not afford transportation to and from school when we confronted the fact that, like many other public school systems, DC Public Schools did not provide discounted transportation fares for people over the age of eighteen; they were not considered students unless they had a documented disability.[5]

Granted, the resources needed to adequately maintain such a robust support system make it even more daunting to consider mixed-age classrooms. To address students' social, emotional, and academic needs, my school was staffed with four counselors plus therapists, in addition to a full complement of classroom teachers. But such supports may be necessary to establish a just educational system.

IMPROVING SOCIAL SUPPORTS

This brings me to the absence of social support I see in this case. We understand that Adahuaris has been tossed around in the foster care system and has witnessed the trauma of seeing her brother shot to death. Research tells us that because of this trauma, Adahuaris has repeatedly revved up her stress pathways and likely suffers from "toxic stress."[6] Indeed, the Centers for Disease Control and Prevention (CDC) has stated that youth living in the inner city have higher rates of post-traumatic stress disorder (PTSD) than combat veterans. Such stressors may preclude any learning from happening. Though we demand our veterans receive appropriate mental health care—as they should—we don't treat ruptures in a child's safety net with the same care.[7]

Rather, when we talk about justice in schools, we commonly expect students to pull themselves up by their bootstraps, or, as the faculty in this case put it, "Other kids have struggled at home, but they pull it together." This statement ignores the grit that we are just beginning to understand kids need in order to overcome the hurdles when "life gets in the way."[8] Some kids develop this grit and others don't. We must have honest conversations about how to help those students build grit instead of faulting them for not inherently bringing it to the table.

To continue borrowing from medicine, we know the best health care systems provide primary care by triaging their patients within a comprehensive, coordinated care model called the medical home.[9] In education, an analogy might be "Response to Intervention" (RTI). Students should be similarly triaged to receive differentiated services to meet their varying needs.[10] We know Adahuaris entered the school reading at the third-grade level. Why was RTI not in place at this time? Because of the Individuals with Disabilities Education Act (IDEA), we are obliged to develop, monitor, and renew Individualized Education Programs (IEPs) for our students with special needs, but what about students like Adahuaris?[11] As in a primary care practice, not all students require intensive care, but we must have protocols and pathways, including rapid identification, for each level of need and type of care.

Our default has been to promote unprepared students and to justify this decision by saying that it is not in the best interests of the child to remain in an environment with younger students. I, too, made this mistake as a guardian. But now, as an educator, I can see that we aren't as helpless as we claim. We can make better choices the minute a student enters our door at whatever grade. But this won't be possible if we insist on operating in the same sclerotic system.

Melissa Aguirre, a bilingual teacher with ten years of experience in education and the nonprofit sector, has worked with youth in Philadelphia, Boston, Washington, DC, and now back home in Queens, New York, where she teaches middle school. She is the proud daughter of Dominican and Argentine parents and feels privileged to work with immigrant youth and their families in the most diverse county in the country.

Toward Pragmatic Educational Ethics

Jal Mehta

As I was reading the case, I felt myself whipped to and fro. As new facts were introduced, I found myself shifting back and forth between thinking Adahuaris should be retained and that she should be promoted. I was torn partly on ethical grounds as different normative arguments presented themselves. But I was also torn on pragmatic, empirical grounds as I imagined best-case and worst-case scenarios and everything in between. I further found myself shifting between the specific dilemma the teachers faced that afternoon—should they graduate Ada or not?—and the broader ways in which the system failed to meet Ada's needs. It was too limited to treat the ethical decision solely as that which was being made in the room that June afternoon rather than as a series of decisions that had been made over time, by people throughout the system, to arrive at this point of reckoning.

Thus, I think we should treat ethical administrative decision making in a different way than most moral and political philosophers do, as a debate among first principles. Rather, we should see educational ethics as requiring a pragmatic approach that tries to find common ground among diverse constituencies, that balances multiple competing priorities in a way that is attentive both to principle and practice, and that looks beyond individual decisions to the health of the system as a whole, since the best hard decision is one that never has to be made.

THE NATURE OF ADMINISTRATIVE ETHICS

The kinds of considerations that shaped my thinking about how to "solve" the dilemma moved across different theories of justice: a consequentialist claim that retention would lead to her dropping out, which would worsen her life prospects; an egalitarian claim that asked how could we bend the rules for Ada and not for other students; a communitarian claim that retaining her would destroy Innovation Academy's collective ethos and commitment to high standards; and an ethic of care claim that promoting her would be the best way teachers could show their love toward Adahuaris.[12] Although they did not explicitly name these schools of thought, the teachers were similarly advancing these different kinds of justice claims.

What does responsible decision making look like when so many compelling, but also competing, principles are at stake? I think it requires balancing among different goods, looking for solutions that might meet multiple objectives simultaneously. It means moving between what is good for the individual, what is good for the organization, and the nebulous notion of what serves the public interest. A lot of the decision making for what Mark Moore calls "public managers" or Michael Lipsky calls "street-level bureaucrats" has this form, where the challenge is to find a workable and fair solution among competing goods.[13]

I would contrast this to the way in which I learned political philosophy in college and graduate school, where different authors were trying to show that their set of philosophical principles was *writ large*, more desirable. But teachers and administrators in the field do not have the luxury of prioritizing one such system. Sometimes they need more deontological or rights-oriented reasoning, and sometimes more consequentialist—and sometimes there are choices one can make that will meet both simultaneously. *Skilled administrators, in particular, excel in ways diametrically opposed to those of political philosophers: they find ways to diminish rather than ignite conflicts around first principles, and they look for solutions that will make multiple constituencies satisfied, even if not for the same reasons.* In this case, it might mean, for example, not promoting Ada, committing to getting her the extra support she needs, and using the stark dilemma she has posed as a way of reconsidering other aspects of the school's policies that led to this situation in the first place.

However, as far as I'm aware, there is much less guidance from the philosophical literature on how to handle such situations. Cases are taught in professional schools because they help students to practice this kind of *phronesis*, Aristotle's term for practical wisdom. In business, public policy, or education school cases, students are frequently asked to apply different social scientific theories and see which ones are particularly useful to understanding a particular case. Law school cases similarly ask students to read fact patterns and discern which set of precedents should apply. There is a little bit of work on case-based ethics, particularly when it comes to bioethics, but there is not a real corpus of work that would help practitioners guide ethical decision making in situations of multiple goods.

Hence the key question is what good ethical decision making looks like in what I am calling administrative contexts, *or where the choice is not between a good and a bad or a right and a wrong, but in trying to find a solution that integrates multiple competing goods.* This will be challenging for at least two reasons: (1) good ethical decision making will be necessarily context dependent in ways that are difficult to anticipate or prespecify; and (2) it will require heavy integration of the empirical and the normative, a combination that historically has been uncomfortable for most political and moral philosophers. I think the example of bioethics suggests that it is possible to develop a field that integrates evolving scientific and professional knowledge with ethical decision making; bioethics could serve as one model for a field of educational ethics.

BUILDING GOOD SYSTEMS, NOT JUST GOOD INDIVIDUAL ETHICAL DECISION MAKERS

Even as I wrestled with the decision I thought the teachers should make, I worried that focusing on this particular decision left out an important part of the story. I am enthusiastic about the idea of building a field of educational ethics. I could imagine a popular course on this subject; I could imagine it becoming part of the regular training of teachers, administrators, and other social service workers; and I could imagine it giving some backbone to the reflection that we are frequently urging thoughtful practitioners to engage in. But I would worry if, in so doing, we cordoned off developing individual ethical decision makers from the larger task of building the kind of good systems that we so desperately need to create more public value; in this case, creating more social mobility for highly disadvantaged students.

Indeed, the challenges this decision poses should push us to think about it from the systemic level as well. Admittedly, building a better system may not help teachers who have to deliberate about other cases like Ada's; they will need to rely on ethical judgment. But keeping a systemic solution in focus will lessen the likelihood that other teachers will find themselves in the position of having to choose between two or more undesirable options. The teachers in this case identify a number of problems that could (and should) be addressed at the systemic level. Would a viable alternative option for students who are not ready for ninth grade but are too old for their cohort in eighth grade mitigate students' dropping out of school entirely? Would creating mixed-age classrooms and cohorts lessen the likelihood of students like Ada dropping out? What supports need to be in place to catch Ada sooner?

In other words, it is as important to develop robust school systems as it is to develop good ethical decision makers. If strong school or district leaders developed these systems, they would not face the kind of stark dilemma that is posed here in an after-the-fact way. What appears in the case is an impossible dilemma for individual practitioners, but what it is arguably really showing us are the myriad ways that the system failed Ada over many years. If we are going to develop a field of educational ethics, it should focus at least as much on the justice of the system as it does on the ethics of individual decision makers.

Jal Mehta is associate professor of education at the Harvard Graduate School of Education. His work focuses on understanding the empirical and normative considerations that are important for developing good classrooms, good schools, and good educational systems.

Humanism and Standards

SIGAL BEN-PORATH

Innovation Academy's eighth-grade team has decided that they will not "pretend to teach while their students pretend to learn." This is admirable. By focusing on explicit and unified academic expectations, teachers can express their beliefs that all students can succeed and can pursue shared practices to reach these goals. When teachers work to clear and common standards, they can also combat inequities based on differences in teacher preparation, students' academic preparation and enrichment opportunities, and other factors that are closely tied to students' socioeconomic statuses. Innovation Academy teachers' commitments to framing a schooling context in which all are expected to teach and to learn, and to achieving a clearly defined set of goals based in knowledge and skills, are hence laudable.

However, teachers who define their role solely in academic terms, and solely with respect to standards rather than students, stand the risk of dehumanizing the children they teach. They risk seeing their students narrowly as a means to achieve "100 percent proficiency" or to "close the gap" rather than seeing them as individuals with valuable skills, interests, and challenges. These teachers also risk buying into the view that every child should be pushed to his or her limit in order to achieve preestablished goals, even as they interact daily with children whose circumstances call for more personal attention and greater flexibility. If teachers' relationships to their students are reduced to one metric of high academic standards, then both futility and injustice will result.

STANDARDIZED VERSUS PERSONALIZED RESPONSE

Virtually all teachers and school leaders care about academic achievement in line with specified standards. But schools serving predominantly middle-class children can work toward standards without sacrificing their responsiveness to personal needs. This is in large part because students from middle-class homes tend to achieve proficiency without much effort on the part of the school because of common parenting practices, better nutrition and health care, and other social factors.[14] Middle-class schools can thus focus their attention on broader considerations than the articulated standards. Furthermore, because these schools meet the standards relatively easily, they tend to be less carefully scrutinized. Rather than fostering a culture of compliance with external standards, they are able to be more intrinsically directed and child oriented. As a result, middle-class students tend to experience a school culture that is relatively robust and personalized, allowing for the preservation of social studies, art, and music. Their schools are also more responsive to individual students' needs and circumstances through established practices or in response to involved (or pushy) parents' demands.

By contrast, externally set standards have an enormous impact on teaching practices in schools like Innovation Academy, in which most students have not yet demonstrated academic success. These schools cannot afford to broaden the content of the curriculum, because many of their students have not mastered the basic content yet. It is quite possible that a student like Adahuaris is failing social studies, for example, because she finds it dull and disconnected from issues she cares about. It is also likely that she has fewer opportunities to engage with project-based learning and other creative approaches.

Teachers' mental, material, and physical resources are also quite limited in high-poverty schools such as I assume Innovation Academy to be. Teachers may be wildly underprepared, as Mr. Beecher, the theater major turned science substitute, certainly is. They often lack basic material resources, whether pens and books or, at Innovation, air conditioning, counseling services, and summer school opportunities for struggling students. They face a barrage of distracting and intellectually and emotionally taxing difficulties every day. Moreover, many teachers in underresourced schools like Innovation Academy feel unable to be flexible about their procedures, as is clear in this case, because they always feel on the verge of a slippery slope leading from high expectations to no expectations and ensuing failure. For all of these reasons, the school days of poor children are marked by much greater levels of stress, rigidity, and tediousness than those of their luckier peers. Decisions about their fate, such as the decision to promote or retain Ada, tend to be marked by rigidity rather than attention to personal circumstances for the same reasons.

"EXCUSES" VERSUS EXPLANATION AND HUMANISTIC EMPATHY

It is similarly inhumane, as well as ineffective, to pretend that students' lives outside school are irrelevant, or to expect schools to solve all the problems born of inequality. Youth like Adahuaris face dire living conditions, unstable family supports, and limited exposure to possible and desirable life plans. It is unconscionable to point to schools—often underresourced institutions themselves in which teachers are struggling with challenging conditions and a lack of supports or models—as the source of students' failure, or even as the essential route to their remediation.

True, some children facing hardships similar to Adahuaris's manage to beat the odds and succeed academically. Some of these children succeed because of the support and mentoring they receive at their schools. In some cases, this is because they have even one excellent teacher who believes in them and is capable of helping them transcend the complexities of their lives and their resulting academic challenges. But such Cinderella stories are far from the norm, and they often require an exceptional talent (the child's or the teacher's) or other outlier conditions that mitigate the hardships that the child faces.

Cinderella stories definitely should not guide education policies, which they do today in some "no excuses" contexts that demand all teachers and students put aside all personal struggles for the eight or ten hours they spend at school each day. It is important that policy makers recognize, by contrast, that the combination of poverty and distressed family life creates unfavorable conditions for learning. Calling those circumstances "excuses" is both inaccurate and demeaning.

CONCRETE STEPS FOR MOVING FORWARD

We thus need to talk about treating both teachers and students as ends in themselves, rather than as means to achieving some abstract social goals like "academic standards" or "closing the achievement gap." Education policy and practice should maintain ample room for the humanization of those who take part in the process of learning and teaching, rather than treating students or teachers as interchangeable cogs in a machine whose settings are beyond their reach.

As a first step, this means actually interacting with the humans whose lives are at stake and asking them how they feel, what they need, what they hope for. In Adahuaris's case, this would mean bringing her into the conversation with her teachers. Adahuaris is fifteen years old; in many states, students at this age participate in their own IEP and transition meetings. The ultimate decision about promotion or retention remains squarely in the hands of Ada's teachers and administrators. But a humanistic approach would demand that she be consulted about her own future. If she were in the room that June day, what would she say she prefers?

Ada's exclusion from the meeting is no surprise. Individuals living in poverty tend more than others to experience loss of autonomy and control over their lives. They are regularly suspected of moral failures or legal wrongdoing, scrutinized before being helped by welfare programs, or required to comply with external limitations on how they can use their resources. Ada's capacity to make independent, reasonable decisions may be circumscribed by the many difficult circumstances she is facing in her life outside school, but Innovation Academy is also limiting her prospects for agency by failing to consult her, possibly (and this is speculation) because her teachers hold limiting social perceptions about her capacities as a young person, as a female, and as a person of color.

To include Ada in a meeting about her future would thus be a mark of respect, a way to acknowledge her humanity, to treat her as an end rather than a means. It also seems likely, as a practical matter, that involving her in the process of decision making at this important junction in her life would have positive consequences. Ada could provide her teachers with essential information they need to make a good decision. Participating in the meeting might also help her feel more proactive about her path; she might feel she owns the decision, and hence have a better chance of following through with it.

Conundrums such as the one presented in this case are faced daily by children and adults in many schools. Our current framing requires teachers to think of their decisions in such matters in terms of the way in which they contribute to an environment of high expectations and in terms of their willingness to see all children as able to succeed on set metrics independent of any external considerations. By contrast, I have suggested a humanistic framing that would enable educators to make decisions in light of their students' needs and abilities, recognizing students' own preferences in the process and bringing their professional knowledge and personal connections with students to bear on the decision. Such a humanistic approach is certainly more just, and likely more effective, than one that clings to ideals about standards and procedures while losing sight of the persons affected by them.

Sigal Ben-Porath is professor of education and political science at the University of Pennsylvania. Her books include Tough Choices: Structured Paternalism and the Landscape of Choice *(Princeton University Press) and* School Choice *(forthcoming from The University of Chicago Press).*

Promotion, Retention, and
the Rights of the Child

WILLIE JR FLEMING

By international standards like the United Nations Convention on the Rights of the Child (CRC), the conditions under which Ada lives might well be considered an armed conflict or a war zone. Not even sixteen yet, she has already been bounced around in foster homes and has experienced the brutal murder of her brother. Unfortunately, her story is common to many urban African American and Latino American children, as is the academic situation in which she is ensnared. Given these circumstances, the question in such moments should not be simply whether to pass or fail Ada. The question should be: how does the educational system respond to children who experience violence, familial instability, and the ensuing and lasting trauma of such tragedies?

THE CONVENTION ON THE RIGHTS OF THE CHILD

One possible response to this question is to employ the framework provided by the CRC. First and foremost, this framework emphasizes what is necessary for the full development of a child. Recalling the Universal Declaration of Human Rights, the preamble to the CRC declares that "the child, for the full and harmonious development of his or her personality, should grow up in a family environment, in an atmosphere of happiness, love and understanding," and should be "fully prepared to live an individual life in society, and brought up in the spirit of the ideals proclaimed in the Charter of the United Nations, and in particular in the spirit of peace, dignity, tolerance, freedom, equality and solidarity."[15] These statements comprise a baseline standard of living that every child should expect. All too often, however, many children are left wanting. Society must begin to look at all the factors that impact a child's ability to learn and adjust accordingly. Our children and students are the future of this nation. We, as adults, parents, educators, and decision makers, must begin to respect, protect, and fulfill the human rights of children and students.

In Ada's case, the sanctity of family and the atmosphere of happiness, love, and understanding she should have experienced have been undermined through a series of volatile relationships and displacement created through the foster care system. Knowing that Ada's rights have been under assault even before she steps through the entrance of a school, how might American educational institutions begin to address Ada's needs? Should the school offer counseling supports or familial-like figures on whom Ada can lean? At the very least, the violent death of her brother should grant her services that enable her to heal the mental and emotional wounds that affect her ability to participate in institutionalized settings for academic achievement. Moreover, the rhetoric surrounding her progress should not focus solely around her ability to learn, but should also include the system's ability to care for her needs.

Unfortunately, the structure of many American institutions that play a part in ensuring children's development—for example, child and family services, educational institutions, and the justice system—does not provide the capacity, training, or understanding to uphold these demands. The current system is set up for the success of particular individuals who have been afforded foundations of capital and privileges of race. Thus, particular race and class backgrounds enable some members of society to benefit from institutional structures whose policies are rigidly constructed to support their success in the first place. Individuals who succeed in this system without the benefits of race and class become poster children for a pull-yourself-up-by-your-bootstraps, meritocratic narrative that serves to demonize and further marginalize those who come from complicated and challenging circumstances and do not find educational or occupational success. Simply meeting the demands of the CRC and ensuring that the needs of all children are met might go a long way to challenging such unjust and flawed institutions and changing such damaging narratives.

THE BEST INTERESTS OF THE CHILD

If teachers must make such decisions about graduation amidst circumstances that fail to live up to the basic demands of the CRC—as they do in this case—they might do well to follow the principle of "best interests" found in Article 3 of the CRC. It states:

> In all actions concerning children, whether undertaken by public or private social welfare institutions, courts of law, administrative authorities or legislative bodies, the best interests of the child shall be a primary consideration.[16]

In explicitly noting "public or private social welfare institutions," Article 3 clearly refers to schools, and thus decisions made by teachers. In this manner, teachers should deliberate about Ada's impending promotion or retention on the grounds that their decision reflects what is in her best interests.

Yet, in Ada's case, her teachers are caught between enforcing the rules of the school and doing what is best for Ada. Indeed, as Mrs. Angly angrily makes clear, the school's standards for promotion do not account for the hardships Ada had to overcome to make the gains that she has made. They have few ways of acknowledging what Ada accomplished over the course of the school year and are forced to make a decision that dehumanizes both Ada and, to some extent, themselves. Because rules for promotion do not account for Ada's best interests, only her achievement, the teachers cannot treat Ada with love, care, and respect—precisely the standards emphasized in the CRC. Forced to make a decision in this manner, Ada's teachers also compromise their own values.

Consider the alternative: what would promotion decisions based on Ada's best interests look like? Admittedly, determining what is in Ada's best interests is not easy. On the one hand, as the case makes clear, promoting Ada may ultimately place her in a difficult position, because she is not academically ready for ninth grade. On the other hand, retaining Ada may lead to her dropping out, as she would be three years older than the vast majority of her classmates. As neither option is overwhelmingly appealing, teachers' experience may be a helpful tool in making the decision. Take Mr. Rodriguez, for example. Mr. Rodriguez identifies with Ada because of his similar experience surviving crime and poverty in his neighborhood as a child. Mr. Rodriguez made his decision based on the impact the decision would have had on him. This connection is key—knowing what it is like to struggle in and through poverty adds significance to Mr. Rodriguez's decision. Indeed, Mr. Rodriguez's awareness of the long-term damage possible through promoting Ada resonated deeply with me.

CHANGING THE RULES

The effects of making decisions in such dire circumstances under such prescribed rules speaks directly to the American education system's lack of structural capacity to support students in the full sense of their humanity. This shortfall is illustrated by the ways in which Ada's teachers deliberated between adherence to institutional rules for promotion and their concern for the personal trauma Ada experienced in moving between various foster homes and witnessing the death of her brother. From my vantage point, the values and principles teachers offered to support different actions to care for Ada illustrate how they all wanted to change the very rules of academic promotion policies.

If we acknowledge that the institutional structures of our schools are flawed by basic instances of unfairness and therefore create and nurture broken relationships with marginalized individuals, we can begin to imagine a new system that allows people to heal, grow, and thrive despite the adversities and challenges of life. I believe that better advocacy, based in part on the basic needs of children laid out in the CRC and by what is in Ada's best interests, is part of a solution to Ada's dilemma. We must have better advocacy for alternative schools and summer programs. These spaces must support the growth and academic needs of children that mainstream institutions could not. There must also be a better system of accountability around qualified teachers to teach academic subject matter, especially when schools task ill-qualified teachers with subjects they have no experience teaching, in effect putting students in a failing position—even at a good school.

We live in a society today that is faced with many challenges for students and teachers. These challenges cannot be met with the same solutions of the past, for they have only furthered the problems that exist today. Grounding such efforts on the principles of the CRC broadens the possibility for children to reach their full potential to develop into human beings who can better serve humanity. Doing so also recommits teachers to the process of bettering humanity. If we are to better our education system, we must ground our practices and policies in a concern for children's rights. It is the children who inherit our work and this world.

Willie JR Fleming is executive director of the Chicago Anti-Eviction Campaign, a community organization that enforces the human right to housing. A lifelong human rights advocate, educator, and enforcer, he serves on the International Covenant on Civil and Political Rights Task Force and the Action Committee of the US Human Rights Network.

The Pedagogical Implications
of Case Study Structure

BRENDAN W. RANDALL

The case study "Promotion or Retention?" ends with a simple and direct question: "What should they do?" The teachers seem to face a binary choice: retain or promote Adahuaris. Either option entails the potential of significant negative outcomes. Retaining Adahuaris likely will result in her dropping out of school, with lifelong adverse consequences. Promoting her before she is ready almost certainly will set her up for failure later and will send a message to other students that academic expectations are meaningless. The teachers face a no-win situation. To make things worse, they are under pressure to act quickly, without sufficient time for further investigation or reflection. They have only ten minutes to make a decision that will have potentially profound and lasting impacts on both Adahuaris and the broader school community.

"Promotion or Retention?" presents a compelling dilemma for the reader because it portrays an unfortunately all-too-common scenario in public education for which there is no obvious answer, at least not from a progressive social justice lens. This combination of uncertainty and urgency provides an excellent foundation for a normative case study, the purpose of which is to identify and examine normative issues through the lens of lived experience rather than abstract theory. As the other commentaries on this case study demonstrate, "Promotion or Retention?" provides substantial fodder for articulation and discussion of timely and critical issues of justice in public schools.

The narrative structure of the case study, however, also merits closer examination. As noted above, the case study ends with a simple and direct question, "What should they do?" This seemingly unpretentious question actually is quite powerful and has significant pedagogical implications. It influences how the reader initially approaches the case study and potentially frames the subsequent analysis of the underlying justice issues. In particular, it invites the reader to make a decision involving a specific situation—whether the teachers should promote Adahuaris—rather than to question the moral legitimacy of the question itself—whether the teachers should ever have to make such a decision. As the other commentaries addressing this case demonstrate, readers are not inherently limited to the initial question. The format of the case nonetheless gives this concrete question primacy, thereby highlighting pedagogical issues associated with the structure of case studies.

THE CASE STUDY AS A PEDAGOGICAL TOOL IN THREE PROFESSIONS

Case studies involving specific situations or problems have gained prominence as a common pedagogy in multiple forms of professional education. In "Making the Case: Professional Education for the World of Practice,"[17] David Garvin reviews the history of case studies at Harvard's law, business, and medical schools. He presents a genealogy of sorts for the case study method, tracing how the case study, as a pedagogical tool, evolved in three different educational contexts.

In each professional training context, the case study method served to promote a particular, albeit different, habit of mind. Garvin explains that the case method originated at Harvard Law School in the late nineteenth century. Rather than memorize legal rules from textbooks, students read judicial opinions to derive essential legal principles. The ultimate goal was to teach students "to think like a lawyer."[18] The American legal system is based on precedent. By examining and comparing various cases and hypothetical scenarios, students develop the ability to identify similarities and differences relevant to the proper application of a governing legal principle.

The case study method spread to the Harvard Business School in the 1920s. Once again, case studies replaced a more prescriptive pedagogy. The pedagogical purpose, however, was fundamentally different. As Garvin notes, unlike the legal profession, business is not governed by precedent. Rather than serving to illustrate general principles, business school cases tended to focus on the particular. They typically placed students in the shoes of a protagonist facing a critical decision. Because delay was rarely an option, these cases fostered a disposition for action, even in the face of uncertainty.

Finally, Harvard Medical School began using case studies in the 1980s. As Garvin explains, case studies replaced traditional preclinical training, which focused on the memorization of extensive and detailed medical and scientific information. Medical case studies, in contrast, were based on patient files and asked students to act as treating physicians. Rather than following previous study on a subject, students faced unfamiliar situations, forcing them to identify and fill gaps in their knowledge. The essential goal of this pedagogy was to foster self-motivated inquiry and problem-solving skills.

SHAPING NORMATIVE INQUIRY IN EDUCATION

In structure, "Promotion or Retention?" closely resembles a prototypical business school case study. Questions such as "What should they do?" are a paradigmatic element of such case studies, linked closely to the goal of fostering a disposition of action, even in the face of uncertainty.[19] Hence, the reader's first inclination likely is to answer the question in concrete terms. Readers must choose between two options—to pass Adahuaris or not—both of which have potentially undesirable consequences. Focusing on the case in such concrete terms defines the relevant normative issues. What sorts of reasons or principles justify the "best" decision? For example, should the team emphasize universals (such as through a deontological theory calling for similar treatment of similar cases)? Mr. Rodriguez's argument for holding Adahuaris to the same high standards as other students reflects such a rule-based approach. Alternatively, should the team accord greater attention to the particular (such as through care theory, which focuses on specific relationships)? Mrs. Angly, for example, responds to Mr. Rodriguez by forcefully arguing that the team is talking about a specific student, Adahuaris, and pointedly asking, "How do we show Ada our love?"

The discussion among the teachers reinforces the reader's understanding of the question "What should they do?" as a fundamental choice between two dichotomous options. This framing is most explicit in the team's consideration of "Actions" and "Outcomes." The teachers identify three possible actions: "Retain [Ada]," "Send Ada to summer school," and "Give Ada passing grades in science and social studies." They reject the second action as unfeasible, leaving only the other two.

The teachers also reinforce an understanding of the final question as an inevitable choice between promotion and retention in more subtle ways. They never seriously challenge the circumstances in which they find themselves. They do not, for example, discuss whether others should be involved in the decision to promote or retain Adahuaris. As they note, the decision has potential implications for the entire school community. If so, should the discussion involve the entire faculty and administration, if not the broader school community such as parents and guardians? Nor do the teachers seriously question the legitimacy of their assigned task. Finally, they acknowledge that factors beyond Adahuaris's control influence her academic performance, but they merely debate how to weigh those factors in their decision to promote or retain her. They do not consider how these factors raise broader systemic issues of social justice and potentially render the very question of promotion and retention inherently unfair. In short, the case study's narrative structure initially diverts the reader's attention away from broader social justice issues.

EXPANDING THE FOCUS

The pedagogical goal of the normative case study, however, is not limited to the concrete concerns raised in the dilemma the teachers face. The potential ethical issues here go beyond the immediate question of whether or not to pass an underperforming student—as the other responses to the case in this collection make abundantly clear. The question, then, is how to move past the concrete concerns of the decision in order to understand the full normative context of the dilemma.

Although the case study's fundamental structure may promote an initial focus on the concrete question of promotion or retention, a facilitator's judicious use of other prompts easily could expand the discussion to other normative questions reflecting a more proactive rather than reactive stance. Indeed, reflecting on the choices one should make in undesirable circumstances helps us to figure out precisely why the circumstances are so undesirable. Here, the conversation would move from a focus on normative questions regarding the proper response to a particular situation—whether to promote or retain a student—to the situation itself: whether the very paradigm of promotion and retention in the context of extreme socioeconomic inequality is just.

Brendan W. Randall is the director of campus engagement at Interfaith Youth Core, a nonprofit organization promoting interfaith cooperation as a social norm in the context of higher education. A former lawyer and teacher with a master's of theological studies, Brendan is also completing a dissertation at the Harvard Graduate School of Education, focusing on religious pluralism as a civic norm.

Systems, Not Individual Saviors, for *All* Students and Schools

Toby N. Romer

Innovation Academy's eighth-grade teachers are clearly well intentioned and caring. But they make two fatal errors as they discuss whether to promote or retain Adahuaris. First, they base their proposals on what they think they know about how the education system *actually works*, rather than on how the system is *supposed to work*. In so doing, they give into unconscious biases and reinforce whatever dysfunctions actually do exist. Second, they see themselves as responsible almost solely to *one individual student*—to Ada—rather than to the needs of *the system*—including the other individuals in the system. As a result, they fail to act as truly ethical professionals within a complex system. By contrast, if they were able to have the vision to act in ways that accord with how the system is *designed* to work and for the best interests of *all* students, their actions would meet a higher standard of ethical behavior.

THE DANGERS OF ASSUMING THE WORST

Consider how many unquestioned assumptions faculty members make about what will happen to Adahuaris given the specific options that they faced. Teachers assert with total confidence:

- "If we hold Adahuaris back, we know she's just going to drop out."
- The alternative school "is the express bus on the school-to-prison pipeline."
- Retention is "the fastest route to poverty I know."

All of the faculty members seem to agree with these statements, and to agree that they are relevant to the discussion.

As a statistical matter, the teachers are absolutely right that retention increases a student's risk of dropping out and remaining in poverty. They also could be right about the outcomes in the particular alternative school in question. But they are mistaken to accept these statistical outcomes as definite and causal for any particular child such as Ada, and therefore to base a utilitarian calculus solely on their likelihood.

By focusing their decision making on their personal assessments of how the system is working, they become prone to accepting and furthering stereotypes. Embedded in their comments are low expectations of other schools and of other educators' abilities to meet the needs of students like Adahuaris. In fact, any alternative school designed solely to serve struggling students is vulnerable to the (often fallacious and certainly circular) judgment that the school is the *cause* of its students' underperformance rather than a remedy. Systematically withholding students who could benefit from the interventions that alternative schools provide only decreases the likelihood of those students getting the support they need. By reflexively ruling out an option like this, the faculty members limit the choices they have and that they accept for Adahuaris.

This problematic decision-making logic doesn't only limit options for students like Adahuaris, it makes it harder for the system to operate as it should for all students. If diligent and needy students like Ada are withheld from enrolling in the alternative school, its ability to create a positive climate and successful "last-chance" environment is restricted. If even needier (perhaps less motivated and more troubled) students are concentrated there in larger numbers, the school will be unable to create a successful class cohort and a positive peer culture as its additional resources become overwhelmed.

And as students like Ada who are academically unprepared and who do need more interventions are enrolled, the high school's chances of successfully pushing for high standards and creating a culture of achievement are also limited. In this case, the system is set up to promote students with passing grades and to remand overage middle school students who do not meet academic requirements to the alternative school. Violating these systemic expectations will undermine the logic of the system and negatively impact hundreds of other students.

For everyone's sake, therefore—for Innovation Academy, the high school it feeds into, the alternative school, and the teachers and students in all of these schools—teachers should make decisions based on how the system is *supposed to* work rather than on any assumptions about how it *does* work. Otherwise, systemic failure becomes a self-fulfilling prophecy.

PRIORITIZING THE NEEDS OF ONE OVER MANY

This point, that individual decisions undermine systemic functioning, leads to my second ethical concern about the logic used by the team. Given the passion that all of the teachers feel for ensuring the best possible outcome for Adahuaris, they never fully grapple with the question of where their ultimate ethical responsibilities lie. Mr. Rodriguez does raise concerns about precedent, and about the problematic message that promoting Adahuaris might convey to other Innovation Academy students. He also points out that their logic in favor of promoting Adahuaris may not stand up when extended to other students, such as D'Andre, Joachim, or Silvania. But the other teachers quickly set these concerns aside. As Ms. Angly responds, and the others seem to agree, "We're not talking about the group here, we're talking about Adahuaris."

By focusing on piecemeal triage, the teachers fail to generate a consistent and strategic theory of action that could support better outcomes over the long term. By prioritizing Ada's individual well-being above all else, the teachers neglect—arguably even sacrifice—their other students and the school system as a whole.

Consider how their reasoning might change were they to take the health of the system, and the well-being of all students collectively, into account. They would then ask questions such as:

- How do high schools respond when less prepared students are promoted? Can they maintain rigorous standards for all students, or do course quality and expectations drop?
- When underprepared middle school students are retained rather than offered placement in summer school or alternative high school, how are middle school peer culture and academic rigor affected?
- When the students who could benefit most from alternative schools are systematically not enrolled due to safety concerns, what happens to students who *are* sent to alternative schools? Can those schools serve remaining students effectively?
- Will funding for summer school and other more effective interventions ever be reinstated if educators compensate for their loss by creating implicit work-arounds and pretending such services are unnecessary?
- More generally stated, what decision will be most likely to prevent this dilemma from recurring in future years? How can teacher practices reduce rather than exacerbate the number of Adas (and D'Andres, and Silvanias) they have to cope with each year?

If the faculty members seriously consider these questions, they would be much less likely to take actions that have unintended (but highly predictable!) consequences that weaken the system as a whole. Given their current emphasis on simply helping their students one by one, there's a good chance that they will unintentionally contribute to concentrating academically underprepared students in one or more schools and reinforcing the current dysfunction of the system. Faculties in these schools will then likely find it much more difficult to create healthy, vibrant academic communities where positive outcomes for all students are probable. Much like the tragedy of the commons, decisions that are made to maximize the outcomes for individual students, or even schools, may serve to make the overall academic environment for all students more challenging.

WE NEED SYSTEMS, NOT SAVIORS

The teachers' professional motivation is what ultimately drives them to ignore the systemic impact of their decision and act solely on the basis of Adahuaris's individual needs. In Mr. Rodriguez's impassioned charge to the group about their team mission, we get a glimpse into their collective desire to be saviors and islands of reform within the wilderness of education. His statement is based on the assumption that everyone else must be playing "the game of pretending to teach" while this team alone stands for high standards and real caring. This savior orientation toward the profession of teaching encourages shortsighted, seemingly expedient decisions on behalf of individuals that do not promote a healthy and balanced system of education over the long haul.

A strong case can be made—and this orientation is largely ignored in the current framing of the case—that an ethical professional response to the dilemma would be to retain Adahuaris based on the principle of ensuring the proper functioning of the system of education and ensuring that all students have equal access to quality education. To put it another way, the decision to retain Adahuaris is the most likely to result in a change in the system and the prevention of this dilemma from recurring.

Such a decision would also need to be accompanied by a genuine effort on the part of the teachers to advocate for systemic change of the factors that created the dilemma. Students who have experienced trauma need consistent counseling and academic supports. Alternative schools for struggling students need to provide a real alternative that is academically rigorous and socially and emotionally supportive, and is not just a holding pen. Districts need to provide meaningful safety nets for students who do not meet the standards, including by providing summer school.

Innovation Academy teachers can see firsthand how their students, the school, and the system as a whole are harmed when these systemic supports are not in place. They should therefore engage in proactive advocacy to improve the working of the system while behaving in a way that is consistent with and that reinforces the system they would like to see in place. This would ultimately redirect the energy of the team in a more sustainable and transformative direction for all students and be aligned with a more robust definition of professional ethics for educators.

Toby N. Romer has served in numerous roles in the Boston Public Schools over the past nineteen years, including teacher, headmaster, assistant headmaster, coach, and teacher-leader. He is currently assistant superintendent of secondary education and special programs for the Newton Public Schools in Massachusetts.

CHAPTER TWO

Rocky Choices

Scientific Inquiry, Discipline, and Mental Illness at Rivers Elementary

MEIRA LEVINSON AND SIGAL BEN-PORATH

K ate was one of the more troubling children to come through Rivers Elementary School, a public K–5 school in a small suburban district that serves predominantly well-educated, upper-income professionals.[1] In a district known for its high academic achievement levels and strong support for schools, Rivers has a reputation for being the "best of the best." Families embrace its high-quality academics, nurturing school culture, and commitment to educating "the whole child." Parents also appreciate Rivers's open-door policy; when Kate was a student at Rivers, for example, school principal Mr. Thomason was known to make himself immediately available when parents had questions or concerns. Classroom teachers were also accessible; many sent home weekly newsletters or posted daily blogs about class activities, and all responded to e-mail.

Kate, the only child of a lawyer and an art history professor, had initially thrived at Rivers. Kindergarten and first grade were a breeze. She was right on target socially and emotionally, and above grade level academically. The summer before second grade, however, Kate became increasingly oppositional for reasons that no one, not even Kate herself, could identify. When school started in the fall, Kate's behavior plummeted further; she regularly disrupted class by shrieking and banging her chair. Other children showed signs of stress in response to Kate's outbursts, looking frightened or starting to cry when Kate lost control. Together, Kate's parents and teachers agreed that she needed to be evaluated for special services; while her exact diagnosis remained unclear, she received an Individualized Education Program (IEP) that included a full-time inclusion aide so she could remain with her regular second-grade class.

Even with an aide and other accommodations, however, Kate's behavior interfered with her learning and other children's learning on a regular basis. That January, therefore, she was reassigned to the Emotional Support class, which met in a separate area of the school. Despite the smaller, therapeutic setting, Kate frequently screamed, cried, kicked, and hit people. Twice she ran out of the school building and straight into the street without looking for oncoming traffic. Kate herself seemed to hate finding herself out of control; one morning, for example, she asked her parents if she could wear slippers to school "so that I won't be able to run so fast."

Often during her outbursts in school, Kate would be placed—or ask to place herself—in the "Think Room," which was a form of solitary confinement used to help children contain themselves. Once there, she might collect herself relatively quickly; other times, she'd continue her tantrum until she fell asleep. Although the Think Room was controversial within the district—many teachers and parents saw it as developmentally inappropriate and punitive, and there was talk of legal action to shut it down—both Kate and her parents were grateful to have a place that she could go to when school became overwhelming.

To everyone's relief, Kate started making significant progress in controlling her emotions and behaviors over the following summer. By late autumn of third grade, she spent part of each day in the regular classroom, and she was fully mainstreamed later that winter, helped by an Emotional Support teacher who sometimes assisted Kate inside the classroom and sometimes pulled her out for special services as needed. Kate was still often disruptive. But on balance, Kate's mood seemed to be stabilizing, and she was even starting to catch up on the academic material she had missed.

Kate's third-grade classmates seemed happy to welcome her back when she was stable. She had been a popular kid in kindergarten and first grade, and she was fun to be around when her mood was under control. Her classmates also felt good about creating the kind of community in which Kate could be successful. Ms. Brown, their third-grade teacher, had led a number of conversations with the students about inclusive communities that honor many kinds of difference. The children had been excited to identify their many differences and to discuss how classroom norms and procedures enabled everyone to "be their best selves."

At the same time, many children privately expressed concern about Kate's continued disruptions. Although they had learned that Ms. Brown was not open to accusations that "Kate messes everything up," they did complain to their parents and each other when an exciting learning activity came to an abrupt end following one of Kate's mini explosions. Some students felt that Kate got too much attention from Ms. Brown, and that Ms. Brown therefore wasn't as available to deal with their own questions or problems. Other students worried about being kicked or hit, and visibly tensed up whenever Kate was nearby. In a few cases, the children were so concerned about setting Kate off that they seemed to concentrate more on mollifying her than on the subject of the lesson.

In light of these concerns, a group of six parents met in March with Principal Thomason to establish clear procedures and expectations about Kate's participation in class. These parents expressed concern about classroom safety and culture. They also questioned the academic rigor of a class that was sporadically disrupted, and they questioned whether Ms. Brown was capable of simultaneously teaching Kate and the other children in the class.

In response, Mr. Thomason expressed support for Ms. Brown's teaching methods. He noted that she was a respected veteran with certifications in general elementary education, science, and special education. He also emphasized that Kate was entitled by law to the least restrictive educational setting appropriate for her, although privacy regulations prevented him from sharing anything more specific. At the same time, Mr. Thomason reassured the parents that all children's needs would be attended to, and he agreed that "it is of paramount importance that every child feel safe and secure in class, ready and able to learn." At the end of the meeting, one of the lead parents, the only father in the group, told Mr. Thomason he felt good about their discussion, but also noted that he was prepared to "take it to the next level" if there were continued problems.

Mr. Thomason met with Ms. Brown the next day to discuss next steps. Ms. Brown was initially upset about the meeting, frustrated that the parents had bypassed her to go straight to the principal. She also suspected that the parents' own concerns were feeding their children's worries. "It's not the kids who are scared of Kate; it's the parents," Ms. Brown explained. "They say stuff to their kids over dinner, about how Kate shouldn't be there or is disrupting other kids' learning, and then the children come in the next day with complaints that they never had and blow things all out of proportion."

In response, Mr. Thomason emphasized that he was responsible for all children and their families. "If you see Kate starting to get upset, I want you to ring for help so an adult can escort Kate to the Think Room," Mr. Thomason instructed. "Remove Kate from the classroom *before* she explodes. That way, Kate can feel some success that she hasn't disrupted another day of learning, and her classmates can feel confident Kate won't be allowed to get out of hand. We can't afford to let this escalate.

No need to get the superintendent involved." Mr. Thomason was firm; although Ms. Brown tried to protest, he made it clear their meeting was over.

The following Monday, Kate arrived at school late, seeming agitated. Her parents explained that she had had a rough morning, but was eager to get to school to learn about rocks—a favorite subject. Students were working in small groups to classify rocks by their sedimentary, metamorphic, or igneous characteristics. Ms. Brown assigned Kate to work with two boys, Philip and Frank. Both boys were welcoming, although Philip, who identified as a "future world-famous inventor," had occasionally gotten upset about Kate's disruptions in the past. It was his father who had threatened Mr. Thomason with "taking it to the next level." Frank was a soft-spoken, reserved child. A struggling reader, he often seemed to disengage from classroom activities if they seemed too challenging. Ms. Brown worried about his self-confidence, reminding him frequently that he was a great thinker and observer, even if "your brain needs extra help matching letters to sounds."

Initially, the group work went smoothly. Frank took on the role of holding each rock up for examination. All three children expressed their opinion about its classification; finding that they were unanimous, Philip recorded the group's decisions on a worksheet. About ten minutes in, however, the two boys began to squabble over the designation of a rock. Philip insisted it was igneous; Frank was sure it was metamorphic. Kate did not take a position in the debate. Instead, she squirmed and moved away, as if trying to shield herself from the conflict. She then returned to the table, but again seemed undone by the boys' vehement disagreement. The boys weren't misbehaving—to the contrary, they were passionately involved in the science task at hand—but their argument continued unabated.

Ms. Brown was across the room, helping a group that was struggling with the classification exercise; they kept trying to organize the rocks by shape and size. Noting Kate's increasing distress, however, Ms. Brown crossed the classroom and quietly asked Kate if she would like to switch groups. Kate refused, seeming hurt. She had already sorted some of the rocks for their group; she did not want to walk away from the important work she had done! Ms. Brown then turned to Philip and Frank. "Why don't you present your debate to Kate, and let her be the judge?" Ms. Brown suggested. But Kate nervously shook her head, feeling pressure at being in the spotlight. Frank, uncharacteristically, also scowled. He was on the verge of convincing Philip he was right, he felt; this wasn't the time to start over!

Ms. Brown could tell that Kate was close to breaking down. She had little time to decide what to do. Should she pursue her tactic of having the boys present their argument to Kate for adjudication, potentially agitating Kate to the point of no return, leaving the other group to founder, and risking censure from her principal? Should she send Kate preemptively to the Think Room, causing her to miss the lesson for which she had worked so hard to get to school? Should she move one of the boys out of the group, effectively punishing them for doing their work, and undercutting Frank's newfound academic engagement and self-assertion? Should she shift to whole-class instruction, scrapping the current lesson plan and perhaps diminishing all children's active engagement in learning? What was the right course of action?

Navigating Rocky Choices
with Practical Wisdom

JOSHUA WAKEHAM

The central dilemma of this case surrounds the practical uncertainty and perceived risk of responding to Kate appropriately. The demands of the parents and the principal have distorted Ms. Brown's perception of the situation with Kate. Yet with some insight and flexible thinking, Ms. Brown may both calm Kate and keep the class lesson on track.

PRACTICAL WISDOM

For Ms. Brown, successfully navigating this fraught situation requires some practical wisdom, or what Aristotle calls *phronesis*.[2] In Aristotle's understanding of ethics, the biggest challenges come from morally complex situations—that is, those situations where competing moral goods are at stake. Being able to both recognize the moral complexity of the situation at hand and to practically realize some greater moral goal are the hallmarks of phronesis. Aristotle contrasts phronesis with both theoretical knowledge (*episteme*) and technical, or rule-based, knowledge (*techne*). Both theoretical and technical knowledge are ill suited for handling morally complex situations, as they tend to impose a kind of rigidity in thinking. Without the insight earned through practical experience, one is likely to be oblivious to nuances and subtle differences that might be morally and practically salient in specific situations. Phronesis is the ability not only to cut through the moral complexity of the situation at hand, but also to act effectively toward some greater goal.

In this situation, Ms. Brown struggles to serve competing goods. As a teacher, she must maintain an orderly classroom, meet the educational goals of the class as a whole, provide an inclusive classroom community for all, respond to the educational needs of individual students, and encourage the social and emotional development of individual students. Ms. Brown, a well-respected veteran teacher, has presumably accumulated some amount of practical wisdom in navigating these competing demands in her twenty-two years of teaching. Yet the circumstances of the case suggest Ms. Brown is unable or reluctant to use this experience to respond to the situation.

CONSTRAINTS ON MS. BROWN'S THINKING

Social forces conspire against any kind of creative response to the situation with Kate. The parents of the other students in the class are justifiably concerned that Kate's disruptive behavior monopolizes Ms. Brown's time and energy. Mr. Thomason is understandably responsive to these parents, who are the most immediate, most vocal group pressuring him. Mr. Thomason's order to preemptively move Kate into the controversial "Think Room" seems unnecessarily constrained by the weight of habit (it has worked in the past) and risk aversion (one of the hallmarks of bureaucratic thinking).

In imposing such a rule, Mr. Thomason attempts to reduce the uncertainty and risk surrounding Kate's unpredictable behavior, thereby narrowing the moral and epistemic complexity of the situation. He imposes an artificial sense of the risk if Kate has another meltdown by mentioning the possibility of the superintendent becoming involved. And by telling Ms. Brown to remove Kate from the classroom, he limits her focus to a particular problem in a larger complex whole and makes only one course of action the "right" one. Thus, he precludes the consideration of courses of action that might both keep Kate calm and keep the lesson on track.

In contrast, practical wisdom requires both moral insight and sufficient practical skill to realize one's moral goals. One way to generate moral insight is, as research by Zhang, Gino, and Margolis suggests, to frame cases such as this with "could" questions rather than "should" questions—that is, rather than asking if Ms. Brown *should* preemptively send Kate to the Think Room, we ask, what *could* Ms. Brown do in this situation?[3] Framing questions in this way tends to generate a wider array of—as well as more creative—responses to the moral dilemma. Being open to a wider array of practical responses thus allows one to consider previously overlooked courses of action that may help one realize more than one goal simultaneously.

The practical skills being put to the test in this case are Ms. Brown's social interactional skills. Whether Ms. Brown can successfully navigate this unfolding situation depends on how well attuned she is to the emotions of her students and how effective she is in influencing her students' reactions. Good teachers manage the ebb and flow of their students' emotions, enthusiasm, and attention to maximize their learning. They often have an ineffable sense of how this works at both the individual and group level. Good teachers have also developed a repertoire of tactics to deal with potentially disruptive group dynamics and individual problems. They have learned when to let the conversation continue and when to step in. They have learned when to lay down the law and when to give kind words of encouragement. Good teachers, in other words, have cultivated practical wisdom.

MS. BROWN'S OPTIONS

If we allow that Ms. Brown is able to draw on her years of experience and acquired skill, we might ask, what *could* Ms. Brown do? I think there are several good options—but I do not necessarily think there is any one right thing to do in this situation.

The first option is not to address Kate, but to change the tone and tenor of Kate's group. If Ms. Brown believes that it is the heated argument between the two boys that is making Kate upset, then simply stepping in, speaking to the boys calmly, and getting them to *calmly* talk through their disagreement could quell the source of Kate's anxiety. Rather than putting Kate on the spot to adjudicate between her two classmates, perhaps Ms. Brown could have the boys calmly take turns giving their argument to her. This not only engages these boys in an edifying experience, but it also signals to Kate that disagreement does not need to produce anxiety.

The second option is to address Kate more directly. Rather than have the boys continue on with their debate, Ms. Brown might ask Kate to explain the disagreement the boys are having. This not only disrupts the boys' quarrelsome dynamic, but it also forces Kate to focus on the intellectual content of their disagreement rather than the emotional tone. Doing so both nudges Kate toward better behavior and models for her an important way of approaching seemingly heated social situations. In other words, this course of action might help Kate keep her emotions under control, if not help her reengage with the intellectual content of the course.

The third option is to do nothing. Ms. Brown might simply drop her line of questioning with Kate, provide some positive words to the group, and then move on. The case reports that Ms. Brown can tell the situation was about to get out of hand, but we should be skeptical of that claim. Kate may, in fact, pull through the situation okay. In the face of anxiety, she may muster some undiscovered inner reserve and get control of herself before she breaks down. Recall that Kate had done something similar to this in order to come to school and classify rocks. She may well do it again.

DEVELOPING PRACTICAL WISDOM

None of the options presented are guaranteed to work. In each scenario, Kate may still explode and end up in the Think Room. However, these options hinge on a very different interpretation of the uncertainty and risk involved in the situation with Kate than is suggested by Principal Thomason's call for preemptively isolating her in the Think Room. Developing and acting on practical wisdom concedes ground to uncertainty (we do not know for sure what will happen) and requires a higher degree of risk tolerance (we might be wrong, and that is okay).

Even if Kate does explode and disrupt the lesson, it is not the end of the world. Handled quickly and professionally, the situation can still work. Kate and Ms. Brown can still pick up the pieces and try again. The other students will still have other opportunities, and they will still face other disruptions to their classroom experience besides Kate.

Enabling teachers like Ms. Brown to develop and enact practical wisdom does dismiss the parents' concerns or the principal's instructions, but it avoids letting them impose an artificial sense of the moral stakes—and thus, an artificial sense of the risk Ms. Brown is taking—on the situation at hand. With emotionally unstable young children like Kate, the goal is not to avoid meltdowns at all costs, but rather to take small steps to help them build the social and emotional skills they will need to self-regulate.

Doing the right thing for Kate means not only having the sensitivity to recognize her crumbling emotional state, but also having the practical skills to direct her back toward learning effectively. The case's suggested options are tactics of avoidance, suggesting that perhaps skilled interpersonal interactions are beyond the responsibilities or skills of Ms. Brown. My own proposed options are based on the assumption that the interactional skills necessary to stave off a meltdown and reengage Kate are learnable and are part and parcel of a good teacher's responsibilities.

In bringing up the notion of practical wisdom, I am also suggesting that situations like this resist rule-based solutions. This is not to suggest that anything goes, but rather to point to the idea that realizing some greater good—in this case, the successful education of Kate and her classmates—requires a kind of practical flexibility. Allowing teachers like Ms. Brown to develop practical wisdom, of course, requires that school leaders give them a tremendous amount of discretion. They need the freedom to make mistakes with students so that they can figure out what works and what does not. On the other side, good teachers must also work toward building a professional environment that encourages active learning and reflection in order to gain from their experiences. Years in the classroom mean little without a deliberate attempt to learn from one's mistakes and successes.

Finally, in emphasizing the notion of practice, my goal is not to minimize the moral stakes of the case, but rather to emphasize the moral richness of the day-to-day work of teachers like Ms. Brown. As Aristotle's moral philosophy argues, the good and the just are not found solely in abstract principles or rules, but rather are lived and made in the messiness of everyday life. The competing demands placed on schools, and on teachers in particular, make the question of justice a complicated one that resists easy answers. Nonetheless, it is important to recognize the role of deep knowledge from practical experience, or practical wisdom, in breathing life into the work of a good teacher and a just school.

Joshua Wakeham is an assistant professor of criminal justice and sociology at the University of Alabama. His research explores issues of morality, justice, and epistemology in the context of bureaucratic organizations, with a particular focus on organizations at the crossroads of social services and the criminal justice system.

Educational Justice in the Inclusive Classroom

Jaime Ahlberg

Teachers often have to make difficult decisions that privilege some students over others, simply because of the plurality of educational objectives and the heterogeneity of students. In this case, Ms. Brown is tasked with educating students with a diversity of needs and interests. Additionally, she is facing some very practical constraints on her actions, including limited resources and pressures from students' parents and the school principal. How is she to come to a well-reasoned conclusion about how to proceed?

This scenario illustrates quite clearly that in overseeing the educational development of their students, teachers must often act as agents of justice. Making trade-offs is inevitable, as not every educational objective and student need can be met. Three clear principles ought to guide teachers like Ms. Brown in negotiating these trade-offs. First, she should aim to be as inclusive as possible, consistent with students' safety. Second, she ought to provide adequate educational opportunities for all students. Lastly, when she has satisfied these two principles, Ms. Brown should prioritize meeting the needs of her least advantaged student(s).

INCLUSION

One of the central moral issues in this case is that of inclusion. In the United States, every student is legally entitled to the least restrictive environment appropriate for his or her learning capabilities. A commitment to the value of inclusion—physical, curricular, cultural—undergirds this legal requirement and has supported the movement to "mainstream" students like Kate, who would otherwise be placed into separate classrooms or schools.

Beyond legal requirements, inclusion is motivated by justice-related concerns. Both students with disabilities and nondisabled students stand to benefit from inclusive learning environments. Children with disabilities have short- and long-term academic, developmental, social, and civic interests at risk when they are physically removed from the standard classroom. Of particular concern is the risk of emotional and social isolation that students may experience when separated from their nondisabled peers. The effects

49

of such isolation are likely felt beyond the period during which the child is removed from the standard learning environment, and thus may affect a student's long-term academic and social growth. Exclusionary policies, then, may deny some children educational goods they have a right to expect.

Nondisabled children are also targets of inclusion policies, insofar as the aims of schooling include moral and civic education. Bringing together children of differing backgrounds and ability levels fosters an environment that identifies the needs of all as important, and prioritizes treating each member of the classroom well and with respect. All children benefit from such an environment, though arguably the children who would otherwise not directly encounter children with disabilities have the most to gain in this regard.[4]

In the case at hand, Ms. Brown has already primed her class with a sense of what makes inclusion valuable. Leading discussions with her students about how classroom norms can facilitate participation across children's differences seems to have guided them toward an interest in including Kate in their classroom activities. Further, Mr. Thomason has communicated to the concerned parents the legal basis for Kate's presence in class and has expressed support for Ms. Brown's methods. Unfortunately, he does not seem to have explained the classroom commitment to an inclusive community or to have had a more general conversation with concerned parents about why keeping Kate with her peers is of value for everyone.

PRINCIPLES FOR JUST INCLUSIVE EDUCATION

Ms. Brown still faces familiar difficulties with implementing inclusive policies. Meeting the interests of different students while also meeting any one student's full set of interests can demand interventions that are not simultaneously compatible.

Consider, for example, students' many different needs in Ms. Brown's classroom. All students have an interest in a safe environment that is inclusive and conducive to learning. Kate has a strong interest in having her intellectual curiosity and contributions affirmed. Frank has a strong interest in developing a sense of self-confidence with respect to his academic ability. Philip has an interest in pursuing his talents as far as possible. Students in the struggling group have a knowledge-based interest in gaining a better understanding of the classification exercise.

How should Ms. Brown adjudicate this variety of conflicting educational interests while trying to promote an inclusive environment? I propose that she treat two goals as fundamental. First, she must ensure that her classroom stays safe. No student can learn in an environment in which she is, or reasonably feels, threatened. A stable, safe learning environment is a precondition of learning. Notice that educating students to be tolerant of difference will support the achievement of this goal, because it may minimize the insecurity and anxiety that students sometimes experience when facing new or unusual behavior from their peers.

Second, Ms. Brown should secure a minimum level of educational opportunities for all of her students over the course of the academic year.[5] Each student has an equally strong interest in achieving the educational benchmarks that will prepare her for adulthood in our world, including, at a minimum: the capacities necessary for democratic citizenship and economic participation; the ability to think critically and reflectively; and the disposition to treat others with respect. Ms. Brown should thus work to secure these capacities, skills, and dispositions for each student.

Assuming she has satisfied these two obligations, however, Ms. Brown then has a further obligation of justice, which requires her to prioritize the needs of her most disadvantaged student(s). The most disadvantaged students are those least likely to flourish in the classroom as well as in the long term. Since all children have an equal interest in living flourishing lives, and since education is central to realizing a flourishing life in a multitude of ways, teachers have an obligation to prioritize the needs of those students who stand to benefit the most from additional attention and/or resources.[6]

SERVING THE LEAST ADVANTAGED

Let's see how these principles apply here. To begin, even if Kate breaks down, there is no indication that Ms. Brown's classroom will become unsafe. It *will* become significantly less conducive to learning, however, because Kate's breakdown will at least temporarily shut down the lesson and lead students to feel alienated. It will also lead to censure from the principal and parents, which threatens Ms. Brown's employment. Given that she has little power over her principal or the parents in this moment (or indeed, at all), it is best if she can find a solution that does not risk their disapproval.[7]

Ms. Brown seems to have good historical, experiential evidence that a breakdown is imminent, and given the high costs if Kate breaks down, it would be unfair to the students and imprudent for Ms. Brown to risk it. She thus needs to find a way to shift the developing dynamic before it leads to a breakdown. If she can do that, then classroom safety and learning can be maintained at appropriate threshold levels, and she can focus on the needs of the least advantaged.

Who are the most disadvantaged students, those whose interests should be given priority, if possible? Kate surely is the most disadvantaged—not only because she is academically behind, but also because she is struggling to overcome her emotional disabilities as she pursues her schoolwork. Frank's needs are also quite serious, though perhaps not as serious as Kate's. He is, apparently, on the cusp of breaking through his withdrawn disposition to occupy a more participatory role in his education and with respect to his peers.

Both Kate and Frank thus have educational interests at stake that are larger than those the simple rock classification exercise addresses. Preemptively moving Kate to the Think Room or undermining Frank's engagement would plausibly have long-term consequences for both students' abilities to develop as learners over time. By contrast, there is no indication that Phillip or the students in the struggling group will suffer in the long term if they receive less than ideal instruction with regard to this exercise.

Here are two possibilities for how Ms. Brown could prioritize Kate's and Frank's needs. She could have Philip and Frank present their disagreement to the class as a model for discussing scientific questions. This would remove pressure from Kate, communicate to Frank the worthiness of his contribution, validate Phillip's and Frank's achievements, and provide a model for the struggling group. Admittedly, this does not offer an opportunity for Kate to actively participate. It does, however, avoid removing her from the classroom, and in that sense prioritizes the importance of her remaining present for the activity. Or, if she thinks Kate could manage it, Ms. Brown could move Kate to the underachieving group. Ms. Brown could even ask Kate to guide the struggling group through the exercise. This option would allow Frank to continue his debate with Phillip, and hopefully would communicate to Kate that she has valuable intellectual talent.

Other possible courses of action undervalue the needs of Kate and Frank. Preemptively sending Kate to the Think Room would set a dangerous precedent of removing her from the classroom rather than teaching her to work through her issues. It would also not take advantage of an opportunity to promote the value of her contribution to the class, which could also encourage her to focus on the value of academics. Lastly, it would publicly undermine the value of including Kate in the class, since she has not yet been disruptive in any way.

Alternatively, sending Frank or Phillip to a different group would risk long-term consequences for Frank's confidence. Seizing on a moment in which his confidence is burgeoning seems critical to his long-term success as a student. Finally, scrapping the lesson plan would compromise the interests of all, and set a bad precedent for group exercises.

BETTER AND WORSE, BUT NO SINGLE ANSWER

In closing, it is important to note that even if there are better and worse courses of action, there is no single right course of action in this case. I have indicated some guiding principles of educational justice that teachers in Ms. Brown's position should have in mind as they move through the school year:[8]

- Be as inclusive as possible while not compromising classroom safety.
- Promote a fruitful learning environment for all.
- In cases of conflict, prioritize the educational interests of the most disadvantaged students.

Undoubtedly, teachers' character and good judgment will be crucial to the appropriate implementation of these principles. Further, it is likely that no one incident will irrevocably sacrifice any one student's interests. If Ms. Brown commits an error in judgment in this incident, or if events unfold in a less than desirable way, there will probably be later opportunities to adjust her approach so that over time she approximates what the principles demand.

Jaime Ahlberg is an assistant professor of philosophy at the University of Florida. Her central areas of interest include ethics and political philosophy, bioethics, and philosophy of education.

Preparing Teachers for
Complex Decisions

Elisabeth Fieldstone Kanner

This case study presents a familiar dilemma for teachers: how to balance the needs of one student with the needs of all the other students, and in particular, how to address the unique needs of a special education student while supporting the general education students. However, the text's simplistic treatment of this important issue undermines its usefulness.

UNDERSTANDING MS. BROWN'S CONTEXT: LET'S GET REAL

First, the case study implicitly pits Kate's needs against the needs of the whole class. This dynamic does not represent the context of most classrooms, where there can be three or four or even ten "Kates," each of whom often requires a specific accommodation at the same time. As far as we know, Kate is the only special needs student in this classroom. This is not realistic.

Even if we entertain the idea that Ms. Brown has the luxury of balancing only Kate's needs with the needs of the rest of the class, the listed options lack a deep understanding of the complexities of teaching and learning. According to the case study, Ms. Brown has the following options: (1) force the boys to present their debate to Kate for her to be the judge, (2) send Kate to the Think Room, (3) move one of the two boys out of the group, or (4) "shift to whole-class instruction, scrapping the current lesson plan." Clearly, there are more than these four options open to Ms. Brown.

For example, reinforcing the value Ms. Brown has already placed on respecting difference, she could talk with the boys about their speaking style, explaining how some people, like Kate, prefer listening to ideas presented calmly. Then she could reassure Kate of her ability to take part in this calm discussion. Ms. Brown could find another adult to go on a short walk with Kate, perhaps with the rocks, so Kate can continue her learning. Or, instead of "scrapping the lesson" when she shifts to whole-class instruction, Ms. Brown could engage all students in the debate that is so captivating to Philip and Frank. We could continue to come up with alternative choices for Ms. Brown. Teachers have an almost infinite number of possibilities to select from at a given moment, and that is what makes teaching so complicated.

Not only does this case study minimize the complexity of Ms. Brown's decision, but it also simplifies the context in which she must act. The text reads as if Ms. Brown has time to consider four options (and we know there are more) and then make the best choice. Keep in mind that Ms. Brown is in the middle of teaching a lesson; she likely has less than sixty seconds to come to a decision (which is considerably less time than you will have spent reading this commentary). And, she has to handle this complicated thinking while also managing the learning of twenty or so additional students.

MAKING INFORMED DECISIONS: LET'S GET MORE DATA

Assuming we forgive the case study for presenting this reductive view of Ms. Brown's dilemma, then can we respond to its question: Should Ms. Brown push Kate to judge the debate, send Kate to the Think Room, remove a boy from the group, or scrap the current lesson plan? That is the question posed, so we can assume the authors believe we have enough information to make a sound recommendation. But, making wise teaching decisions requires more data.

To begin with, how many students have mastered the lesson's objective? If most of Ms. Brown's students have met the lesson's learning goals, moving on might be instructionally sound. If many students are confused, however, like the group that had been struggling with classification principles, Ms. Brown should probably spend more time on this subject.

Does she have time to return to this tomorrow? Will she still have the rocks then, or does she need to hand them off to another teacher? These are all important factors Ms. Brown would have to consider.

We should also want to know more about individual students. For example, does Philip have a history of raising his voice to prove a point? If so, perhaps this is an appropriate time to work with him on developing a less intimidating speaking style.

Answering these questions would yield only a fraction of the information that Ms. Brown should be calling upon when she decides how to proceed. But they are enough to show that no teacher could—or at least, should—be making decisions based solely on the scant data available in the case study.

IMAGINING MS. BROWN'S PREPARATION: LET'S GET SPECIFIC

Without more information, it would be unwise to suggest what Ms. Brown should do. In fact, that is the wrong question even to ask. A more useful question is, What would *prepare* Ms. Brown to make an ethically and pedagogically sound decision? To answer this question, we need to think more carefully about Ms. Brown's training, her professional development, and her collaboration with other educators.

First, has Ms. Brown developed a *stance* that rejects the "zero-sum game" approach that some parents might be assuming (i.e., to help Kate is to hurt the other students, and to help the other students hurts Kate)? It is not helpful, just, or necessary to pit the needs of a special education student against the needs of general education students. Rather, we can and should look at this situation in a way that would allow Kate and the rest of the students to learn something useful, especially if we widen our definition of curriculum to involve not just classifying rocks, but also building social, emotional, and civic skills.

In Ms. Brown's training, has she been shown examples of ways to support the needs of special education students while benefiting all students in the classroom? Universal Design for Learning (UDL), for instance, enables teaching practices that serve all students, just like a ramp into a building benefits more than those who cannot walk.[9] Ideally, Ms. Brown would be prepared to approach this scenario with the understanding that (a) the most just solution is one that benefits Kate *and* the rest of the class, and (b) it is possible to find such a solution. Of course, she should also have ideas of what these kinds of solutions look like.

Second, has Ms. Brown had opportunities to *practice* or *rehearse* making decisions about supporting special education in an inclusive classroom before she has to make them in real-time with real students? Imagine if Ms. Brown had the opportunity to discuss a case study like this one during her preservice training. She could have learned that sometimes students interpret and respond to "debates" differently, especially students with socioemotional disabilities. This knowledge could have helped Ms. Brown anticipate the challenge that occurred during this lesson. As a result, she could have arranged for an adult to be on hand to take Kate for a walk if the classroom situation became "too heated." Or, she might have intentionally grouped Kate with students who would be less likely to argue (i.e., not Philip).

Indeed, preservice teachers, called "residents," in the Boston Teacher Residency (BTR) program, are taught how to predict challenges that might occur in a given lesson and then plan some possible responses.[10] They have the opportunity to get feedback on their ideas before and after they teach. What came up that the resident did not anticipate? How was that challenge addressed? In what other ways could the resident have responded?

Coaching novice teachers through these steps makes it easier for them to manage the inevitable hiccups that arise in any given lesson, and even avoid some of these challenges altogether. Now, imagine that during Ms. Brown's preservice training she investigated not one, but dozens of these case studies. Her decision-making muscle, perhaps weak at the start of her career, would have strengthened considerably with this rigorous mental and ethical "workout."

EXPANDING THE SCOPE: LET'S GET ADMINISTRATORS INVOLVED TOO

Just as regular exercise maintains physical muscles, educators' decision-making muscles should be further honed through school-based professional development. This is as true for administrators as for teachers. Suppose that prior to this situation, both Ms. Brown and Mr. Thomason had been part of a workshop with special educators, other teachers, and perhaps even some parents, where a teacher presented a classroom situation like this one. Think of how much they both could have learned from a rich discussion about different ways to meet the needs of a special education student without sacrificing the learning of the whole class.

Equipped with this understanding, Ms. Brown would be better prepared to make a wise decision when she notices Kate's agitated state. Similarly, Mr. Thomason might have been able to support Ms. Brown in making a better decision. He clearly directs her to send Kate to the Think Room, at least in some part to avoid parental criticism. This situation exemplifies how even the best teacher judgment can be thwarted by administrators who entertain a "zero-sum" stance and/or have not practiced making these kinds of decisions themselves.

Ultimately, therefore, I am suggesting that addressing this dilemma is not about one teacher's decision, but really about how the professional judgment of teachers and administrators is nurtured and developed.

As a founding teacher at the Francis W. Parker Charter Essential School, curriculum writer at Facing History and Ourselves, and now graduate teacher coach at the Boston Teacher Residency program, Elisabeth Fieldstone Kanner focuses on preparing teachers to nurture their students' capacity for critical thinking and ethical decision making. She earned her doctorate from Harvard Graduate School of Education in 2005.

Academic Engagement as Classroom Management

SETH ANDREW, WITH NATALIE GOULD
AND MIRIAM JOELSON

All too often, schools focus on conflict avoidance and behavior management in order to create classrooms in which learning can happen. But this gets the relationship between academic engagement and good behavior backward. In my experience as a charter school network founder and principal, academic rigor and engagement are the best forms of preventative discipline. Furthermore, even when students like Kate do act out or explode, prioritizing their academic needs while also supporting their social and emotional growth is the best way to get them, and the rest of their classmates, back on track.

PRIORITIZE LEARNING, NOT PUNISHMENT

Ms. Brown feels torn between the conflicting priorities of Kate's academic growth and the expectation of a calm learning environment. But when such a trade-off is presented, she must get her priorities clear. Kate's learning should be her most important concern when determining a course of action, both before and after an incident. Furthermore, by focusing on Kate's learning, Ms. Brown can shift from an "either/or" to a "both/and" approach. This is because Ms. Brown's most effective strategy would be to use Kate's intellectual engagement as a way to redirect her energy, and to do so without sacrificing the lesson.

Fortunately, Ms. Brown has every opportunity to intervene gently on a purely intellectual basis without singling Kate out for her emotional instability. Instead of asking her to join a different group, why not say, "Philip and Frank, great discussion! I am so impressed by your knowledge of igneous and metamorphic rocks. This one is a tricky one, though. So let's pause here: Kate, what are your thoughts?"

In this way, Ms. Brown does all of the following:

1. She refocuses Kate on the rock project and away from her emotions.

2. She gives Kate—a third, more silent team member—the chance to weigh in, thereby modeling how healthy debate occurs.
3. She gives the two active team members the positive feedback they deserve while communicating to Kate the value of her opinion and participation.
4. She does not disrupt the class.
5. She does not blame anyone, and no students are punished.
6. She does not refer to or make excuses for Kate's previous behavior.
7. She does not set a precedent of easy class disruption.

A punishment-free course of action is essential, as *none of the students has done anything wrong.* Kate has not yet disrupted the class; instead, she has made a concerted effort to participate. The two boys in her group are doing what they are supposed to do: challenge each other to understand just why they disagree about the formation history of the rock in question. There is also no indication of disruption elsewhere in the class. So punishment is self-evidently undeserved and inappropriate.

Disciplinary action in this scenario would also set an unfair, unpredictable precedent. Classroom disruptions should not be preempted by removing emotional students from the room, as Mr. Thomason maintains, but rather *prevented and managed* through consistent, high expectations for all students. Mr. Thomason's approach, because it is grounded so heavily on Kate's record of past bad behavior, cannot be consistently applied to all students, leaving Kate feeling targeted and less likely to engage in her coursework. Rather, by having each student—particularly Kate—focus on the task at hand, the teacher sets the tone of priorities: focused and engaged learning frequently obviates the need for discipline.

PROVIDE MULTIPLE OPPORTUNITIES FOR INTELLECTUAL REENGAGEMENT

If Kate explodes after the proposed intervention directed by Ms. Brown, it would then be appropriate for the teacher to use whatever strategy has proven effective in calming her down. Sending Kate to the Think Room could be the right solution in this instance, as long as Kate understands why she's been sent there—or rather, what she should be "thinking" about. The consequence then would logically follow the negative behavior, leaving eight-year-old Kate with a clear sense of the "crime" and the "punishment."

However, to the extent possible, Ms. Brown should employ strategies that keep Kate in the classroom. Again, this is because Kate's academic growth is the top priority for Ms. Brown. Rigorous intellectual engagement can be used to curb her tantrums. For example, she might suggest that Kate write out her ideas about the rocks, or select the next set of rocks for her group to identify. These options allow Kate to participate, even if she is not in a space to engage intellectually for a few minutes, and keeps her in the classroom. By slightly modifying the activity to accommodate Kate, Ms. Brown gives her the opportunity to reengage quickly while not disrupting the other students. Sending Kate to the Think Room, by contrast, separates Kate from the lesson material. It should thus be used only sparingly, thoughtfully, and for short periods of time.

Parental complaints or district politics, while valid concerns, should never take precedence over Kate as a learner. School leaders and community members will inevitably have priorities that are motivated by their own interests, leaving Kate vulnerable to forces that could hinder her academic growth. As the only adult in the school specifically responsible for Kate's learning, Ms. Brown has an obligation to be Kate's strongest advocate and to take the most stubborn opposition to any policy that could interfere with her education, even if that sometimes means disagreeing with the principal or superintendent. Ms. Brown faces a more challenging situation when accommodating Kate's needs negatively affects other students' learning. Yet in this scenario too, the teacher would need to evaluate the classroom from the perspective of the least advantaged member of the class, maximizing that student's academic growth. Scaffolding lessons and providing multiple opportunities for reengagement will give all students the academic environment they need to thrive.

SCALE THESE APPROACHES FOR ALL STUDENTS

We know there are thousands of students like Kate in public schools across the country whose behavior problems have left them at risk for losing the rigor and vibrancy of their education. It can be tempting, under the guise of utilitarian maximization of teacher time, to make convenient decisions and sacrifice the learning of the most vulnerable students. But this is a disservice to Kate, her parents, and the classroom community, whose success should be measured by academic growth. A teacher's limited time and attention should be used in such a way as to maximize this growth for the class.

Thirty years ago, I was a third grader with a learning disability in a New York City public elementary school. I struggled with controlling my temper and communicating in writing. Had teachers preemptively moved me out of the learning environment on a regular basis, I wouldn't have been able to persist or develop the coping strategies I needed to succeed in the long term, despite my learning differences. Happily, my teachers didn't write me off. Instead, they accommodated me and gave me unlimited chances to learn the coping strategies that would prove essential in high school, college, and beyond.

My personal experience resonates with Kate's, but more importantly, my professional experience building Democracy Prep Public Schools, a network of urban charter schools now serving more than five thousand students across the country, has taught me that academic rigor and engagement are the best forms of preventative discipline. Avoiding conflict is not a solution—it is an abdication of a teacher's responsibility.

Democracy Prep serves an extremely high need student population and yet outperforms some of the wealthiest suburban schools in America, with academic results that Harvard researchers found to be some of the strongest in the nation. How? We hold our expectations high; we support our scholars in myriad ways; and we embrace the struggle that ensues. In so doing, our citizen-scholars are prepared to *work hard, go to college, and change the world*, regardless of the challenges they may have faced along the way.

Seth Andrew, a product of the New York City public school system, is the founder of Democracy Prep Public Schools and cofounder of the Washington Leadership Academy. He has served as senior adviser to the Chief Technology Officer of the United States as well as senior adviser to former US Secretary of Education Arne Duncan.

Natalie Gould is on the founding team of the Washington Leadership Academy, a next-generation charter high school in the District of the Columbia. She holds a BA from the University of Pennsylvania.

Miriam Joelson is a consultant to the Washington Leadership Academy. She holds an AB from Brown University and a MSc from Oxford University.

Promoting the Values of Inclusion, Learning, and Expertise in Complex Situations

DIANA HESS

Classrooms are complex and morally charged spaces. Consequently, many of the decisions that even the most skilled and experienced teachers need to make are extremely difficult. This is especially true when there are multiple and competing values at stake. While this case is chock-full of ethical dilemmas, two stand out as both fundamental and unusually consequential. The first is the immediate pedagogical dilemma. Should Ms. Brown keep Kate in her current group, move Kate elsewhere, or end the small-group activity entirely? Here, two values—*learning* and *inclusion*—are at stake. Simply put, Ms. Brown should prioritize solutions that address both values. The complexity of this decision also underscores how *expertise* functions as a catalyst for reaching the best solution. But who has legitimate expertise and authority to resolve matters of pedagogical ethics in the classroom? When Principal Thomason directs Ms. Brown to send Kate preemptively to the "Think Room" to avoid an explosion, he asserts his own authority and presumptive expertise. Is he justified in doing so? Can Ms. Brown legitimately substitute her own pedagogical judgment instead? This conflict suggests a second dilemma about the boundaries of pedagogical authority: who in fact should get to decide how to address the first dilemma?

INCLUSION, LEARNING, AND EXPERTISE

A host of values comes into play when considering ethical dilemmas in classrooms. One is the importance of creating *inclusive* communities in which people are not deprived of their rights simply because they are different from the norm. It is critical to remember that state and federal statutes providing students with disabilities the right to be educated with non-disabled children in the "least restrictive environment" are fundamentally civil rights laws. Like other civil rights laws, their purpose is to create a more inclusive and democratic society. The Individuals with Disabilities Education Act (IDEA) and other laws do this by ensuring that students like Kate have equal access to the public good of education. Moreover, the mainstreaming required by such laws has educative purposes for nondisabled students. Ms. Brown recognized this opportunity by teaching Kate's peers about the importance of inclusion and about the many ways in which all students are different from one another. By doing so, Ms. Brown worked to normalize difference in her classroom.

In integrating Kate into the regular classroom, of course, it is essential to ensure that she can receive a meaningful educational benefit (academically and socially). Special education law prioritizes disabled students' right to *learn* in an integrated environment, even if this infringes somewhat on the learning of their classmates. It is important to recall that before the historic special education laws were passed, young people like Kate were routinely treated as second-class students whose needs were almost always deemed less important than those of other students. Clearly, Kate's classmates do deserve a high-quality education, but so does Kate, and it is the role of special education to ensure that her rights are not sacrificed to satisfy the concerns of a disgruntled minority, like the parents of Kate's classmates.

But the educational rights of disabled students and nondisabled students are not necessarily in conflict. They may, in fact, complement each other. Young children learn in school not just about rocks, but also about how to work in groups, even with loud boys and with peers who, like Kate, have challenges that are different from their own. After all, one of the arguments for inclusion was the need to develop citizens who value the creation of diverse and inclusive public spaces and know how to behave in them.

In order to create inclusive learning environments that are educative for Kate and her peers, the adults who construct and maintain these environments need to have deep *expertise*. Now, expertise may not be so much a value on its own as it is a potential contributor to other values, providing assurance that educators apply our best knowledge about students' needs appropriately and consistently. Here, it is easy to infer that Ms. Brown possesses deep expertise; she has certifications in elementary education, science, and special education. In the United States, very few elementary school teachers are as extensively certified as Ms. Brown. Because schools are obliged to provide in-classroom experts when this is necessary for a fully inclusive and meaningful education, Ms. Brown's special education expertise is particularly salient, as there does not seem to be a classroom aide for Kate.

MS. BROWN'S PEDAGOGICAL DILEMMA

Given the important values of inclusion and learning, what should Ms. Brown do when it becomes clear that Kate is close to breaking down? With respect to the value of inclusion, the worst option is to send her to the Think Room; it is entirely noninclusive. With respect to the value of learning, it is also purposely not educative. Isolating her in a non-learning-oriented space cannot provide a meaningful benefit that is in line with the spirit or the letter of special education laws. Nor does it demonstrate the use of special education expertise to adjust to Kate's particular challenges. While it is arguable that options like the Think Room may be necessary as a last resort—and Kate's and her parents' desires to use the Think Room, while not decisive, also carry some weight—this doesn't seem to be a last-resort situation, and it fails to fulfill the values that should be considered here.

Changing the lesson plan to a whole-group lesson would be a better option than banishing Kate to the Think Room because it promotes the goal of inclusion. However, Ms. Brown presumably designed the lesson with small groups because students would learn more than in one large group. The intense academic discussion that was occurring in Kate's group most likely would not have occurred in the large group, simply because there would not be enough airtime for all students to think and talk out loud with one another. Moreover, Ms. Brown was likely using a small-group lesson to teach her students how to work in groups—an important goal in its own right. Changing the lesson robs Kate and all of the students of the chance to benefit from what appears to be a highly engaging and complex lesson.

Moving Kate to another group when she is close to melting down also doesn't seem like it would work; at this point, Kate is probably too agitated to learn well in a new group. Moreover, Kate did not want to exit her group, which was working well for her until the two boys began to argue over the classification of a rock. It is critical to note that Kate started getting agitated when the boys vigorously disagreed with one another. Even though they were not misbehaving, they—and Kate—probably needed immediate coaching to interact in a more constructive way. Given that we already know that Ms. Brown had the option of ringing for another adult to escort Kate to the Think Room, it is likely that another adult (ideally, one of the Emotional Support teachers or a special education aide) could have come into the classroom just as quickly to work with Kate's group. This option promotes the values of inclusion and learning, but to implement it, there must be someone with expertise who could focus on Kate's group.

Mr. Thomason could better support the values of inclusion and learning if he made sure that there were adults with expertise available when quick interventions are necessary to ensure that students like Kate receive the meaningful benefits they deserve. In this case, making greater use of special education experts would seem to be the option that would best realize the values of inclusion and learning.

WHO SHOULD DECIDE?

So, who should make such decisions in cases like this? It depends, of course, on the situation. While it is generally best for teachers to make these decisions, Kate's situation is especially complicated—historically, whether or not she even belongs in Ms. Brown's classroom has been in question. Mr. Thomason brings his own expertise and distinct perspective as a school leader, asserting a general policy about how to handle Kate. However, this sort of expertise may not be suited to making particular pedagogical decisions. Indeed, his expertise may be more political in nature, insofar as he is concerned with managing relationships with parents and thinking about the school in general. It is significant, then, that the school's special education experts seem to be missing from his decision-making process. Mr. Thomason should solicit their input as integral to any general policy.

Moreover, Mr. Thomason should have approached Ms. Brown—an expert in her own right about special education, pedagogy, and her classroom—to discuss the parents' complaints rather than immediately issuing a directive. Mr. Thomason, too, should promote the values of inclusion and learning in how he works with faculty members, and should draw on their expertise in setting policy and practice.

The promise of the IDEA is to provide disabled students with the benefit of a public education to the extent possible. This means not only adjusting content and pedagogy so that students have opportunities to learn rigorous content in ways that recognize their particular needs, but also including disabled students in regular classrooms to the greatest extent possible. Segregated environments not only reduce disabled students' chances of learning at the level of their nondisabled peers, they also eliminate the important opportunity for disabled and nondisabled students to interact, which, ideally, promotes learning of social skills and the creation of a more inclusive, democratic society. Realizing the promise of the IDEA, then, requires recognition of both all the values behind providing an education to disabled students and the importance of the participation of multiple actors who try, from their different positions, to recognize these values.

Diana Hess is the dean of the School of Education at the University of Wisconsin–Madison and the Karen A. Falk Distinguished Professor of

Education. She researches how young people learn about controversial political issues.

Professor Hess thanks Dr. Steve Klein and Mary Ellen Schaffer, two very experienced and savvy educators, for their thoughtful insights about morally complex situations involving special education. She also is appreciative of the extensive feedback that Colin Ong-Dean provided on earlier drafts.

From Interests to Membership

Jacob Fay

In contending with Kate's impending meltdown, Ms. Brown ostensibly faces a choice between prioritizing Kate's interests over the interests of other students in the class, or prioritizing the other students' interests over Kate's interests. She could isolate Kate in the "Think Room" and keep the class going, or she could change the dynamic of either the groups or the entire class in hopes of keeping Kate from losing control. Yet, in my view, approaching Ms. Brown's decision as between conflicting interests ultimately obscures an equally pressing value: membership. She ought to be concerned first and foremost with the status of Kate's membership in the classroom and the effect preemptively removing Kate will have on that status. Once our focus settles on membership, it becomes clear Kate's interests and those of her classmates overlap more than we would likely suppose. Acknowledging such overlap suggests a range of actions that Ms. Brown, and for that matter, Mr. Thomason, might take that emphasize the particular value of membership.

FRAGILE MEMBERSHIP

First, consider what we know about Kate's actual inclusion in Ms. Brown's class. Rivers Elementary placed Kate in an Emotional Support class in second grade, and she began her third-grade year in that class as well. This seems for good reason; Kate was aware that she frequently lost control, acknowledging it as only a child might in her request to wear slippers to school. Yet Kate has worked hard to return to a "regular" classroom, gradually transitioning from the Emotional Support class to Ms. Brown's classroom. Ms. Brown—a strong advocate for Kate—has worked equally hard preparing her other students for Kate's inclusion in class, even spending time talking to them about the importance of valuing forms of difference.

Even so, Kate's inclusion in Ms. Brown's class appears to be, in some respects, *fragile*. That is to say, because of Kate's behavioral volatility, her inclusion in the class seems predicated on whether she has earned and continues to earn her spot in the class through appropriate behavior. Ms. Brown's decision is particularly salient because it can serve to reinforce or undermine the status of Kate's membership in the class.

Now, imagine Ms. Brown decides to send Kate to the Think Room. She could justify this decision on the grounds that it promotes Kate's safety and preempts a meltdown. Indeed, Kate's parents seem to approve of the use of the Think Room as a space for Kate to go when school overwhelms her, and Kate herself finds the room safe. Ms. Brown could also justify this decision based on the interests of the other students; Kate's behavior could potentially change the tenor of the class's investigation of rocks, even derailing the entire exercise. There are plenty of seemingly good reasons to choose this option.

Yet, regardless of the justification, Ms. Brown would seem to throw Kate's already fragile membership further into doubt. In particular, sending Kate to the Think Room *before* an outburst—even though signs are pointing toward one—indicates that she is treated differently than her classmates in a way with which we should not be comfortable.

Preemptive exclusion ignores or devalues two important choices that Kate has made—choices that indicate she is trying to learn how to manage herself. First, Kate chose to come to school even though she had a rough night because she was keen on categorizing rocks. Second, she chose to stay in the group rather than move when Ms. Brown offers her that option. By downplaying the importance of these choices, preemption may undermine Kate's ability to learn how to manage her emotions and behavior.

On perhaps a more fundamental level, Ms. Brown also signals that Kate's presence in the classroom is highly conditional. Kate may remain only if her presence does not conflict with the interests of her classmates and she poses no safety risks to her classmates (or herself). Such reasons, in particular, treat Kate as a liminal problem to be managed rather than a full member of the class.

RETHINKING THE INTERESTS AT STAKE

Surely teachers do not want disruptive or unsafe students in the classroom, and Ms. Brown has to deal with Kate accordingly if and when her behavior becomes disruptive or unsafe. But in sending Kate out preemptively, the ways in which the classroom environment contribute to Kate's sudden downturns remain obscured.

In this instance, for example, Kate's two partners quarreling about whether one particular rock is igneous or metamorphic may be more problematic than we suppose. Their quarrel, while intellectually engaging, has upset a group dynamic in which Kate was engaged and has left her feeling uncomfortable. Why should Kate be excluded so their group work can continue? Does the fact that they are engaged with the substance of the lesson trump the fact that their argument has isolated one of their group members, thus making group work into partner work? This, too, seems to undermine the goals of categorizing rocks in small groups. To question such thinking suggests the importance of thinking about membership; it values Kate's inclusion in the class and locates her struggles in shared social space as well as in her own behavior.

To truly include Kate as a member of the class challenges the idea that Ms. Brown needs to balance Kate's interests against those of her classmates. Rather, taking care of Kate may also mean taking care of the group; taking care of the group may also mean taking care of Kate.

This has implications for Ms. Brown's choice of action. She might talk to Kate's partners about how their behavior has changed the dynamic of their group to the detriment of one of their members. Doing so would call attention to other facets of the lesson that are part of the implicit curriculum—learning to work cooperatively and collectively. Or, Ms. Brown might try to diffuse the quandary by sharing the group's challenge with the whole class, hopefully easing the tension that is agitating Kate. Both instances may support Kate and help her classmates, either through learning about the dynamics of group work or by addressing a potentially challenging example of the genetic classification of rocks. These suggestions are meant to illustrate that there may be no single right action for Ms. Brown to take, but rather a range of options that all recognize the importance of membership.

FROM CLASSROOM TO SCHOOL

Additionally, reframing the case in this matter also has implications for the principal, Mr. Thomason. In the case, Mr. Thomason's directive to Ms. Brown compounds and constrains her possible actions. But given the purposes of a case discussion, it is possible and important to rewind back to *his* decision point: how should Mr. Thomason have responded to the parents' concerns about Kate's participation in class?

Consider the reasons he offers the concerned parents: first, the school is legally bound to serve Kate in the least restrictive environment possible; and second, Ms. Brown is an experienced teacher. Knowingly or not, Mr. Thomason again treats Kate as a problem to be managed and, moreover, legitimizes the parents' perception that Kate's interests are opposed to their own children's interests. If he were to emphasize the importance of membership, Mr. Thomason might alternatively frame his response by drawing on some of the same suggestions mentioned above. He might be explicit about the social and emotional learning that takes place within the classroom, and explain that from such a perspective, Kate and her classmates have much to learn from and about each other. In short, he has a range of new reasons to support Kate's inclusion in the class.

Now, Mr. Thomason suggests that he is responsible not only for the students in Ms. Brown's classroom, but also for all students at Rivers. Thus, it seems plausible to think that his view of membership may play out on a different level—at that of the school—as opposed to Ms. Brown's, whose primary concern is presumably her own classroom. At the school level, it appears that Kate is not a liminal member; she is not at risk of leaving Rivers. Indeed, the school is seemingly accommodating Kate's needs by creating a separate space for her.

However, the notion of membership questions the use of separate spaces. Such spaces, while potentially serving a reasonable purpose, may still marginalize some children when they ought not to. The very structure of "regular" and "Emotional Support" classes perhaps contributes to the fragility of Kate's membership in the first place. Shouldn't all classrooms be emotionally supportive spaces? Thus, even though Mr. Thomason may view this case from a broader perspective than Ms. Brown, a more robust commitment to membership could prompt Mr. Thomason to consider redesigning and reorganizing the school itself to be more inclusive.

FINAL THOUGHTS

In following this line of thought, it becomes clear that the notion of membership is fairly demanding. Not only does the value of membership place pressure on Ms. Brown to make inclusive decisions with regard to the students in her class—including but not limited to Kate—it also suggests that Mr. Thomason should consider how Rivers could be reconceived to be inclusive from the start, and how he should work with parents to understand why this is the case. None of these are easy tasks. Moreover, accepting that Kate is a full member of the class does not solve everything. Kate clearly needs support in ways that her classmates do not. What kind (or what degree) of differential treatment does this merit, and how should differentiation be meshed with membership?

I have suggested that, at the very least, acknowledging the overlap of Kate and her classmates' interests entails molding the classroom environment to support Kate and attempting inclusive solutions before exclusive solutions. However, there is a great deal of subtlety in such decisions, which

I have only begun to explore here. Indeed, such decisions may ultimately derive more from the experiences of veteran practitioners than from abstract analysis.

Jacob Fay is a doctoral student at the Harvard Graduate School of Education whose work focuses on the ethics of education policy and practice. Prior to serving as coeditor of this volume, Fay was cochair of the board for the Harvard Educational Review.

CHAPTER THREE

Stolen Trust

Cell Phone Theft in a Zero-Tolerance High School

KAILEY BURGER AND MEIRA LEVINSON

North High School (NHS) is one of two high schools in a low-income suburb of St. Louis, part of the ring of historically working-class but now increasingly impoverished towns that surround the city.[1] Annual photos of the senior class lining the stairwells tell the story of a school that has undergone significant transition in recent decades. Photos from the 1970s and 1980s show senior classes that are predominantly White; records from 1984, for instance, indicate that NHS was about 60 percent White and about 33 percent African American, with a smattering of other students. About 35 percent of students that year were eligible for subsidized lunch. The 2014 graduating class, by contrast, was about 85 percent African American, 10 percent White, and 5 percent other (Latino, Asian, Pacific Islander, or multiracial). At least two-thirds were eligible for free or reduced-price lunch. Over the same period, as the NHS student body "flipped" from minority to majority African American and from working class to poor, the tax base collapsed. School district revenues plummeted. NHS's academic standing fell, and the school became a known site of gang activity.

In 2003, in response to increased disciplinary problems at the school and a nationwide trend toward rigid control of student behavior following the massacre at Columbine High School in Colorado, the school board adopted a "zero-tolerance" code of conduct for student discipline. This policy mandated specific consequences for defined violations rather than leaving punishments up to teachers' discretion. Students who cursed in class, for example, earned an automatic after-school detention; leaving class without permission was punished by in-school suspension. The zero-tolerance policy also required that teachers immediately report theft, violence—including "horseplay"—and the presence of prohibited substances or weapons to the main office. Depending on the nature and frequency of the offense, students might be suspended from school for a minimum of three days; they also risked being expelled and/or being remanded to the police for potential criminal prosecution in juvenile or adult courts.

Teachers themselves were subject to zero-tolerance consequences for diverging from the discipline code, as they were contractually obligated to comply with these reporting policies. If they failed to uphold the zero-tolerance mandates, they faced sanctions ranging from poor reports in their personnel file to suspension without pay to termination of employment. In the first months of implementation, NHS faculty were frequently "written up" by the administration for such failures, and some even had their pay docked. Two respected, nontenured teachers who openly opposed zero-tolerance policies did not have their contracts renewed at the end of that first year. Faculty members had generally complied with the mandates ever since.

Over the following decade, NHS settled down both disciplinarily and academically. Despite significant decreases in disciplinary issues over time, however, zero-tolerance mandates remained constant. This led to what many teachers viewed as disproportionate punishment for "kids just being kids." Frustrated teachers shared stories with one another about how their "hands were tied" by zero-tolerance policies. They said they felt coerced into reporting students for behaviors that could have been resolved without administrative involvement and without such harsh penalties.

North High School's principal and its dean of discipline were aware of these complaints. They warned teachers against taking them public, however, reminding teachers that they risked being fired for insubordination if they failed to follow the regulations or criticized the zero-tolerance policies in front of students. Principal Jackson also emphasized his belief that NHS's zero-tolerance policies were responsible for keeping disciplinary challenges to a relative minimum at the school. Rather than focus on the few, visible cases in which students suffered "disproportionate" punishment for their actions, Mr. Jackson suggested, teachers needed to recognize the many invisible cases in which students likely would have done wrong under another system, but instead chose to do the right thing because they knew the consequences would be severe if they stepped out of line.

Administrators, teachers, and students all agreed that there was a "race, class, and gender" element to the zero-tolerance policies, although they disagreed about what that meant or how it played out. Researchers consistently find that zero-tolerance policies are far more common at majority-minority and low-income schools than they are at middle-class and/or majority-White schools. They also implicate zero-tolerance policies in the "school-to-prison pipeline," producing rates of suspension, expulsion, and criminalization of Black, brown, and poor children—especially boys—that are wildly disproportionate to those for middle-class and White children. Many of the teachers and some of the students at the school pointed to this data when muttering about the continued imposition of zero-tolerance measures at NHS.

At the administrative level, however, a different analysis was often put forward. As is the case nationwide, the vast majority of NHS's teachers were White, female, and middle class. By contrast, Mr. Jackson, two of the school's four vice-principals, and the dean of discipline all identified as African American men. Mr. Jackson spoke openly at leadership team meetings, faculty meetings, and student assemblies about the dangers young Black men face in a racist society. After Trayvon Martin's death, he invited parents, teachers, and students to an assembly in which he talked about how NHS was trying to keep students safe; the zero-tolerance policy was high on the list. Two years later, Mr. Jackson addressed protests in nearby Ferguson following Michael Brown's shooting death. In a booming voice, he told NHS students, "Take one step out of line, and you may not get a second chance. Boom, you're dead, that's it. I don't want any more Black mothers wailing for their sons who will never return. My goal is to keep you alive, march you across this stage, and into college and career. You don't like the punishments I dish out? Then just follow the rules, gentlemen, follow the rules."

Jennifer Smith was in the auditorium that day and felt she understood where Mr. Jackson was coming from. Ms. Smith—petite, White, twenty-five years old and recently married—was in her third year as an eleventh-grade history teacher at NHS. She had come straight from earning her BA in secondary education at a local college. As an undergraduate, she had spent time observing and student teaching in one middle school and two high schools in the area. The disorder that characterized all three of those schools had left her both exhausted and angry. Neither students nor teachers could ever truly focus on the work of learning and teaching because they always seemed on tenterhooks about whether chaos might break out—if not inside the building, then as students walked to and from home. She herself had been warned not to stay at school past sundown, a restriction she found difficult to follow when the winter sky dimmed to gray black well before five o'clock. Ms. Smith appreciated Mr. Jackson's emphasis on order, therefore, even if she also chafed at the specific rules that made up NHS's code of conduct.

On the last day before winter break, however, Ms. Smith's commitment to the system was shaken. For the first time, she felt she truly understood her colleagues' protests against the zero-tolerance regulations.

It had been a tough semester. Unusually for her, Ms. Smith had struggled that fall to build a positive relationship with a student. She had always compensated for her petite stature—and her risk of being taken as one of the students—by project-ing a bold personality. Funny, empathetic, wise to the ways of adolescents, and on top of the latest cultural references and trends, Ms. Smith was good at con-necting quickly with her students. They liked and respected her, probably because she clearly conveyed that she liked and respected them. She usually found a way to reach students others found challenging, and had never before found herself locked in a power struggle with one, as some of her colleagues had.

Wesley was different. Tall, handsome, seventeen years old, with chocolate skin and a ready grin, Wesley paired a promising intellect with defiant behavior. He had been suspended so frequently in ninth and tenth grade that the dean of discipline had been on the verge of expelling him. He had also had a few skirmishes with the police. But Wesley always seemed to know how to take it to the edge with-out going over. Unfortunately for Ms. Smith, Wesley applied similar insights to her classroom. As often as she reached out to him, he rejected her. He engineered new skirmishes virtually on a daily basis. Ms. Smith tried all her tricks, but to no avail. By midterm, not only had Ms. Smith failed to connect with him, she had also failed to teach him. He earned an F in history on his first-quarter report card.

Fortunately, the risk of having to repeat eleventh-grade history gave Ms. Smith a small opening to convince Wesley to begin staying after school. Wesley seemed shocked Ms. Smith wanted him to stay—in particular for tutoring, rather than for detention. "Don't you just want to get rid of me, miss?" he asked. "You got a nice house and husband to go home to, right? You don't need to hang with hard-head-ed kids like me." Ms. Smith persisted nonetheless, and started meeting with Wesley two afternoons a week to catch him up on the world history he had missed.

The one-on-one tutoring proved a turning point. From the end of October through mid-December, Ms. Smith and Wesley made tremendous strides with re-spect to his grades, his classroom demeanor, and their relationship. They had some bumps along the way, but Ms. Smith understood that for Wesley, testing her com-mitment and her patience was a way of protecting himself. He had not experienced many relationships with adults who stuck by him. He clearly worried about making himself vulnerable to another adult only to watch her reject him if he made a mis-take. So she persevered even when he pushed back—and eventually, he seemed to stop testing her. By December, she felt that they had developed a high level of mutual trust. Wesley confided to Ms. Smith about the adult responsibilities and stress he faced at home. They both knew she couldn't do much directly to help, but even offering him a sympathetic ear seemed to relieve his burdens somewhat.

During their last afterschool meeting before winter break, Wesley was in the middle of talking about his vacation plans when a teacher called Ms. Smith out into the hall. She left the classroom briefly. Then she returned to finish her meeting with Wesley. "So, you were telling me how you planned to work full-time during break to help your mom," she said sympathetically.

"Yeah, it's cool, though. Listen, I gotta get home, okay?" Wesley responded. Ms. Smith was surprised by his sudden eagerness to leave, but attributed it to a typical teenage short attention span. It made sense, too, that he would want to start his vacation—even if that meant double shifts at the local dollar store. So she sent him on his way, then stayed at her desk for another hour finishing up final grades for the semester. Ms. Smith took particular pleasure in marking a B in the grade book for Wesley, who had achieved a remarkable transformation in just two months.

Walking out the door, Ms. Smith reached into her purse for her cell phone. She stopped in her tracks. She knew she had checked her messages right after school and put the phone in the outside pocket of her purse, but that pocket was empty. "Oh no," she thought, turning back toward her desk. She retraced her steps and emptied her bag—still nothing. Ms. Smith was starting to panic now. Fearing the worst, she headed to veteran teacher Laurie Hampton's classroom next door.

Ms. Smith explained the situation to Ms. Hampton, who took a defeated tone. "Ach, Jen, not another one? You know, Mr. Williams had his stolen last week by a ninth grader—the kid is gonna spend the holidays in juvenile court. Why do these kids keep doing this? They know it's an automatic suspension and police report."

Ms. Smith stared at her feet. "It doesn't make any sense," she said.

Ms. Hampton continued, "Look, I know you're more sympathetic than most, but you can't be naive. We all love these kids, but we also need our jobs, and the administration doesn't give us a choice on these cases. We have to report everything. That means major consequences—"

Ms. Smith stopped her, "I know, Laurie, I know."

Ms. Hampton softened. "I'm sorry, I know this is hard. Look, Jen, it may not be fair, but with this zero-tolerance crap, we have to be really careful. The kids are always going to test us, and that's why we have to lock up our phones. Especially your iPhone. What's that worth, $600? That's a class C felony." Ms. Hampton gave a self-conscious laugh. "Listen to me, quoting the Missouri criminal code at you. The things you learn as a teacher these days . . . Anyway, you gotta be proactive. Protect our students by protecting yourself. Let them know that even though we care, our hands are tied."

On the way home, Ms. Smith tried to pull her thoughts together. Wesley had come such a long way. Could he still be testing her? She believed they had gotten beyond that, but maybe he still wondered how far she would stick by him. Or maybe, she thought, he was acting out because he was anxious about spending so much time at home during break. That made sense—but it didn't excuse his actions. Wesley had to realize there were consequences for theft. She didn't want him treated as a criminal, though, which is exactly what would happen if she turned Wesley in. Mr. Jackson would send the case straight to the police, she was sure. Given his prior record, Wesley wouldn't be shown any leniency; as a seventeen-year-old, he would be treated like any other adult in the system. That didn't feel right—especially if he was just testing the strength of their relationship in the messed-up way that teenagers could. And maybe she was at fault, too, for leaving her iPhone unsecured. Had she set him up to fail? No, that didn't seem right, either. She couldn't blame herself for his choosing to steal.

Ms. Smith's thoughts turned to North High School in particular. She really liked teaching at NHS. She admired her colleagues' dedication, and appreciated Mr. Jackson's unswerving commitment to fostering a safe environment where students could focus on learning. She did not believe in the zero-tolerance approach, exactly, but she did feel it was only because the administration ran such a tight ship that she could make a difference in the lives of kids like Wesley. Maybe NHS could adopt a more nuanced discipline policy in the long term, one that permitted more teacher discretion and even student participation. In the meantime, though, she could protect Wesley from likely expulsion and prosecution only by subverting the school's policy. How could subversion be right? Wouldn't she be undermining the conditions that made it possible for her to teach effectively? On the other hand, she thought bitterly, she would not get to teach Wesley anything at all if he was sitting in prison rather than in her junior world history class.

As she pulled into her driveway, Ms. Smith caught sight of her husband nailing a loose board on their front porch. They relied on her income to cover bills, she reflected, while he trained to become a paramedic. They also hoped to start a family soon. It was daunting to think of having her pay docked, let alone losing her job—although she was pretty sure Mr. Jackson would not fire her. They got along well. But that could change, she realized, if she did not report Wesley and the school found out. She was proud of being a teacher. Could she really conceive of sacrificing her professional standing, or even undermining her career, for the sake of a single kid—one who had, after all, stolen her iPhone—even if she thought that the zero-tolerance policy was wrong?

With such high stakes for her and for Wesley, what should Ms. Smith do?

The Challenge of Responding
to Injustice

TOMMIE SHELBY

On its face, Ms. Smith's dilemma seems to be about how to fulfill her formal obligations both to her students and to her administrative supervisors
(school board and principal) within an educational bureaucracy. But this
perspective fails to subject educational institutions themselves—as well as
such institutions' relationships to the broader social order—to appropriate
moral scrutiny. What matters first of all are the injustices that pervade society as a whole. Rather than focusing on Ms. Smith's professional responsibilities within the school, therefore, we should focus on her more general
duties as a relatively privileged member of a profoundly unjust society. Seen
in this context, Ms. Smith must determine how she can do two things: promote the establishment of a more just social order, and ease the burdens of
the unjustly disadvantaged. The first poses practical difficulties, but no deep
moral dilemma. The second is more morally challenging, as it potentially
pits her justified self-interest against her duties to ease Wesley's burdens.

DUTIES IN AN UNJUST SOCIAL ORDER

Ms. Smith and Wesley live their lives as fellow citizens within a structured
social order. The justice or injustice of this social order affects our responsibilities to each other and to the institutions that claim authority over us.
We should, on grounds of reciprocity and civic duty, support and comply
with the rules of a just social order. But we don't have an obligation to obey
the rules of a seriously unjust society or its basic institutions. This is so even
if we have said we would uphold the regulations, as Ms. Smith did when
she signed her teaching contract. Agreement to comply with the rules of
an unjust social practice does not bind one. Before we ask what Ms. Smith
should do about Wesley, therefore, we need to ask whether the basic institutions of US society are arranged in a way that is fair to all who are under
its claimed jurisdiction.

Among the most important social institutions is the public education
system. A just education system enables individuals to participate as equal
citizens in a democratic society, equips students to participate in and benefit

from economic life, and develops their talents and abilities so that they can pursue a life that they find worthwhile. An education system within a just social order also helps to ensure that citizens have roughly equal life prospects. Their class backgrounds, for example, should not inhibit their ability to pursue a meaningful life or interfere with their ability to compete on fair terms for employment and other valuable social positions.

Although educational institutions play a crucial role in maintaining social justice, they are unable to establish a just social order on their own. Dedicated teachers and well-designed schools may be able to mitigate the harms created by injustices elsewhere in society, but they cannot fully cancel them out. We must therefore also attend to the broader social framework within which schools are embedded. We should consider, for example, how schools interact with employment and housing opportunities, neighborhood dynamics, the distribution of wealth in society, and the operation of the criminal justice system.

On all of these grounds, there is overwhelming evidence that the social structure that kids like Wesley face is deeply unjust in ways that far outstrip the unfairness and inadequacies of our education system.[2] In light of this, Ms. Smith's first obligations pertain not so much to her role as a teacher, but to her role as a citizen within an unjust social order, a society that falls below any reasonable standard for tolerable injustice. What should be her posture toward such a society?

As I argued above, she has good reason *not* to comply with the demands of the basic institutions of society, including its education system, when this compliance would clearly exacerbate social injustice and add to the unjust burdens of the oppressed. Knowing the costs to the vulnerable of going along with the rules, Ms. Smith would show a lack of empathy with those most negatively affected by the social order were she simply to submit to these demands out of a sense of professional duty. Such acquiescence would also express insufficient regard for the requirements of social justice.

Under unjust conditions, Ms. Smith's duties are twofold. First, she must do her part to make the society she and Wesley both share a more just one. Second, she should ease Wesley's own burdens if she can, as he is profoundly disadvantaged by social injustices, and her decision will deeply impact his future prospects.

THE DUTY OF JUSTICE

How might Ms. Smith fulfill her first obligation, her duty of justice? She would be justified in registering her political dissent by acting in defiance of the society's rules and expectations provided this would serve some useful purpose. However, she can't reform the society on her own. She needs allies, and perhaps even a social movement, to be able to fundamentally change things.

Therefore, it might be better for her to not risk losing her job and to continue working at the school, fighting to change its policies and counseling her students to avoid breaking its rules. If she were to quit on principle, this would have symbolic value (particularly if she made her objections publicly known), but she would thereby lose her standing as a teacher at the school and within the school district, which would undercut her ability to effect change from within the system. If she stays but conceals Wesley's violation, she risks being found out and thus impairing her relationship with Mr. Jackson, who, while sympathetic to her concerns, will likely feel insulted by her defiance and will probably trust her less in the future.

Her decision should turn on what, all things considered, would most likely enhance just social relations. This is no doubt a difficult question with a number of practical considerations to take into account. But it does not represent a moral dilemma.

THE DUTY TO EASE BURDENS OF THE UNJUSTLY DISADVANTAGED

In regard to the second obligation (her duty to ease the burdens of the unjustly disadvantaged), a moral dilemma remains—namely, how large a self-sacrifice is it reasonable to make to protect the unjustly disadvantaged? This, of course, depends on, among other things, how dire the situation of the oppressed happens to be.

Wesley and his family likely face many forms of social injustice: inadequate access to childcare and health care, lack of employment opportunities, racial and class-based discrimination, an unsafe neighborhood and limited access to affordable housing, substandard public services, and so on. But perhaps the most pertinent in this instance is the operation of the criminal justice system.

There is much research to suggest that the US criminal justice system is grossly unfair in practice, particularly to the Black urban poor.[3] Wesley is vulnerable to many of these injustices if his case is remanded to the police. First, although he is an adolescent whose brain is probably not fully developed, Wesley will wrongly be treated by the justice system as an adult. Second, Wesley is very unlikely to have access to competent legal counsel. Third, if convicted of a crime, he is likely to get an overly severe punishment. Fourth, Wesley faces profound physical, emotional, and psychological risks while incarcerated within a juvenile detention center or, worse, a prison. Fifth, his overall life prospects will be grim if he's convicted of a felony and goes to jail, since without even a high school diploma and with a criminal record, his chances of finding a decent job or even adequate housing will be vanishingly small.

These are the kinds of considerations Ms. Smith must weigh when deciding whether to report the theft of her phone. If the cost to her is simply a reprimand or docked pay, then she should probably run the risk—a small price to pay to save a kid's life.

But I don't believe Ms. Smith has a duty to sacrifice her job and livelihood by quitting or risking termination (which would also negatively affect her spouse, and thus possibly her relationship with him). Wesley, while a victim of injustice, is one disadvantaged student among many, and Ms. Smith's staying at the school and maintaining good relations with its administrators, even under its objectionable zero-tolerance policy, may help other students to escape Wesley's fate.

I would admire Ms. Smith if she did run the personal risk of protecting Wesley despite—actually, precisely because of—her not having the moral obligation to do so. But at the same time, it may not serve the broader cause of justice to lose another committed and effective teacher from a school that serves the interests of poor Black children.

Tommie Shelby is the Caldwell Titcomb Professor of African and African American Studies and professor of philosophy at Harvard University. He is currently completing a book titled Dark Ghettos: Injustice, Dissent, and Reform *(Harvard University Press, forthcoming).*

Thinking Creatively in a Bind

JEFFREY SMITH

The case is presented as a binary one, with two unappetizing choices for Ms. Smith: either violate school policy and let a student (Wesley) steal an expensive item without consequence, or immediately report the student's infraction, a course of action that will likely result in Wesley's incarceration.

The first choice compromises Ms. Smith's integrity by having her stay silent despite her knowing with near certainty that Wesley has stolen her phone. Neither does this choice serve Wesley well; by failing to take action regarding her stolen phone, she would be signaling to Wesley that he can flout rules without consequence.

The second choice compromises Wesley's safety and his future by exposing him to the possibility of prosecution, and even prison. Moreover, it reduces Ms. Smith's ability to forge connections with other students in the building, since after Wesley is expelled, other students will likely label her a snitch. If the theft is reported to police and Wesley is ultimately prosecuted and incarcerated, remaining students would be even less likely to trust Ms. Smith. This does not mean that teachers should never report student infractions, but the consequences of this course of action must be considered.

BREAKING OUT OF THE BINARY

But there is a third possible choice. Ms. Smith can call Wesley and tell him that she believes she has misplaced her phone, but that she is pretty certain that the last time she had it was during their tutoring session. "Have you seen it?" she may ask. "If it's not located in the next twenty-four hours, then I'll need to report it stolen. I'd sure hate to have to do that," she might say, ominously, "because we both know Mr. Jackson is no joke. In any case, have a nice break—call if you need anything. And let me know in the next twenty-four hours if you have any information about my phone."

Practically speaking, this approach accomplishes a few things. It lets Wesley know that she knows he has betrayed her. It gives Wesley a second chance to return the phone without consequence. It also ensures that she is not technically violating school policy, since she is not expressing certainty that he has stolen her phone.

Should Ms. Hampton decide to immediately report Wesley, Mr. Jackson would be unlikely to discipline Ms. Smith for violating school policy since she can say that she didn't want to accuse Wesley of something that she wasn't completely sure he had done—perhaps she had taken her phone on a brief trip to the bathroom or faculty lounge and misplaced it there. That she investigated by calling Wesley to press him regarding her phone's whereabouts would demonstrate that she was doing her due diligence.

Such an approach would not compromise Ms. Smith's core values; she would neither be enabling criminality nor consigning her troubled young charge to a likely prison stint. By calling Wesley to investigate—while implicitly suggesting that she knows he's the culprit and will get caught—she's communicating to him that she's no pushover and does not plan to let him off scot-free simply because they've established a rapport.

On a concrete level, by urging him to call if he needs anything over break, she's implying that if he or his family is in a serious financial bind that led to his theft, he could call her and perhaps obtain help. On a psychological level, she's telling him that she knows he made a mistake, but she still cares about him and won't abandon him.

SMALLER WRONGS TO PREVENT BIGGER WRONGS— AN AUTOBIOGRAPHICAL PERSPECTIVE

Some personal background may illuminate my thinking.

At age twenty-two, while working as an evaluator in the St. Louis Public Schools, I moonlighted as an ACT and SAT test-prep instructor for Kaplan, where I taught a high school senior who was a top-flight Division I basketball recruit. He lived in the projects; his summer league team paid his Kaplan tuition. Despite his 3.0 high school GPA, his original ACT score was lower than the likely score of someone guessing randomly. After months of reading *Sports Illustrated* together a word at a time in his apartment, he earned a high enough score to attend Villanova on a full scholarship and later play pro ball.

Having seen how a single test score could change a kid's life trajectory, I created a tutoring program for disadvantaged high school athletes. My goal was to help them earn scores above the threshold necessary for freshman eligibility so they could take advantage of college scholarship offers. I made copies of Kaplan's copyrighted materials, telling myself that Kaplan was already raking in profits; also, Kaplan wasn't losing business, since these kids couldn't afford a $1,000 class in any case. (I charged $50, the cost of photocopies.) On the other hand, if these students became NCAA Proposition 48 casualties and lost scholarship offers, many would quit high school. The statistics for Black male high school dropouts were grimly clear: unemployment and likely brushes with the law. Here were some kids with the chance to escape, I reasoned, and since Kaplan wasn't losing business, no one was getting hurt.

In five years I taught over a hundred athletes, many of whom went on to earn Division I scholarship offers. In so doing, I violated both Kaplan policy and federal copyright law. I prioritized my values (educational advancement for those in need) over those of the institution (profit and procedure). I did so because I knew that if I were to approach the center director and ask if I could borrow the materials to help poor kids who needed to take the course, at best he would have offered them a $100 discount. But these students could no more afford $900 than they could afford $1,000 for a class.

How can we construct systems and regimens that allow teachers like I was, and teachers like Ms. Smith, to exercise compassion without undermining the system?

Questions such as these made me want to change the system, motivating me to cofound a group of charter schools where I could help create a more flexible system, and later inspiring me to run for office. A decade after my time at Kaplan, then, I was a White state senator representing a largely impoverished, majority-Black district with one of the nation's highest crime rates. Five years later, I spent a year as a prisoner myself after pleading guilty to federal charges of obstructing justice. I thus found myself in a criminal justice system that disproportionately imprisons young Black men because of mandatory minimum and drug sentencing laws that pretend to be color-blind, but operate in color-coded ways.

In both roles, one in which I wielded policy-making power and one in which I lacked basic freedoms, I saw profound unfairness in the treatment of young Black men like Wesley who had committed low-level, nonviolent crimes. Due to the highly publicized 2014 and 2015 police-involved killings of Michael Brown, Eric Garner, Walter Scott, Freddie Gray, Tamir Rice, and other young Black males, the lethal consequences of such inequities are now visible on a national scale.

SECOND—BUT NOT THIRD—CHANCES

Given this context, I believe that Ms. Smith should give Wesley a second chance to avoid entanglement with a justice system that many Americans now realize often operates so unjustly.

But, given the second chance, what will Wesley do? In the near term, there are three possibilities. First, Wesley could return the phone and say that he found it, or invent some other story. Second, Wesley could return the phone and apologize. Third, Wesley could keep the phone.

If Wesley chooses #1, Ms. Smith can refrain from reporting Wesley, but pointedly let him know that she will be keeping her eye on him.

If Wesley chooses #2, Ms. Smith can accept the phone and the apology, reassure Wesley that she will continue to help him, but that she demands honesty at all times, and emphasize that if he violates another rule, she will report him immediately.

If Wesley chooses #3, she must report him.

Each recommendation for Ms. Smith to Wesley's possible responses is different, and yet each comports with a simple principle by which I have always operated as an educator—namely, give second chances, but don't give third chances. I have found this to be a valuable principle to follow, whether overseeing elementary school students at one of the St. Louis charter schools I cofounded, or teaching disadvantaged high school students in college test prep courses, or mentoring relatively privileged graduate students in my current role as a New School professor.

PRIORITIZING THE INDIVIDUAL, NOT THE INSTITUTION

This principle does not offer ironclad guidance in all situations, of course. What if another student—one without the personal connection to Ms. Smith—does something similar to what Wesley did? In this case, Ms. Smith may choose whether or not to apply these principles in a similar fashion. I do think that unless a student's initial offense involved physical harm or danger to another person, she should look for creative ways to give them a second chance without seriously endangering her own job. But I do not believe she is obliged to do so, and every case will present its own wrinkles.

While some may find such differential treatment problematic, these differences are inevitable. Teachers are not assembly-line workers churning out widgets. Rather, they are highly trained professionals operating in a fluid environment, responsible for nonstandardized but extremely valuable human beings. Accordingly, they must be given some discretion in sensitive matters.

Finally, these recommendations are consistent with the principle that teachers should prioritize their individual student's interests when those conflict with institutional compliance and impersonal rules and regulations.

Wesley, for example, would likely learn to do right more from a second chance than he would from an encounter with the authorities, which would likely have a very unwelcome ending.

Jeffrey Smith is assistant professor of urban policy at The New School's Milano Graduate School, having previously served as a Missouri state senator, St. Louis public school evaluator, and charter school cofounder. His 2014 e-book, Ferguson in Black and White, *traces the history of race in St. Louis, and his forthcoming book,* Mr. Smith Goes to Prison *(St. Martin's), explores incarceration from the inside out.*

No Just Outcome

ELIZABETH ANDERSON

I would like to distinguish two levels of moral reasoning that correspond to two levels of moral ambivalence I feel about this case. One concerns the *role morality* of teachers in connection with the zero-tolerance school policy, and the merits of that policy. In her role as a teacher charged with enforcing an education policy with racially unjust outcomes, Ms. Smith faces competing moral obligations. The second concerns *considerations of morality* tied to human relationships independent of particular professional roles, and the tension between Ms. Smith's role as a school official and her personal and civic relationship to Wesley. Here, too, I believe she has duties to Wesley, Mr. Jackson, and her other students and colleagues that are difficult to satisfy simultaneously.

THE DEMANDS OF PROFESSIONAL ROLE MORALITY WHEN TEACHERS ARE TOLD TO ENFORCE UNJUST POLICIES

Let's start with education policy on its own terms. I am ambivalent in this case because the zero-tolerance policy simultaneously promotes one goal of justice while reinforcing a profoundly unjust system of racial subordination.

Schools with high numbers of disadvantaged children are schools with high numbers of children suffering from stress and disorderly home lives. Suffering from such conditions may cause children to act out in school, impairing their own learning as well as that of their classmates. To the extent that strict rules of orderly conduct are needed to create a school environment that promotes learning, they are demanded by justice. They are particularly important given that the children in question already suffer from inferior opportunities to develop their talents. On the evidence, it appears that stricter rules than usual play an important role in promoting learning at NHS. At the same time, the harshness and inflexibility of the penalties for disorderly conduct are hard to square with the demand to promote the interests of *all* children, *including those who misbehave.* Penalties administered by school officials—in-school detentions, suspensions, expulsions—deprive students of opportunities to learn, which can hardly promote the education of those who are punished.

In addition, the penalties are based on a deterrence theory that exaggerates many children's capacities to constrain their behavior through foresight of bad consequences. Such an approach fails to offer students constructive training in self-regulation techniques such as anger management and impulse control. Educators cannot presume that students have well-developed executive functions; rather, they must explicitly teach these skills in school. Disciplinary policies that primarily stress punitive deterrence fail in this task.

Even worse is the fact that the school outsources punishments to the criminal justice system, which, as Michelle Alexander and others have shown, systematically metes out harsher treatment to African Americans than Whites at every stage, and which in practice deprives them of due process protections. The system systematically ruins the lives of African Americans. It does so regardless of their guilt or innocence. It is also willfully indifferent to individuals' immaturity, mental disability, or other factors that would, under other circumstances, be taken into account to diminish their responsibility.[4]

Mr. Jackson justifies excessively harsh punishments on the grounds that, in a racist society, they are needed to protect African Americans from the worst the system metes out. His logic fails in two ways. First, to the extent that the school sends transgressors into the racist criminal justice system, it fails in its own terms. Roto-rooting the clogs in the school-to-prison pipeline is no way to stanch the flow. Second, it makes a false promise to the students. Mr. Jackson implies that if students obey the law and police, they will be protected from racist and other unjust treatment by the system. But even the innocent enjoy little protection from the racism of the system, and the guilty are treated far more harshly than can be justified.

Yet these policy considerations have less bearing on what Ms. Smith should do, qua teacher with professional role responsibilities, than one might think. Yes, the zero-tolerance policy is unjust in its excessive harshness and rigidity. And yes, the same benefits to learning could probably be achieved without such rigidity—in particular, without resorting to involving the police in the vast majority of cases, including this one. But Ms. Smith lacks the authority to make school policy. Her job is to follow it.

As a general matter, those hired to implement policy cannot permissibly violate it whenever they believe the results would be better. In addition, Ms. Smith, in particular, is a relatively inexperienced White teacher. She would reinforce deeply problematic ideas about race and authority if she were to disobey the orders of her superior, a Black principal with long experience in school administration who also carries authority in the Black community. Who is she to insist that she is right and he is wrong?

MORE THAN A TEACHER

Professional role responsibilities do not exhaust the moral considerations at stake for Ms. Smith, for she is not *only* a school official—she is also someone who forged a mutually trusting personal relationship with Wesley that went beyond the call of duty. While her personal relationship is inextricable from her professional relationship to Wesley, she is not merely a school functionary in relation to him. She cares about him personally; she cares about their relationship; and she has a compelling personal interest in trying to salvage it.

Furthermore, Ms. Smith has civic responsibilities separate from her roles as either teacher or mentor. In this civic role, she has general duties of justice to prevent another young African American man from being railroaded into the criminal justice system, which is likely to inflict harms on him that are wildly disproportionate to her loss of her cell phone.

Ms. Smith's other roles, as personal mentor and citizen, generate moral obligations that are in tension with the zero-tolerance policy and her role duty as a teacher to obey that policy. These make me morally ambivalent about the zero-tolerance policy in a second way. On one hand, it has helped to create a space in which some troubled students can succeed, precisely by enabling *supererogatory relationships* (meaning relationships that go beyond what is morally required). By securing order and the conditions for academic success, it frees teachers to do more than the basics for their students and motivates them to do so by giving them reason to believe that doing more will make a difference. On the other hand, it attempts to purge forgiveness and mercy from these relationships, thereby threatening to destroy them just at the points where troubled students need them most. Mercilessness is no basis for securing trust in relationships.

Ms. Smith's civic duties also conflict with the zero-tolerance policy. Justice demands that she oppose institutional racism. Ms. Smith should therefore do what she can to keep the matter out of the criminal justice system. This means advocating with Mr. Jackson not to report Wesley to the police, as I discuss below. But it also means refusing to cooperate with the police about the matter if it does get referred, since her lack of cooperation would likely make prosecution difficult. She has the right to refuse cooperation even if Mr. Jackson expects her to testify, because he has no authority to dictate to her, as victim of a crime, how she responds to Wesley, as the accused, in the criminal justice system.

MAKING THE BEST OF A BAD JOB

On a personal level, Ms. Smith is clearly entitled to an accounting from Wesley as to why he betrayed her trust, as well as an apology and reparations. If she called her cell phone right away, he might answer, and she might be able to persuade him to return it. That would likely be enough to keep the matter out of the courts, as there are no damages.

What about school-based sanctions? Assuming she could keep Wesley out of the criminal justice system even if she told Principal Jackson what she thinks happened, the case for following school policy, however misguided, is fairly strong. The principal has authority over school-based sanctions. Ms. Smith would discredit herself if she lied to cover for Wesley, making her unworthy of the trust the school leadership has placed in her.

Moreover, she has little chance of protecting Wesley by evading the school's disciplinary policy. She already let the cat out of the bag by telling Ms. Hampton of her suspicions. Ms. Hampton is likely to tell Principal Jackson what happened—or to tell other teachers, from whom word will eventually get around to Mr. Jackson.

In addition, if she lets Wesley off the hook, she undermines her authority with respect to her students. Wesley is unlikely to keep his theft and Ms. Smith's deception of Mr. Jackson a secret from his peers. That could embolden them to take advantage of her, leading to a loss of discipline and learning environment in her own classes.

This does not mean that Ms. Smith should merely hand Wesley over to Mr. Jackson and wash her hands of the affair. If Wesley takes responsibility both practically (by returning the phone or paying her back over time if the phone is already sold) and morally (by apologizing to her), she should help him out within the terms of school policy. This could involve making pleas on Wesley's behalf before Mr. Jackson, explaining how far he had come, how close he is to success, and asking for disciplinary actions short of expulsion.

In private conversation with Mr. Jackson, she should also point out the shortcomings of the zero-tolerance policy. She should stress how the disadvantaged, no less than the advantaged, need mercy as well as discipline. She should point out that schools do not protect students from a merciless system by extending the reach of mercilessness to the school's own domain.

She should explain that there is a real distinction between mercy and license, and that she is asking, not to let Wesley off the hook, but that his punishment not be outsourced to an institution that will ruin his life, or, if it is internal, that it not end his prospects for graduation.

If, despite her pleas, he is still expelled, she can continue to reach out and tutor him on the side.

Admittedly, none of these outcomes is fully just. But deception and covering up also have their costs, and some of them are likely to fall on Wesley in any event. There are limits to what teachers can and may do to protect students from the unjust consequences of their rash conduct.

Elizabeth Anderson is John Dewey Distinguished University Professor of Philosophy and Women's Studies at University of Michigan, Ann Arbor. She specializes in moral and political philosophy, social and feminist epistemology, and the philosophy of the social sciences, focusing on issues of inequality and social justice.

Agency, Bias, and Imagination in Doing Educational Justice

DAVID J. KNIGHT

Where does a teacher's agency begin and end in a school? In particular, what opportunities can teachers find or create to promote social justice in schools, given schools' deep history of injustice? As a teacher, I have wrestled with these questions on a regular basis. These questions also confront Ms. Smith as she ponders how to respond to her missing cell phone. These questions ask us to address our *agency* as autonomous decision makers (even in highly regulated settings), our risk of *bias* in assessing our students' actions and identities, and our capacity to *imagine* new forms of action and social relationships in order to disrupt biased and unjust systems. In particular, I believe that, for Ms. Smith, as for all teachers who are committed to justice, her (and our) *ability to create change lies most profoundly in how we choose to see, understand, and imagine our students and their possibilities.* This requires an active approach, in which teachers like Ms. Smith interrogate each step of the decision-making process in order to ensure that each choice truly enacts profound moral commitments.

HOW DO TEACHERS EXERCISE AGENCY?

To begin with, it is essential to realize that every teacher has the capacity and responsibility to exercise agency, even in highly regulated settings. Ms. Smith, for example, certainly faces many external demands and challenges, including St. Louis's and her school's own racialized educational histories and pressure to adhere to her school's harsh zero-tolerance policy. But like teachers around the country, she also retains significant autonomy in how she enacts her professional role day by day. Quite simply, Ms. Smith practices choice by connecting with students' social worlds as someone who is "wise to the ways of adolescents, and on top of the latest cultural references and trends." More importantly, Ms. Smith chooses to reach out to Wesley, to build a trusting relationship with him, and to work with him outside of class to bring up his grade. In short, Ms. Smith has agency because she not only wants Wesley to succeed, but also has taken personal steps to help him succeed in her classroom.[5]

Furthermore, at least at the outset of the case, Ms. Smith has a record of using her agency to promote educational justice. She has worked to disrupt Wesley's cycle of underachievement and disengagement in her class, to reengage him, and to invest in his academic growth. Ms. Smith has thus shown agency in *seeing* Wesley as a student who can succeed, in *positioning* herself as an ally for Wesley's success (as opposed to being a mere deliverer of curriculum content), and in *interacting* with him so as to support his own embrace of this positive portrait. These are dimensions of agency that all teachers possess, but that we also often undervalue. Our willingness to recognize, reach out, and partner with even our most challenging students is often in our control and represents half the battle.

HOW DOES BIAS PLAY INTO A TEACHER'S THOUGHTS AND ACTIONS?

Like most teachers, however, Ms. Smith's exercise of imaginative agency is imperfect, and in this case she all too readily succumbs to implicit and explicit biases that infuse the broader system in which she is operating. Although she sees the best in Wesley as a *learner*, she emphatically does not see the best in him as a *citizen;* rather, her inner dialogue in reaction to her lost phone reveals significant negative bias, in particular by inflexibly presuming Wesley's guilt. "Wesley had to realize there were consequences for theft," she says. Even when questioning her own culpability, Ms. Smith presumes guilt: "Had she set him up to fail? No . . . She couldn't blame herself for his choosing to steal."

It is, unfortunately, not surprising that Ms. Smith defaults to a presumption that Wesley is guilty. Her school context, in particular its zero-tolerance policy, frames students as constantly at risk of infraction or even criminality. Her closest colleague, Ms. Hampton, responds to Ms. Smith's concerns by immediately bringing up examples of other students who stole teachers' cell phones, rather than by asking if her phone might be elsewhere. Ms. Hampton even implies that the state criminal code is something one has to "learn as a teacher these days." The St. Louis metropolitan community, where North High School is located, is now notorious for its treatment of low-income Black youth as dangers to society. On a national level, too, evidence is overwhelming that teachers—especially White teachers—hold low expectations for students of color and poor students alike.[6]

So it is perhaps overdetermined that Ms. Smith ends up viewing Wesley as blameworthy in this instance. But this cannot excuse her bias. In simple terms, good intentions are not enough.

Instead, Ms. Smith needs to interrogate her bias—to ask herself why she presumes him guilty. Ms. Smith might ask herself:

- Are my suspicions about Wesley taking my cell phone consistent with how I've previously viewed him?
- Would I still suspect Wesley took the cell phone if he were a wealthy White student, a student without a disciplinary record, or a high-achieving student? What racial, class-based, or achievement-based biases do I carry, and how might they affect my trust in students?
- Is there a conflict of interest between protecting my job and ensuring justice for Wesley? If so, will/should it affect my decision?

I raise these questions not to apologize for Wesley if he is guilty, nor to suggest that it is uniformly wrong to question if a student is guilty of an infraction. Rather, I raise them because asking oneself what one would do in a variety of circumstances uncovers not only one's biases and inconsistencies, but also one's ethical commitments. If Ms. Smith believed Wesley innocent—if he held the position of a coworker, for instance—she would probably call him to ask where he last saw the phone, and do a much more thorough search, in addition to reporting the phone missing (but not stolen). I see no reason why Ms. Smith should not do the same here. By questioning her own assumptions that Wesley is inherently blameworthy, she opens up avenues for action that reflect a more nuanced and constructive approach.

HOW MIGHT A TEACHER'S IMAGINATION CREATE NEW POSSIBILITIES?

This deliberative process is the start of the imaginative work that is critical to "doing" educational justice. As a teacher, I am regularly humbled by how misguided our assumptions can be about students, especially when we assume misconduct. Doing what is counterintuitive—entertaining what is seemingly the less likely scenario—addresses this shortsightedness. Such acts of critical imagination also enable educators to exercise agency in an active way that reflects one's ethical commitments rather than in a manner that passively reinforces extant social biases and injustices.

I have already suggested that Ms. Smith would likely call Wesley to ask about her phone—and report her phone missing rather than stolen—if she were to imagine Wesley as potentially innocent rather than presumptively guilty. But this is only the first of her options for imaginative agency. As she critically reconstructs her attitudes, assumptions, and actions toward Wesley, she may come to question her need to report her missing phone at all. She may decide that reporting the incident betrays her commitment to Wesley by placing him at undue risk. She could seek assistance instead from Wesley's parent or guardian, or from a minister, coach, or mentor, to better understand his involvement before reporting the phone missing.

True, going this route would require Ms. Smith to step out of her school's sanctioned zero-tolerance policy, putting herself at some risk. But I doubt this is the first or the last time Ms. Smith will violate school policy; certainly every teacher I know (myself included) has made difficult decisions to honor the spirit rather than the letter of school policies in order to meet obligations to students. Besides, Ms. Smith is not breaking the law, only choosing not to follow a school policy. When confronted with dilemmas of justice, teachers must maneuver creatively through school system policies in order to maintain their own integrity and do what is right by their students. This is precisely the act of critical imagination for which I am calling; it enables teachers to overcome bias and exercise ethical agency. By imagining multiple paths and multiple outcomes, Ms. Smith may have a better sense of the opportunity costs present in her dilemma and where justice for Wesley and her own integrity fit in.

It is difficult to do educational justice in a context of uncertainty, strong social bias, and harsh school sanctions. It is perplexing work beyond the binaries of good and bad, right and wrong. Teachers therefore must adopt an alternative logic to what is often business as usual in schools, and reflect on the many possibilities of their actions. By examining their own perceptions and prejudices, in addition to weighing the consequences and opportunity costs of their decisions, teachers may come closer to addressing and redressing injustice, and thus closer to enacting justice for their students and for society as a whole.

David J. Knight is a former high school teacher and current doctoral student in the political science department at The University of Chicago. Focused on the intersections of race/ethnicity, gender, and class and the role of mass media in shaping antiracist politics among youth, he has published in several venues, including the Harvard Educational Review, The Atlantic, *and* The Washington Post.

Three Frames for Good Work

HOWARD GARDNER

By definition, an ethical dilemma is one that it is not easily or decisively resolved. True to type, the dilemma facing Ms. Smith eludes definitive or even satisfactory resolution. At best, any action or inaction that she might consider is flawed—a reason why several people to whom I posed the dilemma tried to rewrite it so that Ms. Smith did not have to make a tough decision. For example, they suggested that Ms. Smith could not be sure that Wesley had taken the phone, and so she is well advised just to forget the apparent theft.

In the end, I'll offer my advice to Ms. Smith based on the certainty that Wesley stole the phone. But before that, I will offer three different suggestions for ways we might conceptualize her situation. In the first, I draw upon Albert O. Hirschman's classic book *Exit, Voice, and Loyalty*.[7] In the second and third, I draw upon frameworks for understanding "good work" that my colleagues and I have been developing in recent years.[8] I suspect that these different analytic lenses may be at least as valuable as the specific recommendations with which I conclude.

EXIT, VOICE, AND LOYALTY

While developed primarily for analyzing encounters in the marketplace, Hirschman's *Exit, Voice, and Loyalty* has proved useful to many readers, including me, who are concerned with the best course of action when facing a conundrum. Here is my gloss on Hirschman.

Whenever a relation of any duration proves problematic, an agent can choose among three stances. She can remain *loyal* to the other party; she can *speak up* and lay out her objections; or in the extreme, she can choose to *leave* the situation altogether—perhaps by exiting quietly, or alternatively, by voicing the reasons for her decision.

In her current situation, it would probably be easiest for Ms. Smith simply to do and say nothing. In the specific instance, this course of action is a bit harder because she has spoken about the theft to Ms. Hampton. But there are various ways in which she could prevail on Ms. Hampton not to speak about the theft—for example, saying that she (Ms. Smith) had been mistaken. A lie, to be sure!

Turning to voice, Ms. Smith could confront Wesley directly about what he had done, and threaten him with consequences if he does not return the phone and reform his larcenous tendency. Or Ms. Smith could elect to report the theft and yet protest against the school's draconian policy—hoping against hope that Wesley would be given another chance.

Finally, Ms. Smith could choose to leave the school altogether, and to do so either silently or with a last hurrah. She is young and employable and can probably get another job—though I doubt that she would want to work again in such a challenging environment. Unless she wants to go straight into politics full-time, such a departure would be unlikely to change policy, though it might clear her conscience.

ETHICAL WORK

My second framework comes from two decades of investigation into what my colleagues and I have termed *good work*. We define *good work* as work that embodies three Es: it is technically *excellent* (the person knows what she is doing); the person is *engaged* (she cares about her work, she finds it meaningful, and she looks forward to another work week); and the person behaves in an *ethical* manner. In the present instance, we will assume that Ms. Smith embodies the first two Es and is struggling about how to proceed ethically in a dicey situation.

As a teacher, Ms. Smith faces competing ethical demands. One aspect of the teacher's role is to nurture students and help them develop into decent, caring adults. Another facet of the teacher's role, however, is to demonstrate that actions have consequences. Ms. Smith wants to support Wesley, but does not want to be seen as condoning criminal acts—let alone abetting their continuation in the long run. Also, she has already gone out of her way to help this one student. Ms. Smith must thus ask herself whether continuing special treatment—especially in the case of a felony—sends precisely the wrong message.

ETHICAL WORK—AND CITIZENSHIP AND PERSONHOOD

What it means to behave ethically in this situation is not easy to delineate. And it is made more difficult because of the third organizing framework. Ms. Smith is not only a worker, she is also a person (as are we all) and a citizen (of various communities, ranging from the school to the school system to broader political entities, like the state and the nation).

If she is to make a comprehensive survey of alternative courses of behavior, she needs to weigh how she should proceed as a member of the teaching profession (good worker), as a member of the school community (good citizen), and as a human being relating to another human being (good person). She will likely, and understandably, find this hard to do.

In a given situation, there is no formula for determining which role takes precedence. To take a vivid example, consider a journalist who is covering a war and gains knowledge about a possible surprise attack against the side that he personally favors. Should the journalist retain the "disinterested stance" of his chosen profession, or abandon his professional obligations in favor of his civic membership and inform the military of the impending attack?

Ms. Smith is certainly entitled to diminish her role as a worker (after all, she is only a novice) and to prioritize other roles instead. But I don't believe that her course of action becomes clearer if she prioritizes the other roles. As a citizen, she may object to the inflexibility of the school system's "zero-tolerance" policy, but she also has an obligation to obey the law or to engage in civil disobedience and be prepared to accept the consequences. And as a person, she has the option of focusing either on the "tough" part of tough love or on the "love" part.

SOME RELUCTANT ADVICE

Good advice is always more easily passed on than followed oneself.[9] I am not sure what I would do in Ms. Smith's situation. But if I were in a position to advise her, I would first lay out the options as I have done. And then, if she pushed me on what she should actually do, here is what I would say:

> I think that you have to report the theft. You don't have to say that Wesley did it, but if you are asked for the circumstances, you need to provide the circumstantial evidence, which is damning. At the same time, you can and should lay out the reasons why you think that the "zero-tolerance" policy is not necessarily the best in all situations, and that the leader(s) of the school should have some leeway in how it is applied.
>
> Finally, and most important, you should attempt to get in touch with Wesley, tell him what you think happened, say that you would like to believe that he was not involved, but that you believe that he was, and that he will have to accept the consequences of his behavior. At the same time, you should say that you think that he has real potential in work and in life, that you were proud to be able to give him a B rather

than an F, and that no matter what happens with the disposition of his case, you are willing to help him become a better student and a law-abiding citizen. In other words, you should treat Wesley as a relative or friend who has done something wrong and needs to accept the consequences, but make it clear that you continue to have faith in him, and indeed that you love him.

Two final comments. First, in laying out the frameworks from Hirschman and from our own work, I readily concede that these do not dictate a course of action. At most, they bring to the fore some relevant considerations. I do not recommend that Ms. Smith simply consider the options in isolation. She should discuss them with trusted friends or perhaps her own teacher-mentors or religious leader, though not with anyone else in the school.

Second, in offering a recommendation, I am revealing my own value system. While I am quite liberal on most issues, I am a stickler for responsibility and for adherence to rules and regulations. I sympathize with Wesley's plight, but feel that he has to take responsibility for his actions. In weighing a perhaps ill-formulated policy against a disregard of it, I come down on the side of adhering to the policy and making my dissatisfaction known in other ways. If that qualifies me as a conservative, so be it.

Howard Gardner is the Hobbs Professor of Cognition and Education at the Harvard Graduate School of Education. The coauthor of Good Work: When Excellence and Ethics Meet *(Basic Books, 2001), he now directs the Good Project, a research project that includes studies of good work and good citizenship.*

Whom Can You Trust When
Everyone Is the Police?

MARY PATTILLO

While the unfortunate dilemma that Ms. Smith faces constitutes the core of this case study, a secondary detail illustrates the widely corrosive effects of zero-tolerance policies. Ms. Smith told only Ms. Hampton of her missing cell phone. But for the possibility that Ms. Hampton will hand over Ms. Smith for failing to report Wesley's alleged theft, Ms. Smith could keep the incident to herself and make a personal decision about how to deal with Wesley (or not). The unstated assumption, however, is that Ms. Hampton will be just as unwavering in her policing of Ms. Smith's behavior as Ms. Smith is required to be in her policing of Wesley's. My comments, then, focus on the norms, practices, and dispositions among the adults in this vignette in order to illustrate the systematic extension of the surveillance state and how this extension undermines schools' educational goals. By revealing such logics, we are able to help Ms. Smith see a way forward by reprioritizing trust and student learning.

THE EXPANSION OF SURVEILLANCE

Ms. Hampton is a pivotal character in this case. She is not completely sympathetic to zero-tolerance policies—calling them "crap"—yet she urges her colleague to comply. Having heard the story of the missing cell phone, she now presumably shares the burden of reporting the alleged theft. Ms. Hampton has no contractual obligation to tell on Ms. Smith, given that Ms. Smith herself did not curse, cut class, get violent, or steal something. And, of course, those prohibited behaviors trigger responses only when students do them, not faculty or staff members. Yet a big part of what motivates Ms. Smith's predicament is the likelihood that Ms. Hampton will go to the principal herself with the information that Wesley allegedly stole Ms. Smith's cell phone, and that Ms. Smith did not report it.

Zero-tolerance policies thus create a culture of surveillance, deterrence, and punishment that extends far beyond the teacher-student relationship, infecting even adults' relationships with one another. Will the school board need to write a subsequent set of guidelines for teachers' conduct in cases like this one, which involves only secondhand knowledge of students' infractions? The expanded reach of policing—including the mandate for people to police each other—is obvious here. The rabbit's hole of codes, violations, and sanctions has particularly pernicious effects when it turns teacher against teacher.

The ideologies that generalized surveillance produces is made explicit in Ms. Hampton's admonition to Ms. Smith: "Protect our students by protecting yourself." This statement does not make logical sense. There is no way in which Wesley is protected if Ms. Smith reports the missing cell phone. He will, at the very least, be suspended or expelled; possibly, he will be imprisoned. Perhaps, then, Ms. Hampton is referring to protecting other students from Wesley's allegedly thievery. But if Ms. Smith and other teachers exhaustively report commonplace teenage misconduct, many of these other students will also suffer. Ultimately, there will be fewer and fewer of "our students" left to protect.

Even though Ms. Hampton's statement is not fully logical, it nonetheless creates its own logic by serving as a powerful mantra for following the rules. Teachers must convince themselves that their own best interests align with those of the students—even when that hope is a fiction, as in zero-tolerance regimes. Every time a teacher protects herself by turning in a student, that student misses hours or even days of learning, gets closer to expulsion, and potentially becomes entangled with the law. "Let them know that *even though* we care," Ms. Hampton continues, "our hands are tied." The "even though" exposes Ms. Hampton's knowledge that these policies create adversarial relationships, not collaborative ones. An ethic of care is replaced by an ethic of policing and punishment.

THE EXPANSION OF MISTRUST

The norm at NHS seems to be that faculty members protect themselves first when it comes to following zero-tolerance rules. But at what cost? Suspicion, silence, and fear rule the day. Teachers mistrust students, and thus they advise each other to lock up their valuables. Teachers do not trust each other. If they did, Ms. Smith would not worry about Ms. Hampton reporting her. And teachers do not trust the school leadership to listen and respond constructively to their reasoned arguments about why the policies are problematic. They share hallway critiques, frustrations, and general feelings of powerlessness, but no one dares to raise these things with administrators.

Research clearly shows that trust is a crucial ingredient for fostering effective school cultures and for boosting student achievement.[10] Other important dimensions of successful educational organizations include teacher empowerment and collective efficacy, shared support for school goals, and leadership that is considered legitimate.[11] These are all undermined by the covert complaining, self-censorship, tip-toeing, and suppression of dissent that characterizes the daily workings of NHS's disciplinary policies.

CONFORMITY AS FALSE PROTECTION

What about school leadership? Mr. Jackson is a charismatic, committed, and formidable school figure whose straitlaced strategies follow in a clear tradition within Black politics.[12] Historian Evelyn Brooks Higginbotham describes the "zealous efforts of black women's religious organizations to transform certain behavior patterns of their people" in the nineteenth century.[13] This "politics of respectability" both then and now aims to prove Blacks' readiness for and worthiness of the benefits of citizenship by demonstrating strict compliance with whatever are the prevailing "mainstream" norms of comportment.[14] Furthermore, it is the job of other Black people to police and enforce that conformity.[15]

"Take one step out of line," Mr. Jackson warns the students, "and you may not get a second chance." Tellingly, Mr. Jackson's message comes at an assembly about Black youth's vulnerability to police violence, as illustrated by the killing of Michael Brown in nearby Ferguson, Missouri. In other words, Mr. Jackson's job is to make his students so respectable that no police officer would have the occasion to shoot them.

But this reasoning is clearly faulty. No more than a month or two after Mr. Jackson must have held that assembly, Cleveland police officers took two seconds to pull into a park and kill Tamir Rice, a twelve-year-old Black child who was playing with a toy gun. What could be more mainstream in the twenty-first-century United States than a toy gun?

A CULTURE OF SUSPICION

A final pernicious effect of zero-tolerance policies is the way they produce a culture of suspicion that sits atop conscious and unconscious racial bias. There is nothing in the narrative that confirms that Wesley stole the cell phone. I don't raise this as a legal issue about how to prove that a crime was committed, although that is surely a relevant point. Instead, the story simply makes me reflect on times when I thought I lost my gloves only to find them in another coat pocket, or when I looked for my car in one place only to realize that I had parked on a different street. Every missing item does not raise the suspicion of a theft, but Ms. Smith's search was remarkably cursory before she headed to confer with Ms. Hampton. Why?

Psychologist Phillip Goff and his colleagues find that subjects in their experiments generally regarded Black youths to be less innocent, more culpable, and older than White youths.[16] Could Ms. Smith not fathom Wesley's innocence? Teachers at NHS know that the punishment burden of zero-tolerance policies is borne disproportionately by Black, Latino, and poor children; they even lament the dire consequences of this fact. They seem less aware, however, of how such policies likely affect their own routine interactions and interpretations. The phone might be in Ms. Smith's desk drawer, under some papers, or in some odd and accidental place like the garbage can. The facts of the case are fully apparent to neither Ms. Smith nor the reader. Yet Wesley is no less draped in a veil of suspicion and guilt.

REWRITING THE STORY

So what should Ms. Smith do? Well, before she does anything, she better turn that classroom upside down and thoroughly search her coat, pockets, and all the compartments of all of her bags. Assuming the phone does not turn up, the tough decision remains. Her thoughts on her drive home clearly lean toward not reporting the alleged theft. And so she must return to Ms. Hampton to learn if the zero-tolerance policies have stolen all trust, elevating the job of punitive policing above the profession of teaching.

> Could she really conceive of sacrificing her professional standing or even undermining her career for the sake of a single kid—one who had, after all, stolen her iPhone—even if she thought that the zero-tolerance policy was wrong? Luckily, Ms. Smith neither had to jeopardize her career nor burden Wesley with the mark of a criminal record.[17] She called Ms. Hampton as soon as she got home and invited her for coffee. She explained the progress she had made with Wesley, told her about his earning a B in her class, and appealed to Ms. Hampton's commitment to educating kids. Ms. Smith asked for Ms. Hampton's discretion in the matter, assured her that no one would know that she had any knowledge of the situation, and reminded Ms. Hampton of the widespread discomfort with the policy. Ms. Hampton complied.

That's how my story ends.

Mary Pattillo is the Harold Washington Professor of Sociology and African American Studies at Northwestern University. She studies urban politics and policy and Black communities and is the author of the award-winning books Black Picket Fences *(University of Chicago Press, 2013) and* Black on the Block *(University of Chicago Press, 2007).*

CHAPTER FOUR

Inflated Expectations

How Should Teachers Assign Grades?

MEIRA LEVINSON AND ILANA FINEFTER-ROSENBLUH

Adina Heschel smiled as Terry Morrison and Leah Stein poked their heads into her office and then, barely waiting for her nodded welcome, plunked themselves down on her couch.[1] Dr. Heschel had been in her new job as academic dean at Hamaskil Jewish Day School for only two months, but she had already learned that Dr. Morrison and Ms. Stein were among the most respected teachers at the school. As science department chair, Dr. Morrison had inspired a new level of energy and innovation in what had been a rather lackluster department. Ms. Stein, who taught Jewish history and intermediate Hebrew, was known as a fierce advocate for increasing the academic rigor and status of Jewish studies at Hamaskil. In a faculty known for easy collegiality, but little true collective vision or collaboration, Dr. Morrison and Ms. Stein stood out.

"Good morning. How can I help?" Dr. Heschel asked in a soft Alabama drawl.

"Adina," Ms. Stein immediately launched in, "you know how you're preparing your teaching and learning assessment for the Strategic Vision Committee next month? You mentioned in the faculty meeting last week that you were looking for insights into the hidden curriculum of the school—what happens here that we all know or do but don't talk about. Well, we have something that needs talking about: grade inflation. It's rampant at Hamaskil. It's embarrassing. It undercuts our integrity as educators. And it's got to stop."

"We've been trying to have a real discussion about this for a long time," Dr. Morrison inserted, "but the administration has always pushed back, swept it under the rug. And why wouldn't they? They've been complicit in it, along with the parents! Well, I'm sorry, but not all kids here are A and B+ students. I appreciate that they may do a lot of homework, but that's not the same as doing high-quality work. Parents refuse to hear that, though; they push us to reconsider grades even when their kids can't design a simple lab experiment to demonstrate principles we've been studying all semester—"

"—or read and write about a simple story in Hebrew," Ms. Stein added bitterly.

"—just because it's something we haven't directly taught them," Dr. Morrison finished. "Parents cry foul—and the administration sides with them—if we ask their kids to apply their knowledge and skills in a novel context. As if the only thing they should be held responsible for is knowing the answers to exactly the questions we posed in the past and not the challenges they will face in the future. They've got to be held accountable! Where are our standards?"

"All right, Terry, calm down!" Ms. Stein laughed. "I think Terry's point is that many of our students actually *could* learn more if they didn't think they could slide through with a shoddy understanding. We're preventing them from discovering the true extent of their capacities by rewarding the barest glimmers."

"Not to mention the kids who really do excel," Dr. Morrison took over again. "It's not fair to them that they do this amazing work, really take things to the next level to earn that A, and then other students get a B+ or A– for barely exercising their brains. I don't even know what our grades *mean* anymore!"

"Wow," Dr. Heschel exclaimed. "This is quite an indictment. Do other teachers feel this way?"

"Definitely," Ms. Stein affirmed. "We've been trying to bring this up for so long. Talk to almost anyone on the faculty. They'll tell you the same thing."

Over the following few weeks, Dr. Heschel embarked on a "listening tour" among the faculty, meeting individually or in small groups with most teachers at Hamaskil. As Ms. Stein and Dr. Morrison had promised, many teachers shared their frustration about grading practices at Hamaskil: in particular, they talked about the "shame" and a "lack of integrity" they felt when assigning grades they believed did not accurately communicate students' true mastery. In one meeting, a young English teacher burst into tears while talking about a student she had taught the previous spring. "Despite all of my trying and his trying, he was still failing, but I was supposed to pass him anyway. So I just passed him. But I will be so embarrassed later on if somebody notices that it's my name attached to this pass," she continued. "I don't know what this pass is; it does not in any way reflect my feeling that the student has mastered any of the material. It was just thrust on me."

Teachers also consistently mentioned the sense of "entitlement" that parents and students brought to conversations about grades. Veteran history teacher Horace Finley told Dr. Heschel, "Generally speaking, the parents feel that they deserve it. They're paying, and they deserve for their kids to get an A+." He explained he felt his authority was undermined when parents questioned grades on report cards. "It's like the reification of privilege; they're entitled to money, to good schools, and now they're even entitled to success itself. It's not just that Hamaskil gives them a great academic foundation so they can be successful later on, but they feel entitled to be successful here. It's like entitlement squared."

His colleague Melanie Horowitz elaborated, "I want to say to them, 'I'm the teacher; I see your child in class and I read their papers and grade their tests. I'm the professional. I don't tell you how to do your job; don't tell me how to do mine.' But then you have to ask yourself, how much is this worth, the constant battle back and forth? Sometimes I'll keep fighting. But more often, I'll just give in. It's just not worth my time, especially if I know the administration won't back me up."

"And after all, it's true, the parents do pay the bills," Mrs. Horowitz continued, veering off in a direction Dr. Heschel had not expected. "They're paying my salary, and the salaries of all of us. I guess that's what they're paying us for too: to get their kids into good colleges, and to teach them well enough to succeed once they're there. If I were them, with the $35,000 a year to pay for a private education, I'd want that too. I resent the pressure, but I can't really blame them."

"Do you feel you are preparing students to succeed in college?" Dr. Heschel asked. "I mean, are parents getting what they pay for, if that's what they do care about?"

"Oh, yeah," Mrs. Horowitz responded. "I mean, they're good kids, and they work hard—most of them, anyway—and they definitely seem to be successful. They come back and visit us all the time when they're home on vacation and tell us how great they're doing. Our alumni are big boosters."

"They love Hamaskil," Mr. Finley affirmed. "They talk about how supported they felt, and cared for. You know how our nickname is 'The Haven'? That's because Hamaskil is a little haven from the outside world. We give them the support and love adolescents need to figure out who they are, find their passions, grow into ethical leaders who will make the world a better place. We're good at that, protecting them from the crazy competition."

As Dr. Heschel continued meeting with teachers, she heard similar expressions of ambivalence or even self-contradiction regarding the effects of grade inflation. Teachers who decried the "loss of standards" agreed that students were successful in college—almost all highly selective, four-year institutions. Many faculty members also celebrated Hamaskil's ethic of "care," commitment to "supporting the whole child," and "emphasis on learning rather than on competing." Even Leah Stein, the Jewish studies teacher, acknowledged that grade inflation could be understood in the context of a culture of care. "One of the things that's really good about this school is we encourage personal relations between the faculty and the students. We've created an environment in which we try to find success for kids. I like that. So I feel bad, too, if there's a kid who I know is going to be devastated by her grade, especially when she's worked really hard."

Hannah Abrams, the Tikkun Olam Outreach Coordinator, suggested that this ethic of care also radiated outward; it was not just about helping students feel cared for, but helping them learn to care for others. *Tikkun olam,* a Hebrew phrase meaning "repairing the world," is central to Hamaskil's mission statement: "Our mission is to inspire, teach, and empower Jews who are passionate, intellectual, critical, original, and ethical in all parts of their lives, so as to bring about *tikkun olam*: a more just and caring world in which Jews and all human beings will flourish with dignity and joy." As coordinator, Ms. Abrams oversaw Hamaskil's extensive community service learning initiatives, sophomore trip to Holocaust sites in Poland, junior "social justice internships," and senior trip to Israel and Jordan.

"One of the most important things we do at Hamaskil," Ms. Abrams commented, "is to help our students realize they *aren't* the center of the universe, and that they need to use their considerable resources and talents to be leaders in bringing about a better world. I think we do that by helping them find their successes rather than focusing on their failures. I agree that we give out As really readily—certainly more often than when I was a kid. But when our students are in a good place themselves, they can focus on the bigger picture, orient toward others' needs. They are ready to take a role in healing the world. That is so important."

The dean for Post-Secondary and College Placement took a different tack in emphasizing Hamaskil's and students' embeddedness in the wider cultural context. "Our kids are being evaluated against other high-achieving kids from everywhere. It's not just how our students stack up against each other at Hamaskil, but how they compare to students at public and independent schools across the country. There's incontrovertible evidence that grades have inflated all over," he explained, citing by heart multiple studies from the ACT, College Board, and US Department of Education. "We shouldn't unfairly penalize Hamaskil students by deflating their GPAs compared to other schools'. It's a coordination problem. If we all deflated, fine. But there's no advantage in being a first or solitary mover."

As a Princeton alumna, Dr. Heschel understood the problem firsthand. In 2004, Princeton commenced a decade-long experiment in grade deflation. Faculty adopted a policy meant to "provide common grading standards across academic departments and to give students clear signals from their teachers about the difference between good work and their very best work." The heart of the policy was a recommendation that no more than 35 percent of the grades awarded across all courses in a department be As and A–s. This was intended to permit significant variation among courses within a single department, but students generally interpreted the policy as a hard quota in each class.[2]

Evidence mounted that the negative effects were numerous and the positive effects nonexistent. Undergrads described the atmosphere on Princeton's campus as competitive rather than collegial. "Classes here often feel like shark tanks," one student wrote; even faculty likened the campus culture to "a pressure cooker." There was evidence that high school students who were admitted to Princeton disproportionately matriculated to other Ivies because of concerns over competition for scarce A and A– grades. Students at Princeton also worried that they were losing out in graduate school admissions and hiring. Students and faculty alike agreed that the new grading policies had not clarified or systematized grading standards. "Grade compression," the narrowing of the range of grades that most students received, did not change appreciably after the deflationary policy was adopted. Hence professors could not give clearer "signals" about the quality of student work. Furthermore, anxiety over grades seemed to *reduce* students' attentiveness to other forms of feedback from professors. In 2014, therefore, Princeton faculty abandoned their deflationary policies.

Head of School Esther Cohen was also a Princeton alumna, and referenced the university's experiences to justify her disinclination to end grade inflation at Hamaskil. "Whom does it help to lower grades? No one! It increases student and teacher stress levels, destroys school culture, is developmentally inappropriate for vulnerable adolescents, and hurts students' college acceptance rates. Hamaskil would take a nosedive in the eyes of parents and prospective families. How on earth would we market ourselves, with two other highly regarded Jewish day schools less than five miles away from us? If Princeton couldn't figure out how to keep matriculation up, how could we?"

"Grade deflation also rightly raises parents' suspicions about teachers' dedication and competence," Rabbi Cohen continued. "We admit great kids and great families. Everyone here cares about education. That is in our lifeblood as a Jewish school! When kids aren't performing, maybe the teachers need to look at themselves and ask where *they* are going wrong. Why aren't kids motivated to learn in their classes? Are the assignments structured in ways that are confusing to students, or under- or overdemanding? Are the teachers disengaging? Low grades don't prove that a teacher has high standards. They prove the opposite, that this is a teacher who does not have sufficiently high expectations for their own pedagogical practice. They need help engaging students, but instead they respond by inflating imagined 'standards' over the developing minds of human beings there in the classroom with them!"

"Terry and Leah certainly are right that faculty are out of sync with the administration," Dr. Heschel thought as she left Rabbi Cohen's office. No matter what else she accomplished as academic dean, she reflected, one of her primary goals had to be to foster a coherent academic vision that administration and teachers could collectively embrace.

Back at her desk, flipping through results of a school academic climate survey that had been administered the previous spring, Dr. Heschel realized that parents, too, were divided about grading practices at Hamaskil. She glanced at some of the parent comments she had highlighted:

- "Work with my child so he improves. Don't just mark him down. Let me know what he needs so I can help him be successful."
- "Arbitrary standards and expectations. I don't know what a B means. Nor does my son. Don't play around with his life like this."
- "I see how hard she works. She's doing homework until all hours. I can't believe that with all that work, she still only got a B+."
- "Need higher standards, more differentiation. My daughter worked really hard to do well in that class. Cheapens it if everyone else gets an A, too. NOT EVERYONE CAN BE A WINNER."

Dr. Heschel sighed as she opened up the agenda for the Strategic Vision Committee in two weeks' time. They had set aside a full hour to talk about her teaching and learning assessment. Rabbi Cohen and the Hamaskil board chair had asked her to accompany her assessment with a set of concrete proposals for improving academic coherence and rigor over the next three years. Dr. Heschel knew she needed to address grading as part of her larger report. What should she propose, and why?

Putting School Mission First

REBECCA E. YACONO

Dr. Adina Heschel has quite a dilemma on her hands. As the new academic dean at Hamaskil Jewish Day School, she has been charged with the task of assessing teaching and learning and making recommendations for the school's goals of "improving academic coherence and rigor." Hamaskil is in the midst of their strategic planning process, a process undertaken regularly by independent schools as recommended by the National Association of Independent Schools.[3] If accepted, Dr. Heschel's report and proposal will impact the academic future of the school.

As a college preparatory school, Hamaskil is grappling with the tension between the culture of grades as a retail commodity in an expensive private school market and the meaning and purpose of grades as they reflect student learning and the academic status of the school. It would not be enough for Dr. Heschel's report and proposal to put forth a grading structure of numbers and a list of admonishments about higher standards. On the contrary, the strategic planning process offers her an opportunity to bring coherence to the curriculum by anchoring academic standards in the school's mission and existing culture.

HIGH STANDARDS IN PRACTICE

On her "listening tour" of the faculty and administration, Dr. Heschel discovers pervasive dissatisfaction among the faculty with the lack of consistency in Hamaskil's grading policies. Indeed, she hears feedback about the absence of any kind of coherent philosophy or policy about how grades are determined or communicated, and she hears widespread concern about the resulting effects on faculty integrity.

At the same time, faculty members are confident about and proud of the success of their graduates at prestigious four-year colleges and universities. They also acknowledge the community's reputation as "The Haven," due to the care and support extended to the students by the faculty.

Faculty members would also likely bristle against standardization for its own sake. When science department head Dr. Morrison adamantly poses the question, "Where are our standards?" he is really asking, "What are our benchmarks for excellence?" The "where are our standards?" mantra is common among teachers bemoaning the state of inflated grades. None-theless, those same teachers in independent schools balk when they perceive "standards" to mean the establishment of externally imposed benchmarks of student learning. Standards like these are viewed as threats to teacher autonomy, which is one of the main reasons many teachers give for prefer-ring to teach in private schools.[4]

The way out of this standoff is to recognize that, as Peter Gow puts it, "The actual high standards of which teachers and schools may be justly proud are those that students, teachers, and the community understand as worthy and consistent."[5]

Mr. Finley, a history teacher at Hamaskil, gives insight into this process when he acknowledges teachers' high standards of student support: "We give [the students] the support and love adolescents need to figure out who they are, find their passions, grow into ethical leaders who will make the world a better place."

And the students at Hamaskil demonstrate the results of the school's high standards by their actions. They "figure out who they are, find their passions, [and] grow into ethical leaders." Hamaskil graduates attend "almost all highly selective, four-year institutions." And Mrs. Horowitz, also in the history department, tells Dr. Heschel that students "definitely seem to be successful. They come back [from college] and tell us how great they're doing."

"Judge the school not on what it says, but on how it keeps."[6] Hamaskil has a culture of success both socially and academically. While the school lacks an explicit purpose and coherent protocol for measuring that success, it already has a foundational set of principles on which to build one: its mission.

IDEALIZING THE MISSION

At first blush, Hamaskil's mission seems to say little about academics. The institution aspires "to inspire, teach, and empower Jews who are passion-ate, intellectual, critical, original, and ethical in all parts of their lives, so as to bring about *tikkun olam*: a more just and caring world in which Jews and all human beings will flourish with dignity and joy."

How is a school with a mission that is ostensibly anchored in social justice supposed to have high standards for academic rigor? How does a faculty seeking the integrity of a grading system that holds students to a mastery level of performance reconcile that with a mission that is hardly measurable by quantitative criteria?

One option that Dr. Heschel could propose for exploring the answers is an exercise described in Grant Wiggins and Jay McTighe's book *Schooling by Design*.[7] In the "Picture the Graduate" exercise, members of the faculty and administration are charged with describing "what exemplary graduates of the school should look like, act like and sound like if the school has been successful in achieving its mission."[8] The school can define categories of descriptors, depending on the categories of desired outcomes or community values—for example, "Habits of Mind, Behavior, Academic Accomplishment, and Personal Accomplishment."[9]

Hamaskil teachers and administrators could consider using categories such as Content Knowledge, Academic Skills, World View, and Community Engagement. From that point, any conversation between Hamaskil's faculty and administration about curriculum, rigor, and standards should have its foundation in the resulting ideal.

In her proposal, Dr. Heschel should recommend that follow-up steps include departmental participation in the same exercise, as well as grade-level team meetings to "picture the graduate" at each level. Once those steps have been taken, faculty members will be better positioned to discuss the grading standards they yearn for, and the resulting standards will have the integrity they seek because those standards will be rooted in the mission and values of the school.

As a faculty, their process will be to survey the territory and to map a more coherent and rigorous academic environment within the fundamental values of the community. As they map their curricular route, they will answer the questions: "Where are we going? How are we going to get there? How will we know when we've arrived?"[10]

MISSION IN PRACTICE

It is in answering this last question—"How will we know when we've arrived?"—that faculty members at Hamaskil will define their grading rubrics. One step in that process will be deciding what grades will represent in their community. Should they reflect the extent of student mastery of skills and content? Should they indicate individual progress toward the stated goal? Do they provide a scaled rating of the quality of student performance on a school-defined Likert scale?

Included in the definition of purpose should be the audience for grades: Is the message to the student, his/her parents, and his/her future teachers about the student's growing edges? Is the message for colleges and universities about the caliber of work the student can be expected to produce? Is the message to parents about what a Hamaskil education is worth?

Regardless of the answer, the agreement about the purpose of grades at Hamaskil should reflect exactly what grades represent at Hamaskil and for whom, and it should be stated explicitly. From there, teachers and administrators can move forward in setting policies, format, symbols, and ranges.[11] Hamaskil's student handbook can then be revised to include the school's grading philosophy and common practices. Individual course policies, as articulated on syllabi and implemented in practice, should also be revised if necessary to be consistent with collective decisions.

Going through a mission-driven process for developing grading policies has a host of advantages, particularly if the group uses a collaborative or consensus decision-making model. It gives participants a voice—and consequently, an investment—in the result. The dean for Post-Secondary and College Placement can include with confidence the school's grading philosophy in the high school's profile that accompanies students' transcripts. And based on the feedback from faculty members, the process's most significant outcome is in securing the integrity they seek in the grading process, provided that they hold themselves and each other accountable for maintaining the policies and practices they lay out.

Dr. Heschel is fortunate to have her assessment and proposal fall under the auspices of Hamaskil's Strategic Vision Committee. The committee has positioned her proposal for realistic success, too, by predefining it as a three-year plan. By rooting the grading system in the big picture of the school's mission and values, and by bringing all faculty members and administrators into the conversation, Dr. Heschel can take the community on a journey toward a coherent academic culture of clear and consistent standards.

Rebecca E. Yacono teaches eighth grade Central Subject (humanities) at the Shady Hill School in Cambridge, Massachusetts, building on twenty years of teaching and administrative experience in middle-level and secondary education, primarily in independent schools. She holds an MAT from Boston University and a BA from the Plan II Liberal Arts Honors program at the University of Texas at Austin.

Three Ways to Grade

ROB REICH

What should Dr. Heschel propose in the face of faculty members' concerns about grade inflation? To make sense of the competing perspectives in the case and evaluate potential proposals that Dr. Heschel might make, we need an understanding of what might justify the assignment of particular grades in the first place. Without this understanding, we cannot appreciate what objections there might be to grade inflation.

Of course, Dr. Heschel could propose a portfolio assessment system and dispense with grades altogether. (See Deepa Vasudevan's commentary in this chapter recommending exactly this approach.) Assuming she is committed to grading, however, Dr. Heschel should decide what purpose grades are meant to serve. Three distinct goals come to mind: communicating subject mastery, sorting students, or tracing student growth and/or effort. Assuming faculty members comply with the new policy, grade inflation may cease to be a problem. Grade inflation will be impossible if grades are assigned on a curve to sort students. Or, it will not be problematic if high grades result from all students performing to their potential and/or doing objectively exceptional work.

THREE PURPOSES OF GRADING

Simplifying greatly, we can identify three distinct ways of allocating grades. A teacher could assign grades relative to independent standards of performance (e.g., subject matter standards), relative to the performance of a set of peers (e.g., in the classroom, grade level, or school), or relative to the potential, effort, or past performance of the student (e.g., the student worked to her full potential or improved her performance over time and therefore deserves a high grade). Let's consider each in turn.

1. Grading Relative to Independent Standards of Performance

An intuitive and obvious way of understanding the purpose of grades is to see them as a measure of individual performance: did a student master the material? Teachers, district or state leaders, textbooks, or initiatives such as the Common Core may define what counts as mastery in a particular subject. Students attempt to demonstrate their knowledge of the material through classroom participation, homework, tests, and other tasks. Grades are assigned accordingly.

Note several things about this allocation method. First, grades reflect a measure of absolute rather than relative performance. Student achievement is compared to an independent standard, not to the achievement of fellow students.

Second, as a consequence, this allocation method permits, without any damage to the integrity of grading, every student to receive the same grade. If all students master the material, then every student should receive an A. Think of an elementary school classroom that is learning multiplication tables. One way to assess performance is simply to mark students on the basis of correct answers to the problems; if all students can answer correctly in the assigned period of time, then all students earn the same grade.

Grades on this view represent a mechanism to communicate to students, parents, and others—such as college admissions committees or potential employers—the extent of a student's mastery of various subjects or skill sets. Performance across students is differentiated not as an intended feature of the allocation system, but only to the extent that students actually demonstrate different levels of performance. Differentiation, or sorting of students, by contrast, is the intended and built-in function of the next view of grading.

2. Grading Relative to Peers

An alternative manner to assign grades is to generate a distribution of performance among the students in a class (or grade level or school). This method is known more popularly as "grading on a curve" and begins from the assumption that relative comparisons of performance, rather than absolute measures of performance, are what matter.

The aspiration is to differentiate performance in the classroom for the purpose of providing an easy-to-understand signal of relative student performance across different classrooms or schools. One reason to use a curve is to handle the problems of interpreting students' grades when teachers frequently deploy vastly different standards of good performance. Grading on a curve can reliably identify top and low performing students, independent of what grading standards are used by particular teachers.

Note several things about this grading scheme. First, there is no possibility of a classroom of students earning identical grades. The presumption is that differentiation is the purpose of grading. Second, and as a direct consequence, grading on a curve reflects no intrinsic connection to subject matter mastery. If in a classroom of thirty students the highest grade on a test is 40 percent, reflecting poor subject matter knowledge, the student with 40 percent earns an A as the top performer in the class. What the A represents is top position in the distribution of performance, not subject mastery.

3. Grading Relative to Individual Potential, Effort, or Past Performance

Finally, a third mechanism for assigning grades is meant to take account of performance relative to an individual's potential, effort, or past performance. These arguments are frequently invoked in relation to particular students or groups of students, such as those facing significant adversity. Those who advocate a developmental perspective also often raise this approach to grading. Think of situations in which teachers, students, or parents believe that high grades are warranted when a student's performance improves over time, has shown exceptional effort, or where a student has worked to his or her full potential.

What's essential in this grading scheme is either establishing an initial baseline of performance (grades earned at the beginning of the year based on either of the first two allocation designs) or making an evaluation of a student's potential or capability. Grades on this view may be differentiated across students, but this will not be by design, as in grading on a curve. Nor will differences be due to different levels of performance relative to independent and external subject matter standards, as in the first scheme. They will instead be due to different levels of student effort or growth.

EVALUATING ALLOCATION MECHANISMS

Each of these grade allocation designs should seem familiar and have some intuitive appeal. In my experience, individual teachers frequently use more than one of these designs. Students and parents also often appeal to elements contained within each scheme. We can see such appeals in the various comments about grade inflation in the case study. And yet, these three allocation designs are not mutually compatible or realizable. In many respects, they pull in different directions.

To evaluate whether grade inflation is a problem, Dr. Heschel first needs to decide what grade allocation scheme, or combination thereof, is most defensible. Or to put it less as a theoretical question, she needs to decide what grading standard is most suitable for Hamaskil Jewish Day School.

In making this decision, she will also need to take a few facts into account. Hamaskil's grading scheme does not exist in isolation. As is recounted in the case study, deflating Hamaskil students' grades might penalize them in postsecondary competitions for entry into selective universities. Grades do indeed matter for such competitions, and deflating grades at Hamaskil, even for good reasons, could have unintended and adverse consequences. Therefore, even if Dr. Heschel were to decide to endorse grade deflation because she thought it was merited, she faces a collective action problem. It would be better for her to act in concert with other elite prep schools; she has little incentive to be the first mover, potentially punishing her students and her school's reputation.

There are several other facts mentioned in the case, such as the status of Hamaskil as an expensive and elite private school, its ethic of care, and pressure from parents to see high grades because they feel entitled to them on the basis of the hefty tuition bills they pay. I do not see any of these facts as relevant, however, to the decision Dr. Heschel faces. At best, they present political concerns for a school leader, not concerns about the merits of grade inflation or deflation.

MATCHING PHILOSOPHY AND ACTION

So what should Dr. Heschel propose?

The answer depends, I submit, on her philosophy of grading. And each of the grade allocation designs described above has something to recommend it; each can be defended. So she will need to decide, ideally in conjunction with the school's board and faculty, what approach to grading Hamaskil should take.

The essential point, in my view, is to decide whether Hamaskil should see grades primarily as a mechanism to indicate absolute performance, indexed to particular measures of academic achievement, or instead as a sorting mechanism, intended to send a simple signal to the external world about relative performance and position of a student. If the latter, then grade inflation is an embarrassment and a violation of the underlying purpose of grades, which are meant to provide a wide distribution of performance. But if the former, then a large number of high grades is no necessary embarrassment *so long as student performance is genuinely strong*. Of course, if high grades are being given out in the absence of strong performance in order to accommodate demanding parents or to protect the school's reputation, there is no good reason to defend high grades.

Grades are one of the most familiar aspects of schooling, and their existence is woven into our expectations about what schools are for and how teaching and learning work on a day-to-day basis. In this respect, there are few things more important at Hamiskil, or at any other school, than articulating and enacting a grading policy. Dr. Heschel has a consequential decision to make, one that will affect both her faculty members and students, including students' families and students' prospects for admission to higher education and entry into the labor market. For these reasons, she should take the time, above all else, to develop a clear philosophy of how and why to assign grades.

Rob Reich, a former sixth-grade teacher at Rusk Elementary School in Houston, Texas, is professor of political science and, by courtesy, education, at Stanford University, where he also directs the Center for Ethics in Society. He is the author of Bridging Liberalism and Multiculturalism in American Education *(University of Chicago Press, 2002) and coeditor, with Danielle Allen, of* Education, Justice, and Democracy *(University of Chicago Press, 2013).*

Grade Inflation as a Tragedy of the Commons

Jennifer Hochschild

The case ends with a trick question; it has no correct answer. Grade inflation in an individual school, or across the educational system, is a collective action problem, or, more dramatically, a tragedy of the commons. No
single person, school, or even school system can solve it. Many scholars,
and even more advocates and activists, have tried to resolve commons' tragedies, and I will discuss a few work-arounds below. But they are indeed
work-arounds, not solutions.

THE CHALLENGES OF COLLECTIVE ACTION

Mancur Olson offered the canonical explication of collective action problems: "The firms in a perfectly competitive industry . . . have a common
interest in a higher price for the industry's product . . . But a firm in a
competitive market also has an interest in selling as much as it can [typi-
cally by lowering the price for its product] . . . In this there is no common
interest; each firm's interest is directly opposed to that of every other firm
. . . Profit-maximizing firms in a perfectly competitive market can [thus] act
contrary to their interests as a group." The crucial, generalizable point is
that "though all the firms have a common interest in a higher price for the
industry's product, it is in the interest of each firm that the other firms pay
the cost . . . needed to obtain a higher price."[12]

One can find endless analogies to competitive firms in a competitive
market. Cattle owners all benefit from a common grazing area, but each
owner will benefit even more by bringing in a few extra cows so long as
no one else does. Roommates all prefer a clean kitchen, but each is better off postponing the dishwashing in the hopes that another resident will
break down and do it. Citizens may embrace the presumed outcomes of
government expenditures on policing, social assistance for children and the
elderly, and environmental protection, but each individual is better off if
others pay their taxes while he or she does not. And, most teachers would
prefer to use a range of grades to signal students' actual achievement, effort, and initiative, but each individual (or private school) is better off if

others resist grade inflation while he or she succumbs to it. When the costs of action are concentrated and the benefits are diffuse, individuals benefit from what harms the group.

A GRAB BAG OF STRATEGIES

Scholars and activists have worked out a variety of responses to this basically insoluble problem. Economists, for example, focus on two strategies: privatization and rules. *Privatization* seeks to eliminate the commons: each cattle owner also owns a fenced-off plot of grass; each roommate is responsible for his or her own dishes; each homeowner pays for the level of garbage collection or home security desired; each teacher grades according to criteria that he or she finds most compelling. As these and a myriad other illustrations suggest, dissolving the collective can be beneficial or not, depending on whether its effect is to force the free rider into washing dishes or paying for garbage collection, or to require each teacher separately to face the wrath of parents or the anxiety of students confronted with a grade lower than an A–.

Rules reinforce rather than dissolve the collective, and they, too, can be beneficial or harmful, depending on context and participants. Each owner of cattle is permitted only a certain number of cows on the commons; each roommate can have designated days of the week for washing all dishes; each wage earner can be required to pay a certain level of taxes; each teacher can be given a quota of A grades or a set of criteria to be attained before a student is given an A. Rules work if they can be enforced or if enforcement is seldom needed, and rules are good if they are deemed fair and reasonable. But those observations simply push the problem back one step—enforced by whom and how? Good for whom, and reasonable and fair by what standards?

Political scientists and political activists focus on three somewhat different strategies: particularized benefits, norms, and changing the size of the group. *Particularized benefits* seek to right the imbalance between individual loss and collective gain that comes from working for the common good. Donors to the World Wildlife Fund get a tote bag; precinct workers received a government job in the era of machine politics; teachers who spearhead a reform get a Teacher-of-the-Month award. The goal in this case is not to dissolve the commons, but to enhance individual incentives to contribute to the group or the common good.

Norms are widely shared practices and beliefs. They provide an answer to the problems of rule acceptance and enforcement. If people can be persuaded to believe in the mission of the organization, as in the ethic of care at Hamaskil Jewish Day School, they will more readily wash the dishes, pay the taxes, oversee the community service learning initiatives, or otherwise relinquish individual gain in favor of collective well-being. Public visibility, repetition of the values underlying the norms, and clear cues from leaders may all contribute to individuals' willingness to actually abide by, not just give lip service to, norms.

As you should now be able to anticipate, particularized benefits and norms can both work for either good or ill. If the World Wildlife Fund gives me a nicer tote bag in response to a larger donation, both of us benefit and no one loses. But if a prosecutor tears up the indictment of a campaign donor, we call that corruption. Nazis had norms with underlying values, as did 1960s civil rights activists, and as do the teachers at Hamaskil.

Political scientists and activists also focus on the *size of the group* defined as the collective. Here, too, there is no clearly right answer for all occasions. Olson portrays small groups as "more efficient and viable than large ones" because members are able to encourage, socialize, and monitor each other—and can also identify and punish those who do not contribute to the common good.[13] As group size increases, free riding becomes easier and the ratio of rewards to costs for a given individual of collective action becomes smaller. Others, however, point to the ability of large diffuse interests to overcome narrowly focused groups: the Food and Drug Administration and Environmental Protection Agency are institutional manifestations of concern for the public good overriding pharmaceutical manufacturers or polluters, while the Voting Rights Act and food stamps are policy manifestations of shared public commitment to override oppressors of previously despised and powerless minorities.[14]

APPLYING THEORY TO PRACTICE AT HAMASKIL

What does all of this tell us about how Dr. Heschel should address the issue of grades? In my view, the substantive decision is not difficult: inflated grades are not morally or pedagogically justified, whether for privileged students at Hamaskil (or in my classes at Harvard) or for disadvantaged students in inner-city schools. Inflated grades provide little useful information to students, parents, or university admissions officers. They undermine teachers' efforts to encourage deeper thinking or more intense preparation. They make it difficult to distinguish between a genuinely caring community and one that promotes "self-esteem" as a shallow substitute for real effort or connection. I can see an argument for no grades (or a simple pass-fail system, which is how I was graded for all but one semester in college) in order to reduce unproductive anxiety and competition among students, but that requires a somewhat different conversation.

If one accepts my starting (and insufficiently defended) premise, the scholarly literature on collective action problems offers a few suggestions to Dr. Heschel. First, privatization is clearly not appropriate; no Hamaskil teacher can or should tackle grade inflation on his or her own. Second, personalized benefits are probably not in tune with the school's commitment to an ethic of caring and respect for all, although they might be helpful at the margin if carefully used. Students could, for example, be publicly recognized for an extraordinary accomplishment, sustained improvement, or an exceptional level of effort; teachers could be publicly recognized for doing an exceptionally good job of explaining grading criteria and helping students and parents accept them.

Rather, it seems most essential for Dr. Heschel to help create clear and perhaps consensually developed rules growing out of but also modifying extant norms. An explicit set of rubrics to guide grading will help teachers to make distinctions, provide a framework for discussion with distressed students and parents, and help students see how more work does not necessarily mean better work or genuine achievement. The school's explicit rules can also be attached to transcripts or included in letters of recommendation to colleges in order to blunt concern about the role of grades in taking the next step in schooling.

Norms need to be closely aligned with rules in order for the latter not to feel arbitrary or unfair. But Hamaskil already has a strong set of appropriate norms, including rejection of a sense of entitlement, a commitment to developing genuine leaders, and respect for each individual. Developing them in the direction of genuinely informative, even if occasionally painful, grading decisions should not be a monumental task.

With regard to group size, perhaps Hamaskil can benefit from the advantages of both smaller and larger groups. On the one hand, it is small enough for teachers to deliberate with and bolster one another around rules and norms, and to offer support in the face of an angry parent or disappointed student. On the other hand, school leaders should work hard to get the competing Jewish schools in the area to foster the same new policies, just as firms as a whole benefit more from monopoly than from a competitive market. Presumably the nearby schools are wrestling with the same worries and parental pressure; if Hamaskil can lead the way in promoting a new era of interschool collective action, it might be able to reduce both grade inflation and competition on the wrong dimension with nearby rivals.

Jennifer Hochschild is the Henry LaBarre Jayne Professor of Government and a professor of African and African American studies at Harvard University. She holds lectureships in the Harvard Kennedy School and the Harvard Graduate School of Education, and is president of the American Political Science Association.

Inflated Expectations in a World of Hypercredentialing

PETER DEMERATH

Hamaskil Jewish Day School faces a challenge shared by many parochial, independent, and public schools in the developed world: how to preserve authentic student learning in an increasingly competitive environment. Like many of these schools, Hamaskil has a unique tradition and set of values that are being eclipsed by the focus on student competitive success. At its core, therefore, this case is about nothing less than the purposes and ethics of schooling within a neoliberal global regime. This does not mean, however, that Hamaskil is powerless. To the contrary, confronting these challenges in a thoughtful way can ensure that Hamaskil students acquire habits of effective lifelong learning and that the entire community is drawn together around a renewed sense of the educational purpose that is deeply rooted in the school's enduring mission.

STAKEHOLDERS' COMPLICITY IN THE INSTRUMENTALIZATION OF EDUCATION

To look at the very big picture here, neoliberalism is a political-economic ideology that, in David Harvey's words, seeks to "bring all human action into the domain of the market."[15] One of its key effects, as I explain below, is to "responsibilize" people for their future class status.[16] How people respond to this environment, however, depends very much on their own socioeconomic status, as well as the cultural and social capital they have at their disposal—much of which is inherited. Thus neoliberalism can serve to reinforce and reproduce existing societal inequities.

Understood in this context, the various stakeholder concerns at Hamaskil certainly make sense given their relative positions in the neoliberal order. *Parents* are well aware of competitive higher education markets and the need for a record of high academic performance on the part of their children. Furthermore, many of them seem to have a proprietary relationship with the school, where they expect to influence policy and practice. Although the school *administrators* are responsible for upholding institutional core values, they are also complicit in this proprietary relationship with parents, in part because the school's well-being is contingent on parents' continued financial support.

The *students* are also aware of increasing educational competition. Furthermore, they are likely to be at least implicitly aware that neoliberalism "responsibilizes" their generation for their own future class status. They cannot trust that the same social safety nets that were there for their parents' generation will be in place when they are adults. Indeed, current economic restructuring and the "flattening" of global markets make it likely that middle-class children will have a lower standard of living than their parents'.[17] Parents share these worries with their children, of course. Many middle-class parents are preoccupied with fear of "downward mobility" or "fear of falling" for their children.[18]

Hamaskil *teachers* are torn. Some see it as their job to get their students into the best college possible, while others embrace a broader vision of teaching and take a more critical view of this instrumental role. Individual teachers also ambivalently embrace conflicting perspectives. Melanie Horowitz's plea to be recognized as the "professional" succinctly captures many teachers' fears that they are coming to be seen as cogs in a machine rather than as professionals doing complex work. From this perspective, she firmly rejects what some researchers have come to describe as the "deprofessionalization," and even "clericalization," of teaching.[19] On the other hand, she then credits high-net-worth parents with having the right to expect her to produce specific, measurable academic outcomes. Dr. Heschel, too, implicitly limits the purpose of education at Hamaskil to a narrow and instrumental project when she asks Ms. Horowitz whether she felt parents were "getting what they pay for" in terms of "preparing students to succeed in college."

HYPERCREDENTIALISM IN AMERICAN SCHOOLING

Like schools in many upper-middle-class communities, Hamaskil thus seems to have become enmeshed in an "unwritten curriculum" for student success that conceives of education primarily as a private good. As in schools in similar communities, this unwritten curriculum is rooted in the local class culture and is deeply anchored in the ideology of American competitive individualism. It also, though, has evolved new features to provide youth the additional advantages demanded by a neoliberal era.[20] One of these is building up students' academic worth through inflated grades.

Grade inflation is part of a contemporary pattern of *hypercredentialing* in schools: the production of artificially high credentials intended to strengthen students' positions in education and job markets.[21] While hypercredentialing has the very real effect of bolstering students' academic profiles, it also contributes to students' psychological capital by building up their sense of self-worth and their confidence and by helping them to think of themselves as successes-in-the-making.[22]

In this view, the Hamaskil parent's comment that "not everyone can be a winner," is telling. While this may be the case, the policies and practices of many schools serving more affluent and achievement-oriented students and their families are geared, in part, to make as many students as possible *feel* like a winner—especially in regard to the possible futures they envision for themselves. This confidence may be an important kind of psychological capital in its own right.

Hamaskil's status as "The Haven" is thus terrific for its own students, but is also potentially a means of positioning them for further success. On the one hand, we should celebrate Hamaskil's capacity to give students "the love and support adolescents need to figure out who they are, find their passions, grow into ethical leaders who will make the world a better place." These are laudable educational goals. On the other hand, Mr. Finley's comment that the school's unique climate protects its students from "the crazy competition" is ironic. While the school certainly provides an important nurturing environment for students, it also simultaneously prepares them for individualistic competition by enhancing their psychological capacities to see themselves—and to take action—as winners. And of course, their high grades don't hurt, either.

GRADE INFLATION ON THE OTHER SIDE: REDUCING FAILURE RATHER THAN REWARDING SUCCESS

While this kind of "institutional sponsorship" of students by schools is fairly common in more affluent communities in the United States, it is palpably absent in areas that are more disadvantaged.[23] This sentiment was succinctly put by a student forty years ago who told researcher Jay MacLeod that there "ain't no makin' it" in his community (a phrase that became the title of MacLeod's book).[24] Since then, other researchers in similar settings have described class cultural ideologies marked by lack of belief in equitable opportunity structures, low expectations for success, and disengagement in school.[25]

In my current research in an urban high school, I have repeatedly heard a guidance counselor say the school's mostly disadvantaged students get "beaten at every turn" and have low expectations for future success. His approach is to work with them on what they need to do to start their own "winning streak"—a comment on the importance of confidence and seeing oneself as a "winner."

This is not to say that grade inflation is absent in schools serving disadvantaged students. Rather than enhancing high achievers' credentials, however, it is used to boost the assessments of lower-achieving students so they can pass courses, earn credits, move to the next grade, and eventually graduate. Grade inflation in both settings thus similarly masks students' real learning and achievements, and legitimizes schools as institutions that "sort" students for future opportunities. Consonant with the neoliberal context, however, grade inflation legitimizes very different futures for low-income versus high-income youth.

THE ETHICS OF GRADE INFLATION: ALTERNATIVE VISIONS

A relevant question for progressive-minded educators, then, is the extent to which grade inflation contributes to educational inequity. In my view, it does so in two disturbing ways. First, not all schools engage in hyper-credentialing. Hence, students who emerge from schools that *do* enhance assessments inequitably and unjustifiably benefit in the college admissions process and financial aid process. If a school identifies forty-odd "valedictorians," for instance, each of these students is eligible for a valedictorian scholarship, instead of just the one student from a nonhypercredentialing school. In this respect, grade inflation *directly* promotes inequity.

Second, and more insidiously, hypercredentialing *indirectly* promotes inequity by masking the role such schools play in reinforcing social reproduction. By assessing students from different social-class backgrounds in consistently different but unacknowledged ways, hypercredentialing schools maintain the pretense that more advantaged students simply *are* more meritorious and higher achieving, and that less advantaged students are doing well simply by making it to graduation. It is in these two senses that there is an ethical dimension to grade inflation that extends beyond Hamaskil itself.

In such an increasingly neoliberalized world, it is more important than ever to consider alternative, and arguably more ethical, educational visions. Consider, for example, Lisa Delpit's marvelous interview with a Yupik Eskimo elder, who told her that the purpose of education is "to die satisfied with life."[26] Such a broad perspective opens up the conversation about the diversity of educational purposes and puts the current hypercredentialing fever into perspective.

Similarly, consider the school's timeless and inspirational Hebrew motto, *tikkun olam*—"repairing the world." Parents presumably chose Hamaskil in part because of its mission. (After all, there are two other Jewish day schools in close proximity that they might have chosen instead.) Perhaps they can come to see how their intensifying pressure to extract individual goods from the school in the form of inflated grades rubs up against the school's prosocial purpose of preparing graduates to serve others.

There is even a chance that parents could be led to recognize the ethical and intellectual harms their own children potentially suffer in hypercredentialized settings. Recent research demonstrates the benefits of students' taking on "growth" mindsets with regard to intelligence. They benefit from seeing the brain as a muscle that can be developed, and from coming to understand that intelligence is malleable rather than fixed.[27] Such attitudes are potentially more easily learned when grades come hard rather than easily. Relatedly, students benefit when they learn to treat mistakes, shortfalls, and failures in school as opportunities for further learning.[28] Leah Stein's comment that the school is preventing students "from discovering the true extent of their capacities by rewarding the barest glimmers" speaks to the relevance of this new research.

Indeed, a primary problem with such an emphasis on grades is that it does not attend to one of the most important objectives of secondary education: enabling students to acquire knowledge about how they themselves learn. In an era of "ratcheted" educational credentialism, where most of these students will go on to pursue not only college, but graduate education or training in their chosen field, acquiring the habits of learning is more important than ever.[29]

If parents at Hamaskil can learn to recognize grade inflation as harming their own children's intellectual and ethical development—in addition to seeing how grade inflation harms the broader social order by exacerbating educational, social, and class inequities—then Dr. Heschel may find it easier to help foster a more coherent, educationally rich, and ethically defensible educational vision and practice.

Peter Demerath is an associate professor in the Department of Organizational Leadership, Policy and Development, and an affiliated faculty member in the Department of Anthropology at the University of Minnesota. His 2009 book, Producing Success: The Culture of Personal Advancement in an American High School, *is now in its second printing with the University of Chicago Press.*

Grades Miss the Mark

DEEPA SRIYA VASUDEVAN

Hamaskil Jewish Day School's new academic dean, Dr. Heschel, faces the apparent task of resolving issues related to grade inflation. On the one hand, grade inflation seems to compromise some teachers' sense of integrity, undercut academic standards, and reinforce students' and parents' sense of entitlement because they are paying for school. On the other hand, grade inflation seems to offer assurance to hard-working students and to preserve the school's external reputation for academic excellence; it also does not seem to adversely affect how well students perform in college. Evidence from Princeton's failed experiment with grade deflation also seems to strengthen the case for Hamaskil's continued grade inflation, insofar as it harmed students' well-being, decreased yield, fostered a toxic culture, and failed even in its primary goals of focusing students on learning and professors on rigorous teaching and assessment.

Herein lies the challenge. Once we start untangling the arguments regarding grade inflation, a larger lesson emerges from the endless knots along the way: grades, and debates about grades, are at best disconnected and at worst antithetical to the essence of education—that is, teaching and learning. The problem that Hamaskil faces is not grade *inflation*. It is *grading*. If Hamaskil's primary goals are to engage young people in learning and inquiry and to instill shared values of care, inclusion, and equality, then the rationale for using numerical or letter-based grades is completely flawed. In order to preserve Hamaskil's purpose, I recommend that Dr. Heschel eliminate grades as the mode of academic feedback for students and parents. Instead, Hamaskil teachers should use narrative feedback to offer holistic and meaningful information to adolescent learners and their parents.

A REGRESSION TOWARD THE NORM: DEFAULTING TO GRADES

Unlike Hamaskil's intentional approach to many other aspects of its practice, its policy of assigning students letter grades likely represents an unreflective default to the norm. Letter grades are a fairly new system of measuring performance, having been introduced in schools only in the 1870s as a way to coordinate evaluation systems across institutions.[30] It is now, of course, hard to find a US high school or college that does not use a similar model for reporting student performance—which likely explains why Hamaskil uses grades as well. For although grades and grade point averages (GPAs) theoretically offer comparable performance benchmarks across schools and universities, Dr. Morrison's complaint that he does not know *what grades mean anymore* illuminates how arbitrary and political grading practices, meanings, and value can be.

The meaning of a letter grade varies greatly depending on the context, the evaluator, and the recipient. A grade is an empty signifier; it is teachers, parents, students, college admissions staff, and employers who ascribe meaning to it. For example, an A can signal "high performance," "the highest performance," "achieved mastery of learning objective," "observed hard work," "completed assignments," "creative thinking," "followed the rules," or perhaps even "students' parents complained." The meaning of an A may shift in cases of inflation; thus, for students at elite universities, receiving a B– may feel like receiving an F at another school. An A does not necessarily "lose value" if everyone receives an A; as Hamaskil's Head of School Rabbi Cohen points out, high grades may be widespread because motivated and talented students are achieving great things under the tutelage of high-quality teachers. But because grades represent some level of expectation, performance, or effort, they can lose their significance when high grades reflect merely a lowering of expectations or standards. Insofar as Hamaskil's grading practices seem to represent a default to societal expectations rather than an intentional means of achieving their educational goals, they are particularly vulnerable to such questions about their meaning.

NEGATIVE EFFECTS OF REWARDS: WHAT LEARNERS MISS WHEN ALL EYES ARE ON THE PRIZE

Defaulting to grades threatens the integrity of Hamaskil because grades suggest that learning and academic achievement require extrinsic rewards to make them worthwhile. Both teachers and parents reflect this notion of grades as a form of currency. For example, Dr. Morrison raises questions about who is "deserving" of an A; history teacher Melanie Horowitz concludes "that's what parents are paying us for"; and a parent declares that "NOT EVERYONE CAN BE A WINNER." Such attitudes contradict what Hamaskil stands for and more generally undermine schools' educational missions.

The use of extrinsic rewards in schools, whether it is grades or pizza parties for high test scores, is both commonplace and problematic. Questions

of grade deservedness can distract teachers, students, and parents from focusing on *learning* to focusing on *achievement*. Alfie Kohn has argued, for
example, that the use of grades tends to lessen students' interest in learning,
encourage learners to choose the easiest tasks to meet the standard, and
decrease the quality of students' thinking.[31] Research also demonstrates
that grades lead students to focus on avoiding failure rather than seeking success. Unsurprisingly, they also therefore increase student anxiety
and shame, and negatively affect all but high-achieving students' interests
and performance.[32] Even in the workplace, high financial rewards tend
to have detrimental effects on employees' performance.[33] Thus, although
"[r]ewards are often successful at increasing the probability that we will do
something," we must recognize that "they also change the way we do it."[34]

Behavioral science has inspired a bevy of short-term strategies for both
children in schools and adults in the workplace, but meaningful, long-term
learning and identity construction depend instead on schools' cultivating
students' intrinsic motivation: motivation driven by interest, enjoyment,
and connectedness. Extrinsic rewards that only reinforce control and pressure rather than lead students toward self-regulation or autonomy fail to do
this.[35] Dorothy De Zouche, a Missouri teacher, posed this choice emphatically seventy years ago: "If adults would come to realize that the real and
permanent satisfactions in life are the satisfactions that come from doing
things for the sake of the things themselves, and not for the reward tacked
on, we might be able to sell our young people on the same idea, and we
should have a less ugly, jealous, vicious world."[36]

POSITIVE OUTLIERS: ABANDONING GRADES FOR TRANSFORMATIONAL EDUCATION

Given that Dr. Heschel is participating in a holistic strategic planning process, she is perfectly placed to address the issue of grades in light of her
school's primary aims. Hamaskil's mission is "to inspire, teach, and empower Jews who are passionate, intellectual, critical, original, and ethical
in all parts of their lives, so as to bring about *tikkun olam*: a more just
and caring world in which Jews and all human beings will flourish with
dignity and joy." This profound statement matches the desires of Hamaskil
educators, who emphasize "learning rather than competing" and offer "the
support and love adolescents need to figure out who they are, find their
passions, and grow into ethical leaders who will make the world a better
place." Hamaskil educators aim to foster a rigorous learning environment
for their students, one that encourages curiosity and creativity and that

upholds values such as equity and inclusion. They take pride in their school being a "haven," a safe space for development and growth, and an incubator for civic engagement and democratic participation. With a vision for holistic development, some teachers remark that grades feel inconsequential, perhaps even a distraction from the "bigger picture" where students can focus their attention. Hamaskil staff members do not believe that students need to engage in "real-world competition." Instead, they aspire for their students to become *healers* and *ethical leaders*.

In this model, Hamaskil's ultimate goal is not transactional; it is *transformational*. Teachers' resounding vision for Hamaskil is to offer a safe haven of noncompetitive individualized learning. But their concerns regarding grading practices have little to do with—in fact, are antithetical to—inspiring learning and ethical leadership. Rather, they reveal the school's hidden market logics of competition, commodification, and individual gain. A traditional grading system inherently assumes these logics, along with the logics of punishment and reward that focus on measures of control rather than autonomy. Thus, grades seem woefully misaligned with the mission of the school.

Hamaskil should instead follow the example of some other independent schools and use narrative evaluations to communicate essential formative and summative feedback to students and their parents, including benchmarks for academic progress. Montessori schools, for example, assign "no grades, or other forms of reward or punishment, subtle or overt. Assessment is by portfolio and the teacher's observation and record keeping. The test of whether or not the system is working lies in the accomplishment and behavior of the children, their happiness, maturity, kindness, and love of learning and level of work."[37] The Youth Initiative School, a Waldorf Education–inspired school in Wisconsin, provides weekly narrative evaluations to provide timely formative feedback, along with summative narrative evaluations accompanied by a pass/fail indicator on transcripts. These practices accord with their belief that "learning should not be a competition and that knowledge is its own reward."[38]

There are also a few selective colleges that provide solely narrative feedback as well, such as Evergreen State College and Hampshire College. At Evergreen, once described by *U.S. News & World Report* as the top learning community in the country, faculty members have designed a set of six "Expectations" regarding skills and habits of mind that frame their narrative feedback.[39] In response to questions of how colleges without grades prepare students for future careers and graduate school, Hampshire President Jonathan Nash argued that "rigor in education is not about being told how well you did, but about being told what you need to do next in order to improve," and noted that two-thirds of Hampshire graduates go on to graduate school.[40]

Dr. Heschel and her colleagues have a unique opportunity to dismantle grading at Hamaskil Jewish Day School. They would not be alone in this endeavor, and hence need not worry about the costs of being the "first mover." Additionally, since attending a private school is an educational advantage for the few, it seems all the more important that Hamaskil leaders leverage this privilege by taking this risk and accepting some of the possible backlash. This change could model the transformative and ethical leadership they wish to inspire in their students. As Richard Shaull reminds us in the foreword of Paulo Freire's *Pedagogy of the Oppressed*:

> Education either functions as an instrument which is used to facilitate integration of the younger generation into the logic of the present system and bring about conformity or it becomes "the practice of freedom," the means by which men and women deal critically and creatively with reality and discover how to participate in the transformation of their world.[41]

Hamaskil is committed in principle to *tikkun olam*; abandoning grades in favor of narrative assessments can help put it into practice.

Deepa Sriya Vasudevan is an EdD student at the Harvard Graduate School of Education. Broadly interested in school-community relationships, youth development, and organizational culture, she is currently researching how youth workers understand their occupational identities and practices in community-based nonprofits.

Protect Teacher Integrity

Doris A. Santoro

In her earliest days as academic dean, Dr. Heschel faces a potentially intractable dilemma about how to address her colleagues' conflicting approaches to grading and grade inflation. But this challenge also presents an opportunity—namely, to address teachers' underlying moral concerns that are central to their work. Rather than focusing directly on grading practices, Dr. Heschel should start by addressing the issue of teachers' *professional integrity*. By doing so, she will help Hamaskil faculty members recover their sense of professional moral purpose, stave off demoralization, and create a space in which teachers can enact their professional roles—including their grading responsibilities—with integrity.

MIXED MESSAGES

Like those at Hamaskil, educators around the world, from kindergarten teachers to graduate-level professors, view assigning grades as one of the least favorite aspects of their work. In large part this dislike is because grades can convey many different messages—and educators know that signals often get crossed. Those who assign grades disagree with one another about the meaning they convey; those who receive grades may interpret them in yet a different way. Often these messages are at cross-purposes with one another.[42]

For example, consider the misunderstandings that can result when a teacher assigns a grade in regard to one of the following aims, but students and their parents interpret the grade as serving a different purpose:

- indicate performance
- highlight effort
- communicate progress
- identify capacities
- predict future performance
- rank and sort performance within institution
- enable entry into next level of schooling
- provide access to special goods or services
- offer special recognition

- measure the school's performance
- measure the teacher's performance
- evade or avoid conflict
- foster a sense of well-being among students
- attenuate competition among students
- encourage competition among students

We see such crossed signals at work in "Inflated Expectations." Teachers, parents, and administrators disagree both across groups and among themselves about whether grades should be used to reward student effort, to indicate rigorous academic performance, to sustain student motivation, to indicate caring, to attract new families, or to create a competitive economy based on good grades as a scarce commodity. They also know that no matter what teachers at Hamaskil decide about grading practices, students' futures will be shaped by grade point averages (GPAs) that serve as currency in the higher-education market.

THREE DIMENSIONS OF TEACHER INTEGRITY

It might seem that the best way to resolve these misunderstandings is for someone like Dr. Heschel to establish a single vision for grading across the school community. But this is a Sisyphean task—especially since it is, in fact, reasonable for grades to serve more than one aim.

Instead, Dr. Heschel needs to address teachers' more fundamental concerns about threats to their integrity. Ms. Stein expresses this concern directly when she argues that grade inflation "undercuts our integrity as educators." So do her colleagues when they complain "about the 'shame' and a 'lack of integrity' they felt when assigning grades." Dr. Morrison raises it indirectly when he indicts his colleagues for being "complicit" in the practice of grade inflation. One is "complicit," after all, only in a practice that is in some way wrong, or at least morally compromised.

When teachers like Ms. Stein or Dr. Morrison raise concerns about integrity, they are drawing on three intersecting dimensions of teacher integrity: *personal integrity, integrity of teaching,* and *professional integrity.*[43]

In the dimension of *personal integrity,* teachers ask themselves: How is who I am expressed in my role as a teacher? How does who I am as a person enhance who I am as a teacher? Is this the work that I am called to do? Some teachers may cultivate personal integrity in contexts that fall mostly outside their identities in schools. However, many teachers enter the profession and stay because they find personal moral value in their work.

They feel able to cultivate the qualities that they believe make them good people in their work. Teachers may realize a passion for their subject area, for their commitment to social justice, or for religious or secular beliefs. On the other hand, if teachers believe that their work leads them to be dishonest, untrustworthy, or unkind, they may find that it jeopardizes their personal integrity.

Teachers who are concerned about the *integrity of teaching* ask themselves: Is what I am doing reasonably called teaching? Would others consider my actions to be those of a teacher? In this regard, some faculty members at Hamaskil wonder, if I assign grades based on parental demands, may I rightfully be considered an educator?

Hamaskil's teachers seem to disagree about the answers to this last question. Such disagreements are reasonable, since the work of teaching has a long history peppered with debate, disagreement, and innovation. Consider the following: Should teachers provide students with a core base of cultural knowledge, or encourage students to determine the path of their learning? How should teachers balance the needs of individual students in relation to the well-being of the entire class? When should technological instructional aids supplant human educators? Across time, educators have claimed that how we respond to these questions could bring an end to teaching as we know it. For some, such an end would be a victory; for others, it would be a tragedy. Regardless of the answers, questions about the integrity of teaching provide opportunities for teachers and school communities to articulate core values about education.

The third dimension of teacher integrity, *professional integrity,* lies at the intersection of the integrity of teaching and personal integrity (see figure 4.1).[44] When teachers ask questions about professional integrity, they are *situated* in a particular context and *embodied* by a particular person. They ask questions such as "What does it mean to act in the best interests of students in this case?" and "How am I honoring students' needs and teaching the subject responsibly in my role at this school?" In trying to realize their professional integrity, teachers take personal action as teaching professionals in a specific educational space.

Threats to professional integrity thus affect both personal integrity and the integrity of teaching. When a teacher takes actions that undermine what she believes is the best work she can do, she may experience corrosive effects that diminish how she feels about herself (personal integrity) and how she feels about her contributions to her profession (integrity of teaching). For example, when the young English teacher cries while relating her embarrassment over passing a student, her sense of embarrassment

FIGURE 4.1   Model of teacher integrity

Personal integrity contributes to the integrity of teaching. The integrity of teaching enhances personal integrity. The overlap results in a unique professional integrity.

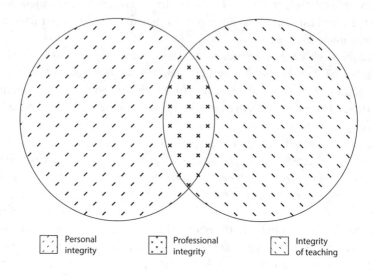

| | Personal integrity | | Professional integrity | | Integrity of teaching |

indicates that her diminished professional integrity bleeds into her sense of personal integrity.

When teachers experience emotions such as "guilt, shame, anxiety, embarrassment—the emotions of self-assessment—and sometimes fear, sorrow, and even pain," they often are suffering from the corrosion of their professional integrity.[45] Teachers at Hamaskil are clearly experiencing such emotions and signaling these concerns to Dr. Heschel; they need her help.

DEMORALIZED FACULTY

They are right to seek help. This is a dangerous place for Hamaskil to be, since teachers, students, and schools all suffer when teachers feel that policies and practices corrode their professional integrity. Many teachers enter the profession with a sense of moral purpose that sustains their work over time.[46] Even in a school like Hamaskil that articulates a clear moral vision in its mission, teachers may interpret and enact their moral purposes differently. The teachers at Hamaskil place emphasis on distinct dimensions of their moral work: facilitating human flourishing, working for social justice, and providing access to intellectual traditions, just to name a few.

Professional integrity and the sense of doing good work go hand in hand. Teachers enact their understanding of goodness, rightness, or justice as individuals in a professional capacity. This work contributes not only to the teachers' livelihood, but also to their moral identity.[47]

Teachers become *demoralized* if they can no longer access what makes their work good, such as developing strong relationships with students or engaging in rigorous study of religious texts, and if they feel forced to engage in behaviors that undermine their vision of goodness.[48] The costs can be substantial. To uphold the moral motivations that brought them to teaching, teachers may leave the school, or even leave the profession altogether.[49]

TAKING ACTION

Dr. Heschel has ample reason, therefore, to be concerned that teachers in her school remark repeatedly about the ways grading impinges on their professional integrity. Her "listening tour" provided significant material for her assessment of teaching and learning. In her recommendations to the Strategic Vision Committee, she needs to articulate a plan to address moral concerns with the school leadership and its faculty.

The school's commitment to *tikkun olam* provides a natural and convenient starting place. Dr. Heschel can connect the faculty members' concerns about grading with the school's mission to bring about "a more just and caring world in which Jews and all human beings will flourish with dignity and joy." In facilitated conversations, faculty members could address issues such as how grading practices demonstrate this principle for students, for the subjects studied, and for the school.

Faculty members are unlikely to reach consensus on grading practices, but Dr. Heschel may soften discord among teachers through these conversations. Teachers at Hamaskil may find that discussing their grading practices using the language of the school's mission provides a shared vocabulary about the purposes of formal assessment. Through these discussions, teachers may bring their grading practices into better alignment with the mission, or, at the very least, see that their colleagues' practices are not arbitrary or intentionally undermining their own.

Hamaskil's faculty members identify the greatest threat to professional integrity in the students' parents. Teachers feel pressured to assign or revise grades because of the expectations of parents who pay hefty tuitions for their children's education and, by extension, pay teachers' salaries. Dr. Heschel can defend teachers' professional integrity by serving as the buffer between teachers enacting their professional obligations and parents who understandably act in what they see as their families' best interests.

School leaders like Dr. Heschel can enable teachers to enact professional integrity. The best question to start with could be, "What do teachers need to enact their professional roles with integrity?" Dr. Heschel can make a commitment to the teachers at Hamaskil—to enable them to work from a place of professional integrity. That commitment also comes with the responsibility for faculty members to provide good rationales for how and why they assign grades that align with the school's mission.

Doris A. Santoro is an associate professor at Bowdoin College, where she teaches courses in educational studies and teacher education. She researches teachers' moral concerns about their work and their moral arguments for resistance.

CHAPTER FIVE

Is Pandering Ethical Policy?

Power, Privilege, and School Assignment

MEIRA LEVINSON

How should access to public elementary schools of variable quality be distributed within a school district? What are the characteristics of a distributively just school assignment system when some district schools are much worse than others? These are questions that the Boston Public Schools (BPS) faced when it attempted to reform its school assignment system in preparation for the 2014–2015 school year.[1]

Boston Public Schools' "Home-Based Plan" is a novel elementary school assignment policy. All children entering kindergarten (called K2) are assigned baskets of ten to eighteen elementary schools to which they can apply through a BPS-wide lottery.[2] Each family's basket includes all schools that are less than a mile away from where they live, all citywide elementary schools, the nearest Early Learning Center, and any elementary school that the child's sibling(s) already attends. In addition, the basket must include at least two schools rated in the top 25 percent in the city (Tier I schools), at least two more schools rated in the top 50 percent (Tier I or II schools), and an additional two schools rated above the bottom 25 percent (Tier I, II, or III schools).[3] Most families will have some of these schools already within a mile of their house; others are added as needed. Families' baskets also include one or more "option" schools—meaning schools that are traditionally underchоsen and hence very likely to have space to accommodate all applicants—to ensure that every child entering K2 and above is guaranteed a seat at one of the schools in their basket. Exhibit 5.1 summarizes families' basket construction.

Families have until early February to submit a rank-ordered list of their school choices and enter the first round of the lottery; a computer then runs an algorithm to assign children to schools. Students already attending a school for prekindergarten (called K1) are guaranteed a K2 spot. Children with siblings at a school then have priority access; after that, children are assigned in order of school preference and their randomly generated lottery number. The assignment algorithm does not take into account demographic features of the children (e.g., to ensure a race/ethnicity, gender, or income balance), nor does it control for distance from the school other than by the initial basket construction. All kindergarten seats are made available to be assigned in this initial round; hence, popular schools are filled by the end of the first round. Families who enter later rounds of the lottery—because they move to Boston during the spring or because they were unaware of, disorganized about, or overwhelmed by the process of entering the initial lottery—thus have much more restricted school choices.

Families who do not like their assignment, or who did not enter the first round, can enter the lottery in later rounds throughout the spring and summer. They operate just as round one did, except that there is also now a "parent compacting" option, which enables groups of families to join together and enter the lottery for an underchosen school (i.e., one that still has a number of seats available) as a group.

EXHIBIT 5.1   Kindergarten access: Home-Based Plan

Each child is assigned a customized basket of schools based on home address.

- Basket includes the closest:
  - Two Tier I schools (top 25%)
  - Two next Tier I or II schools (top 50%)
  - Two next Tier I, II, or III schools (top 75%)
- The basket also includes all schools within one mile of home, citywide schools, siblings' schools, nearest Early Learning Center, and "option" (historically underchosen) schools.
- Other schools may be included for ELLs and children identified with special education needs.
- Tiers are based on standardized-test proficiency and academic growth scores; a proposal to include school climate survey, attendance, discipline, and other data in calculating tiers has been adopted but not implemented.

EQUALITY OF OPPORTUNITY

There are a number of different principles at play in BPS' Home-Based school assignment plan. One indisputably important principle is that children should have an *equal opportunity to access a quality education.*

The Home-Based Plan promotes equality of opportunity most notably by limiting the correlation between neighborhood residence and school access. If students were assigned to schools solely on the basis of their home address, then "geography would be destiny." Wealthier, more informed, and better-connected families would rent or buy homes near high-quality neighborhood schools. Poorer and/or less informed families, often especially new arrivals, would be consigned to neighborhoods that feed to poorer-quality schools. The Home-Based Plan attempts to counteract this pattern. Although the plan relies on students' addresses to construct their baskets of choices, it also explicitly tries to realize the principle of equal opportunity by ensuring that every family has at least four *high-quality schools* (which I define as Tier I or II schools—those in the top 50% in the city), and at least six *quality* (defined as Tier I, II, or III) schools, in their choice basket. In this respect, even the most isolated and impoverished families can be confident that they will have the opportunity to list some high-quality schools on their lottery form.

The Home-Based Plan also promotes equality of opportunity by *limiting* the overall number of schools that are in each family's basket. By restricting families' choices to ten to fourteen schools, on average, the Home-Based Plan paternalistically makes it more likely that every family can learn enough about the schools in their basket to make reasonable choices that reflect their true preferences.

At the same time, BPS' Home-Based Plan limits equality of educational opportunity in some significant ways. First, the Home-Based Plan provides all families an *equal minimum* set of options, not an *equal maximum.* Families are "leveled up" to at least four high-quality schools, but they are not "leveled down" to a predetermined ceiling. High-quality schools cluster in particular, wealthier neighborhoods; families who live less than a mile from these clusters, therefore, may have as many as seven high-quality schools in their baskets, while other families have only four such schools.

Second, simply being able to list schools on a lottery form isn't really what opportunity is about. Opportunity is far more reasonably understood as one's *chance of getting a seat in a high-quality school,* which varies significantly depending on the *size* and *competitiveness* of the high-quality schools in one's basket.

Consider, for example, two prospective kindergartners: "Celia," who lives in the solidly middle-class neighborhood of West Roxbury, and "John," who lives in the lower-income Dorchester neighborhood. West Roxbury has a child poverty rate of 5 percent; Dorchester's child poverty rate is 29 percent, nearly six times higher than West Roxbury's. Using Boston's online tool (www.discoverbps.org) and a residential address within the neighborhood, we found that Celia has thirteen schools in her basket, including six high-quality schools that in 2013–2014 had a total of 339 K2 seats. John, by contrast, has fourteen schools in his basket, including five high-quality schools that in 2013–2014 had a total of 268 K2 seats. Already it is clear that John's family faces a slightly greater information burden and has access to 21 percent fewer high-quality seats than Celia's family does.

These differences between Celia and John's *formal* versus *substantive* equality of opportunity are further exacerbated by the number of other children competing for the same K2 seats. Competition for seats is a function of the population density of young children living in the neighborhood and their likelihood to enter the BPS lottery, both of which make John's tenuous situation worse. As in any city, Boston's population is not spread evenly among neighborhoods. Lower-income neighborhoods are generally denser than middle- and high-income areas and also have more families with school-age kids. These differences in density and population age, along with differences in the size and location of high-quality schools, mean that competition for high-quality school seats varies considerably across neighborhoods.

West Roxbury, for example, has a population density of 700 young children (ages nine or under) per square mile, while Dorchester's population density is triple that: 2,135 young children per square mile. This means that John is likely competing against three times as many children for the seats in his basket than Celia is competing against for the seats in her basket. Not surprisingly, these competition disparities track both income and race. Children of color from low-income families face significantly stiffer competition for high-quality school seats than do middle- and upper-income White children in Boston.[4]

The baskets could be constructed so as to achieve more substantive equality of opportunity. BPS could "level down" choices by taking extra high-quality schools out of some families' baskets and also potentially inserting more low-quality schools into their baskets. Census data and prior school demand data could also be used to calculate a competition index for school seats. Families' baskets could then be built so as to equalize seat-level competition rather than school access. The lottery algorithm itself could also be revised. In San Francisco, children from neighborhoods with low average test scores (a sadly reliable proxy for income) are given weighted priority in the lottery. In Cambridge, "controlled choice" mechanisms ensure that every school reflects the broader socioeconomic demographics of the city. If the lottery results in a school that has a disproportionately high or low percentage of low-income children as compared to the system as a whole, then they are reshuffled (before the assignments are finalized) so as to ensure a more equitable distribution of children among schools—and more equitable distribution of schools among children. Both of these systems could be used in Boston. In fact, BPS engaged in balancing procedures for many years to ensure that schools were racially and ethnically diverse, until it ended the policy in 2000–2001.

"GROWING THE PIE" BY ATTRACTING MIDDLE-INCOME FAMILIES INTO PUBLIC SCHOOLS

On the other hand, leveling down and other policies designed to give poor children an equal shot at accessing high-quality schools may directly conflict with a second principle—namely, that Boston's school assignment policy should *foster an overall increase in the number of quality schools available in the district.*

The best—really, the only—way education and social reformers know to improve urban schools at scale is to eliminate hypersegregation of low-income children of color. Fifty years' worth of studies have demonstrated that children of all socioeconomic backgrounds tend to do better in lower-poverty schools; more recent studies have shown convincingly that, when it comes to academic achievement, school composition may trump even family background. The effects can be profound: low-income children who attend low-poverty schools, for example, do better on average than middle-income students do in high-poverty schools. These patterns are replicated internationally.[5] Furthermore, the magnitude of these school composition effects on the achievement of low-income children may be larger than the magnitude of other, currently popular education reforms such as teacher hiring and firing, curricular shifts, data-driven instruction, or longer school days.

In particular, no other intervention in schools serving hypersegregated low-income students of color has proven replicable and reliable at scale. A study of over sixty-two thousand US public schools, for example, found that less than 1 percent of low-income schools—and only 0.3 percent of low-income schools serving over 50 percent students of color—achieved even decent academic results, defined by at least two-thirds of students demonstrating proficiency on state standardized tests in two subjects in two different grades over two years. To be clear, this amounted to thirty-nine schools *across the entire country.* This is compared to about a quarter of low-poverty and low-minority schools—or 10,174 schools across the United States.[6]

BPS elementary schools exemplify this persistent, stubborn relationship between hypersegregation and academic struggle. Tier I schools have a student body that is, on average, 28 percent White and 36 percent nonpoor; option schools, by contrast, are on average 5 percent White and 16 percent nonpoor. Similarly, only three of the eighteen Tier I schools have a student body that is over 80 percent low-income, while only two of the nineteen option schools have a student body that is *under* 80 percent low-income.[7]

There are a number of reasons that schools that serve a critical mass of middle- and high-income students, as well as White students, tend to be higher quality. Such schools tend to have more parent involvement, fewer discipline problems, higher levels of homework completion, lower levels of both student and teacher mobility, higher percentages of children who enter school "ready to learn," fewer suspensions and expulsions, more extracurricular activities, more whole-child supports like guidance counselors and nurses, fewer interactions with law enforcement, fewer students who are battling homelessness or chronic illnesses, more experienced teachers, and larger per-pupil expenditures, thanks to both regular budget allocations and school-based fundraising.[8]

Some of these school characteristics follow from the characteristics of the families themselves. Wealthier parents, for example, tend to have greater capacities to donate money to the Parent Teacher Association (PTA), to maintain more stable living situations, and to expose their children to academically enriching opportunities from birth onward. Many of these school characteristics also derive from the social, cultural, and political capital these families are able to deploy both within and beyond the school in order to serve their own children. For a variety of unjust but nonetheless politically and socially potent reasons, higher-income and White parents are more likely to be successful in lobbying officials to limit or reverse school budget cuts, for example, or to change a school policy that they believe is harming their children.

Nor do White and nonpoor parents necessarily even need to deploy such capital, as their children are often preemptively served better by schools and districts. The cultural congruence between overwhelmingly White and middle-class educators' expectations and White and middle-class students' behaviors, for example, can create a virtuous circle that nurtures academic achievement, teacher and administrator stability, developmentally appropriate disciplinary policies, and other aspects of a strong and positive school culture. To say that socioeconomic and racial integration is a key factor for improving schools at scale, therefore, is not to suggest that low-income children and families of color are intrinsically educationally deficient, nor that they intrinsically benefit from simply sitting next to middle-class and White children. Rather, it is to say that there are multiple, persistent, and significant *instrumental* benefits to having a critical mass of White and nonpoor children in one's school.

THREATENED EXIT

To create lower-poverty schools, however, districts must actually attract nonpoor families into the system—and equally important, not *push* middle- and higher-income families out of the system. Leveling-up approaches are far more likely to attract and retain such families than are leveling-down policies that families interpret as a direct assault on their educational rights and interests. If leveling-down policies induced well-resourced families to exit BPS when they might have stayed in under a leveling-up policy like the current Home-Based Plan, then that might be a good reason to trade maximum equality for minimum equality.

Boston has good reason to be concerned about White and middle-class flight. Only 74 percent of all school-age children—and only 53 percent of White children—living in Boston attend BPS schools. Although almost half of Boston's school-age children are White and the majority are middle class, 87 percent of children who do attend BPS are non-White, and about three-quarters are from low-income families. Furthermore, many nonpoor and White Boston families flee the city before their children even reach school age.[9] About one thousand children under age five move out of Boston to surrounding suburbs every year; the vast majority are from households with high levels of education and income.[10]

Families with economic means, therefore, hold a trump card with Boston Public Schools: that of *threatened exit*. BPS knows that privileged families will and do exit to the suburbs preemptively. Furthermore, even if these privileged families remain in the city, they can and will exit into charter, parochial, and other independent schools. If BPS wants to convince such families to stay in Boston, enter the lottery, and then actually enter the school system, it must offer inducements to them to not engage in preemptive exit. These inducements include address-based basket construction, a lottery unweighted by demographic characteristics, absolute priority to first-round lottery entrants, and the back-end reassurance of parent compacting. Taken together, these inducements offer privileged families some extra assurance that they will win rather than lose the lottery, and hence that it is worth sticking around to play the lottery in the first place.

By inducing families to stay and play the lottery, BPS keeps high-quality schools integrated by race and class, but also "grows the pie" by inducing families to enter even low-quality schools. Many Tier III schools, Boston officials argue, are "hidden gems" that feature committed teachers, families, and school leaders. Middle-class families who have invested time, energy, and hope in entering the lottery may be convinced to embrace the "gem" to which they have been assigned, especially if they meet other middle-class families also entering kindergarten at the school. School and district integration will thus increase, quality metrics will likely rise, and middle-class families may well be induced to use their disproportionate capital in service of not only their assigned school but also the district as a whole.

THE ETHICS OF PANDERING

In pandering to privileged families in this way, BPS violates the principle of equal opportunity by giving them a better opportunity to access high-quality schools—

while simultaneously upholding the principle of increasing overall school quality by enticing them to stay in Boston and enter the system. How, then, should we assess the ethics of pandering? Can it be just to offer already-privileged children and families unusually high odds of accessing a high-quality school, and conversely to deny poor children of color an equal shot at attaining a good education? If not, can it be just to promote school assignment policies that likely reduce the overall number of quality schools, simply on the grounds that they at least offer all children equal opportunities to access these limited number of seats?

It should be emphasized that this is an ethical dilemma about *pandering* to privilege, rather than one of either *compromise* or *unjust coercion*. BPS does not face a question about what compromises it should make because privileged families do not have a legitimate claim to special treatment. Middle-class families themselves recognize this. They do not say, "We should get priority in accessing quality schools because otherwise we'll leave." Compromise requires competing reasonable claims on both sides, and school assignment policy in Boston does not involve such claims. But at the same time, privileged families' capacities to threaten exit are not unjustly coercive. It is appropriate—perhaps even obligatory—for parents to do what they can to ensure that their children attend a decent school. They have BPS over a barrel, but not because they're behaving immorally.

We return, then, to the questions: What are the ethics of pandering in Boston's case? How much pandering is too much—or too little? Where does an ethical policy land—and how would we know and be able to justify such judgments to others?

Can Pandering Promote Equality of Opportunity?

ANDRÉE-ANNE CORMIER

The Boston Public Schools' "Home-Based Plan" raises the question of how access to public schools of variable quality should be distributed among children and their families. In my view, the case study raises important questions about equality of opportunity in the context of establishing just public policies, but it mischaracterizes its content and justification as well as its relationship with pandering. First, the sort of opportunity that we should be most concerned with equalizing is not the opportunity to get a seat at a high-quality school, but the opportunity to attain more fundamental goods. Second, once we recognize this, then pandering is no longer in tension with equality of opportunity. More specifically, in the context of threatened exit by middle-class families, pandering seems both to promote equality of opportunity to fundamental goods and to increase the number of high-quality schools. But third, pandering still may not be morally justified. Even if it is consonant with equality of opportunity, there might be other compelling reasons of justice not to pander—reasons that policy makers ought to carefully consider.

EQUAL OPPORTUNITY RECONSIDERED

The idea that children should have an equal opportunity to attend a high-quality school has a lot of intuitive appeal. However, I would like to challenge the claim that equality of opportunity to access a quality school is a key requirement of justice. Rather, or most importantly, justice requires us to equalize people's opportunity to attain more basic goods, such as flourishing (as a child and later in life), developing one's talents, or getting desirable jobs and positions of power. After all, that seems to be why attending a high-quality school itself matters: so children can flourish, develop their talents, or move up in the world.

Different people may well hold conflicting views about exactly which fundamental goods are truly important from the point of view of equality of opportunity. I will not take a position on that question here. I shall simply use the letter x as a placeholder for whatever goods are included in the list of fundamental goods. But in any case, insofar as justice demands equality of opportunity, it seems to demand equality of opportunity more for basic goods than for schooling.

If this is true, however, then, all other things being equal, a just school assignment plan may not be one that equalizes children's opportunity to attend a high-quality school. Indeed, a system premised on equality of opportunity to attend a high-quality school may actually *conflict* with the realization of equality of opportunity for x. Here is why.

Children from middle-class families have so many advantages over their lower-class peers that even if they all receive the same quality education, the former children are still more likely to flourish, develop their talents, or get desirable jobs later in life. Setting aside the problem of threatened exit for the moment, it thus seems that equality of opportunity for x entails giving low-income children *more* chances to attend a high-quality school than their wealthier peers.[11] In other words, policy makers ought to prefer, all other things being equal, a system that gives *priority* to less advantaged children over a system that gives every child an equal chance to access a high-quality school.[12]

STILL, WHY PANDER?

But what about when all other things are not equal? In particular, what about a context where there is a risk of middle-class families exiting the public school system—a risk that policies that give priority to lower-income families would undoubtedly exacerbate?

In such a context, the normative analysis of policy options shifts. It may appear that (a) providing children with equality of opportunity for x conflicts directly with (b) increasing the number of available high-quality schools *if (a) is still interpreted as giving less advantaged students greater access to high-quality schools,* since middle-class families would leave and hence lower (b). But that just means that (a) has different policy implications when middle-class parents can threaten exit. In particular, under those conditions, I believe that both (a) and (b) support pandering, and the conflict between the two criteria disappears.

Let me explain. Consider two possible school assignment plans. In the first, middle-class families are not given priority and they exit the public school system. In the second, they are given priority and they do remain in the system. In the former case, it is likely that the number of quality public schools will drop, and less advantaged children's opportunities for x will also therefore be reduced, because they will have fewer opportunities to access high-quality schools. By comparison, advantaged children would still have many opportunities for x, because they have access to quality private and suburban public schools, and they remain advantaged in ways that transcend school access (e.g., more stable home lives, access to summer camps and violin lessons, etc.).

Under the second plan, by contrast, the number of high-quality schools in the public system *and* the worst-off children's opportunities for x are likely to be higher thanks to pandering. These children would now have more opportunities to access a high-quality school in the public system. Moreover, it is plausible to think that advantaged children's opportunities for x would not vary significantly in one direction or the other. Indeed, advantaged children are likely to access a high-quality school whether Boston panders or not, and their other advantages are likely to remain more or less the same.

Clearly, there is considerable inequality of opportunity for x between advantaged and less advantaged children in either scenario. However, if pandering makes such inequality less significant, then criterion (a) recommends pandering. Of the two options, pandering minimizes the opportunity gap. When this happens, criteria (a) and (b) are in agreement.

OTHER MORAL CONSIDERATIONS

Suppose that both (a) and (b) recommend pandering in this way. Should we conclude that pandering is fully justified? This conclusion is too quick. Indeed, there may exist additional morally relevant—and potentially weightier—principles or considerations that count against pandering.

For instance, it is plausible to maintain that educational justice requires us to give every child a minimally decent education. It is also possible to imagine scenarios under which pandering would undermine this goal. Advantaged children, remember, will likely access decent schools under any school assignment system. It may be that more disadvantaged children would gain access to at least minimally decent schools if they were given school assignment priority; even if the number of high-quality schools went down, their access to at least decent schools might increase. If this is the case, and if the goal of providing each child with a decent education turns out to be more important from the point of justice than increasing the number of high-quality schools and equalizing opportunity for x, then pandering would not be justified, all other things being equal.

Here is another plausible argument against pandering. Even if we agree with Levinson that all parents have a right (and perhaps even a duty) to seek a decent education for their own children, it does not follow that parents can exercise this right in any way they see fit. For instance, if there are ways of exercising this right other than exiting that do not undermine equality of opportunity for x and that do not require parents to sacrifice other significant values, then it is perhaps morally wrong for those parents to exit.[13] It is unclear to me whether such alternative options are currently available. But if they doexist, it is far from obvious why the state should protect and legitimize those parents' exit threats by pandering.[14]

In response to the last point, one might object that such abstract moral considerations are irrelevant to policy making insofar as there is no political will in the United States to limit parental freedom to choose in this way, even in the name of justice. And, the objection goes, that justifies pandering here and now. This seems plausible to me. However, it does not make the considerations from parental rights entirely irrelevant. In fact, if it is true that many parents are behaving in an unjust and morally impermissible (although understandable and probably nonblameworthy) way by exiting, then pandering should be accompanied by an additional and important effort—namely, the effort to promote the development of a better sense of justice in the community.

Andrée-Anne Cormier is a postdoctoral fellow at the Center for Research in Ethics (CRE), in Montreal. She is especially interested in issues of political legitimacy, the rights of children and parents, and justice in education.

Don't Pander, Go for Growth!

MICHAEL J. PETRILLI

The complexity of Boston's Home-Based Plan reflects its many competing goals: to ensure equal access to schools that are high quality today; to grow the number of schools that will be high quality tomorrow; to bring middle-class and affluent families into Boston and into its public schools; to reduce transportation time and costs. With so many conflicting objectives, a Rube Goldberg design was practically inevitable.

To simplify the plan—and make it work best for Boston and its young people—policy makers need to clarify their priorities. At the top of the list should be an unambiguous goal: to create a dynamic that turns all of the city's education options into good options. To do so, they must define "good schools" appropriately. They should also embrace neighborhood schools and school choice simultaneously in order to meet the needs of parents of all income levels and to compete with the public schools in Boston's suburbs. These steps aren't easy, but they are doable. Let's explore.

HOW TO DEFINE A "GOOD SCHOOL"?

This is a critical question. The fundamental mistake of the Home-Based Plan as it was originally constructed is in using proficiency rates to judge school quality. To be sure, notions of "proficiency"—or better yet, "college and career readiness"—can be very helpful to parents and educators in order to communicate whether students are on track for success in life. However, proficiency rates themselves are terrible measures of school quality. That's because they are tightly correlated with schools' demographics.[15]

Figure 5.1 shows average scale scores on the National Assessment of Educational Progress (NAEP) by eligibility for a free or subsidized school lunch (FRPL) at the state and school levels. (Students whose families are below 130 percent of the poverty line qualify for free lunch; those below 185 percent qualify for a reduced-price lunch.)

This doesn't mean that "poor children can't learn." It does mean, rather, that there's long been a robust relationship between low "socioeconomic status" and low academic achievement.

Measures of school quality must therefore control for student demographics or, better yet, students' incoming performance levels. Then analysts

FIGURE 5.1   Average scale scores on the NAEP by eligibility for FRPL

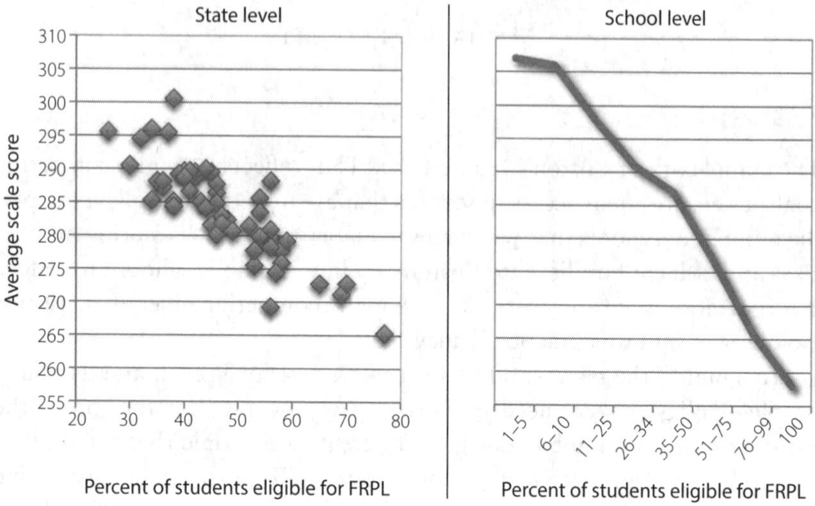

Percent of students eligible for FRPL (State level)

Percent of students eligible for FRPL (School level)

can ask which schools help students make rapid gains over the course of the school year This is a much fairer measure of school effectiveness, as high-poverty schools can in fact demonstrate strong student growth, while, as Levinson indicates, it's almost impossible for them to demonstrate high proficiency rates. And a well-designed growth measure—like the "Colorado Growth Model," now in use in more than a dozen states—gives schools credit for helping all of their students make progress—those at the bottom of the performance spectrum, at the top, and everywhere in between.[16]

Most importantly, using growth measures to define school quality would send better signals to parents. (And not just parents of low performing students—all parents.) It would encourage them to enroll their children in schools where they are likely to make rapid progress over time.

As originally designed, Boston's Home-Based Plan does the opposite. Because its school ratings system gives much greater weight to proficiency rates than to growth, it concludes that high-quality "Tier I" schools are overwhelmingly low-poverty ones. Again, that's because poverty rates and proficiency rates are so tightly correlated. It sends the message that the only "good" schools are those that serve mostly middle-class or affluent students. Thus, the scarcity of such families in Boston is a major impediment to improving schools. Therefore, we must "pander" to such families in order to eliminate this scarcity.

Change the focus to growth, as Boston's School Quality Working Group recommends, and this entire chain of logic evaporates.[17] Any school—even a high-poverty one—can help students make rapid gains, as many of Boston's "no excuses" charter schools have demonstrated.[18] School integration becomes a "nice to have" instead of a "must have." And the scarcity problem disappears—if Boston officials are willing to close down or turn around low-growth schools and replace them with high-growth schools (including charter schools) instead.

BUT HOW CAN HIGH-POVERTY SCHOOLS BE HIGH-QUALITY SCHOOLS?

This is an essential question, since integrated schools surely expose low-income students to peers who are more likely to be academically high performing, to have college aspirations, and to have social networks that may help them to get a foothold in today's economy. The evidence that they *learn* more, however, is less compelling, because most of the research has two fatal flaws. First, many of the studies are based on proficiency rates or one-time test scores, and thus they can't examine the progress that low-income students are making over time. Second, almost all of the studies suffer from selection bias, as low-income students who attend low-poverty schools may be different in immeasurable ways from their peers who attend high-poverty ones. Almost surely these immeasurable differences exist and explain some if not all of the differences in achievement.[19] Studies that can address these potential biases—such as ones with randomized controls—are exceedingly rare; I am aware of just one.[20]

Again, this is good news for the children of Boston and elsewhere. That's because turning every urban school into a low- or mixed-poverty public school is a daunting challenge, especially considering the paucity of middle-class and affluent children in most urban neighborhoods. Turning every urban school into a high-growth school, on the other hand, may someday be doable, as evidence from New Orleans and elsewhere demonstrates.[21] And it means that Boston can have lots of good schools, even if its leaders can't convince middle-class and affluent families to send their kids to schools far from their homes with lots of poor kids.

But this all starts with measuring school quality accurately—and that means focusing on growth.

EMBRACE NEIGHBORHOOD SCHOOLS AND SCHOOL CHOICE SIMULTANEOUSLY

Boston's Home-Based Plan and Levinson's case study assume that neighborhood school assignment is inherently unfair and unjust. It is, if many neighborhood schools are low-quality and parents have no option but to send their children to them.

But eliminating neighborhood schools outright is not the only solution to that problem. Nor is it the best solution, since parents of all income levels love neighborhood schools, and since middle-class and affluent families especially will continue to flee to suburbs offering neighborhood schools.[22] As parents, we like sending our kids to school with the kids in the neighborhood and having our children close by. We want our kids to be able to walk, bike, or take a short bus ride to school. Most importantly, we enjoy the peace of mind of knowing where our children will be going to school until the day they graduate from high school. "Lotteries" are understandably unsettling and terrifying.[23]

For these reasons, cities like San Francisco that have eliminated neighborhood schools and moved to an "all choice" system have struggled to retain middle-class families. This is unfortunate, as middle-class and integrated neighborhoods help grow the tax base, strengthen the city's political constituency, and most importantly, increase social mobility and other positive social outcomes for lower-income residents.

A better option, then, is to do "both, and" rather than "either, or." The nation's capital is a model in this respect. Almost half of Washington's children attend charter schools, which are relatively high performing compared to those in other cities.[24] Meanwhile, its public school system, which maintains a parental right to neighborhood schools, is improving rapidly—and gentrifying rapidly as well.[25] Both neighborhood and charter schools are becoming mixed income. No doubt some neighborhood schools in rapidly changing communities will eventually "flip" and become exclusively middle-class and upper-middle-class schools. But those with some stock of affordable housing (and protections for keeping it that way) should remain well integrated into the foreseeable future.

CONCLUSION

Boston's Home-Based Plan deserves to be given a chance to work. Over the next few years, analysts should be able to determine whether its efforts to "pander" to middle-class and affluent families has succeeded in keeping more of them in the city and in the public schools. We will also see how the greater focus on growth affects school ratings and the preferences of families once some high-poverty schools are shown to be the quality institutions that they are.

I strongly suspect, though, that Boston's efforts won't be enough to compete with the lure of the suburbs. I predict that most parents with financial means will continue to choose school districts that offer neighborhood schools and the peace of mind that comes with them.

If that situation comes to pass, the City on a Hill should look to its swampy neighbor to its south. For I suspect that Washington, DC, will, by then, have more of what Boston wants: more integrated neighborhoods and neighborhood schools, more middle-class and affluent families, more high-quality schools in both the district and charter sectors, and more improved achievement, especially for the neediest children. DC may not have true "home rule," but it does have a true "home-based plan" worthy of emulation.

Michael J. Petrilli is president of the Thomas B. Fordham Institute and research fellow at Stanford University's Hoover Institution. He is the author of The Diverse Schools Dilemma: A Parent's Guide to Socioeconomically Integrated Schools *(Thomas B. Fordham Institute, 2012).*

School Assignment Lotteries

What Should We Take for Granted?

JENNIFER M. MORTON

If we grant the facts as represented, the Boston Public School (BPS) lottery is a good solution to the compound problem of increasing the number of high-quality elementary schools and increasing low-income students' access to those schools. The lottery does so by sweetening the deal for middle-class and upper-middle-class parents so that they will stay in BPS—effectively granting them a leg up in the lottery. However, in reaching this solution, BPS authorities seem to be capitulating to a group of parents who are able to demand an unfair advantage because they are in a position to threaten exit. I want to raise questions regarding the extent to which we should take for granted this psychological fact about middle-class parents.

TREATING PARENTAL ATTITUDES AS FIXED

Policy makers must take for granted a variety of factors that are beyond their immediate control. These include facts about existing larger political institutions, federal education policy, housing policy, and human psychology. For example, those considering the proposed school lottery policy plausibly assume that the executive branch of government will continue to be gridlocked, neighborhoods will continue to be socioeconomically and racially segregated, BPS' budget will remain roughly the same, high-poverty schools will underperform, and so on. Though the individual members could, of course, campaign to change those political and institutional realities, they have to deliberate given these assumptions when making decisions concerning what is under their direct control.

The fact that middle-class parents will exit BPS if they are not offered some assurance that they will be able to enroll their children in a sufficiently good school could also be taken as just one more of those assumptions. These policy makers are not pandering; they are just taking certain well-supported facts about the psychology of parents for granted—parents will use their resources to make sure their children have a good education. A parents' blog, *Braving the BPS Lottery*, which was active during the previous iteration of the BPS lottery, offers a glimpse into what middle-class parents are thinking. A middle-class parent whose child did not get into her family's top-choice schools and who is now considering moving to the suburbs writes:

> We were moving. It was March 2008. We just received our lottery results for the Boston Public School lottery . . . We had put all this hope in the system and it had failed us. I cried, my husband was angry. Boston was flawed. The lottery was flawed. I looked out my window and saw a school my child could not go to. I saw my best friends [*sic*] children in good schools they got into by luck, and we had none. Why should sending your child to a good school be a matter of chance?[26]

The frustration expressed in this post could come from the mouth of any parent from any socioeconomic class. Middle-class parents just happen to have resources that enable them to opt out of the system if they can't be assured that their child will receive a good education within it. Therefore, the newly conceived lottery could be seen as expressing acceptance of this very general fact about parents.

DEMANDING UNFAIR ADVANTAGE

On the other hand, some might see BPS authorities as being complicit in what amounts to middle-class parents holding the system hostage. If there are a limited number of seats in high-quality schools, the fairest policy would seem to be one in which every child has an equal chance in the lottery for those seats. However, because not every parent has the chance to opt out, the lottery aims to appease those who are in a position to opt out if they don't get what they want. The new policy appears to express acceptance of middle-class parents' demanding an unfair advantage.

The problem is that, for middle-class parents, demanding an unfair advantage is one of the resources available to them in seeing to it that their children receive a good education. This gives rise to a thorny ethical question: is using any legal resource to ensure that one's child receives a good education morally acceptable if it might negatively impact other children's educational opportunities? I will not discuss this incredibly difficult question here.[27] However, it is important to note that not all parents share the same attitude. Another middle-class parent writes in the very same blog:

> For all of the effort and dollars now focused on trying to fix public schools, sometimes I wonder if the most meaningful and impactful

thing we could do—and that any family with choice could do—is to stay put. It is one of the few incontrovertible levers for lasting school reform—when more and more parents are more and more engaged, schools get better. Way better. Neighborhood and sense of community gets richer, too.[28]

This parent realizes that giving his child a good education is not the only consideration in choosing a school. He also considers the effect his decision would have on the school system and his community as a whole. If more parents had this attitude, the situation confronting BPS would likely be different.

CHANGING PARENTAL ATTITUDES THROUGH SCHOOL POLICY

In light of these divergent views, the question I would like to consider is whether it is *within the long-term control* of BPS to cultivate this kind of attitude in future parents as a long-term solution to the problem it now confronts. In other words, rather than treat parental attitudes as fixed, as a model based on pandering seems to do, does it make sense to understand these attitudes as variable and within the reach of district action to address? It is reasonable to assume that parental attitudes are not within the immediate control of BPS. BPS could engage in a media campaign to attempt to change current parental attitudes toward public schools or to connect with middle-class parents in town hall or PTA meetings in order to persuade them to enroll their children in public schools. However, the effect of such campaigns is likely limited. That is why BPS is resorting to pandering.

However, BPS has another tool at its disposal—the education it offers current students, many of whom are potential future parents. If BPS has the power to cultivate attitudes in future parents that will support a more just and equitable school system—for example, through civic education—it should pursue this as part of a long-term solution. Of course, to pursue this strategy, these must be attitudes that can be influenced by education. Establishing whether this is possible and how to do it surely requires empirical evidence—for example, research into the effectiveness of civic education in cultivating attitudes of this sort in future citizens. However, historically, the variety of parental attitudes toward schooling—across different nations and even among Boston's parents—suggests that these attitudes are neither psychologically necessary nor recalcitrant. Of course, it is quite possible that schooling may have only a limited impact on cultivating parental attitudes that support a just and equitable school system. Economic, cultural, and social factors outside of school might have a stronger effect. Nonetheless, if BPS can have some effect on the attitudes of future parents, it would be a piece of the solution that should not be left unexplored.

This might strike some as a far-fetched ideal solution with an uncertain payoff far in the future. But if BPS aims to be able to carry out a fair lottery that gives everyone an equal chance at a good school without having to pander, then it must either change middle-class parents' attitudes toward their community schools or attempt to remove this choice from parents' hands. If BPS fails to pursue either of these options, pandering will not be a short-term fix, but the long-term strategy.

One important point to note is that, in order for BPS to change the attitudes of future middle-class parents through education, it needs to have those future middle-class parents in BPS classrooms. Given the current intergenerational entrenchment of advantage, this means having middle-class students in BPS classrooms. So here we have a different reason to make sure that middle-class children stay in the BPS system. Doing so would allow BPS to provide those students with the kind of civic education that could potentially cultivate attitudes that would support a more just and equitable school system. It should also be noted that this line of thought is compatible with a call to invest more heavily in the school system—better schools would entice middle-class parents to enroll their children in the public school system. However, this should not divert us from acknowledging the need to cultivate attitudes that would support a more just and equitable school system in future parents. Consequently, if BPS is to do more than pander as a short-term solution, it must consider how to change parental attitudes toward public schools as a long-term solution.

I have argued that we need to reexamine the assumptions undergirding public policy solutions—as in the case of the BPS lottery—so as not to lose sight of possible long-term solutions that require fostering the necessary institutional, political, and psychological conditions needed to enact a fair lottery without diminishing the availability of high-quality seats for everyone. Pandering to middle-class parents is a short-term solution to a serious problem that partially rests on middle-class parents' attitudes concerning their civic responsibility in sustaining public schools. We need to consider whether those attitudes are ones that can potentially be shaped through the civic education that middle-class children—who are likely to become middle-class parents—receive in public schools. If so, this would be an important piece of a long-term solution and should be explored.

Jennifer M. Morton is an assistant professor of philosophy at the City College of New York–CUNY. She has published on educational inequality, character education, and moral philosophy in various venues, including the Journal of Political Philosophy, Social Philosophy and Policy, *the* Chronicle for Higher Education, *and the* European Journal of Philosophy.

Pandering in a Context
of Limited Choices and Costs

Andres A. Alonso

This case plunges us into what Meira Levinson has rightly called "the messy, contextual, decidedly non-ideal and even unjust circumstances of the here-and-now."[29] It does so in a complex way that does admirable justice to the nature of the dilemmas involved.

Missing from the case, however, are four interdependent elements: the *political nature of decision making* in districts, the *complexity of districts as organizations*, the *diversity of poor students* within districts, and poor students' *interaction with the dynamics of power* at the local level in the American political system. The absence of these perspectives results in a reductive opposition of two principles—equal opportunity to access a quality education versus increasing the overall number of quality schools—in service of a single, district-level policy mechanism: allocating elementary school seats via Boston's Home-Based Plan. By contrast, by taking politics, organizational complexity, student diversity, and power dynamics into account, we can gain a more expansive understanding of the interplay among ethical principles and decision making at multiple levels. In doing so, we can also recognize some of the costs of policies like the Home-Based Plan and the potential benefits of other, more neighborhood-focused approaches that serve children in poor communities.

ETHICAL DILEMMAS OR CONTESTED POLITICS?

Let's start with the importance of taking a *political* perspective. The case assumes a deliberate, technical rationality in district decision making that simply does not match my experience of practice. Districts are hotbeds of internal and external politics. Virtually every decision is fought over by multiple stakeholders. They publicly uphold a logic of principled action, akin to what Jal Mehta has called "the allure of order."[30] But many decisions—most saliently the establishment of school assignment and zoning lines, and choices about the creation, location, and admissions criteria for special programs such as gifted and talented classes or special education services—are often ultimately left to a highly politicized process in American local governance.

The point is not a "realist" one that politics trumps ethics. Rather, it's that even when a moral principle like distributive justice is on the table, the principle itself is subject to political contestation. It is a contested subject of debate rather than a moral imperative, making the ethical dilemma itself contested rather than normative.

ISOLATED INITIATIVES OR COMPLEX DISTRICT REFORMS?

This complexity brings me to my second point, that school improvement must be understood from a *system-level organizational* perspective. Urban districts are highly bureaucratic but also unstable, as employees draw on limited information, uncertain authority, and conflicting individual incentives to make decisions that rarely transcend their siloed perspectives. Many and entangled hands pull in different directions within the bureaucracy, while external stakeholders such as parents and business leaders further add to the diffusion of focus. These organizational circumstances exacerbate the ethical contestation at stake.

In this organizational context, for example, what is needed to improve the education of poor kids will essentially be contested. The case advocates pandering to privileged families on the explicit grounds that "the best—really, the only—way educational and social reformers know how to improve urban schools at scale is to eliminate hypersegregation of low-income children of color." This "only" dismisses the possibility of multiple routes to school improvement. It sets up an opposition between two choices when that opposition might be false.

The studies that suggest integration is "the only" option were conducted prior to the full onslaught of systemic reform initiatives and experimentation with governance that have characterized the past decade.[31] The large urban districts participating in the Trial Urban District Assessment (TUDA) since its inception, for example, improved significantly across demographic and categorical groups between 2003 and 2013, a result mostly ignored by both the advocates (looking for urgency!) and critics (not willing to give the Devil his due!) of modern reform.[32] These districts acted within new federal and state policy frameworks that focused on new standards, accountability, attention to student data, and human capital reforms. But the changes made within the different districts varied remarkably. School integration, by contrast, was not high on the list.[33]

In this light, it is also important to consider trade-offs among appealing but expensive reforms. Boston's Home-Based Plan costs tens of millions of dollars yearly for transportation alone. Consider other potential initiatives, such as expanding early childhood programs, increasing guidance and support to teachers in engaging students in deeper learning, or lengthening the school day and year for targeted students. There is good evidence that these kinds of programs have brought real progress in many American schools. Shouldn't trade-offs in resource allocation be included in how we think of justice in this case? Too often and inexplicably the actual sufficiency and interplay of costs are absent from the policy and research discussion.

Ultimately, because districts are complex systems with many obligations and moving parts, no policy initiative (like the Home-Based Plan) can be evaluated in isolation, as the case study attempts to do. Rather, as we evaluate potential strategies, we must always take broader contextual considerations into account. These include questions of cost, comparative efficacy, and what we actually know about variability and the actual content of implementation in particular settings.

SOME CHILDREN OR ALL CHILDREN?

Even if integration is adopted as a goal, it provides no guarantee that students will have equal access to programs and opportunities.[34] Roughly a fifth of students in Boston Public Schools have diagnosed special needs, and 30 percent are English language learners. Many of these students are not encompassed in the Home-Based Plan—and the case study explicitly leaves them aside as well. That exclusion speaks volumes about the complexities and challenges of integration. It is very much the orientation in American schools to exclude students for whom schools have no certain answers, *within schools as much as across schools*. The arguments for the benefits of greater integration stop short of wrestling with what this resilience of exclusive practices means at the level of the school.

They also stop short of wrestling with what they mean at the system's level. Is there thirst for integration across district lines, for example? What characterizes many urban settings is the hypersegregation across an entire system. In Baltimore, for example, where 93 percent of public school students were African American or Latino, and students were overwhelmingly poor across all ethnic lines, no pandering *within the district's span* could have led to true class and racial integration. The public good should transcend political jurisdictional lines—but interdistrict desegregation strategies are very rare.[35]

In this light, it is also important to consider the dangerous messages that *exclusively* prointegrationist arguments may convey about the relative moral worth of poor and middle-class children and communities. The argument that breaking down concentrations of poor students is the best or only strategy is likely to reinforce people's rampant belief that school quality and the capacity for improvement are indistinguishable from the nature of the kids and their families. This again runs the risk of reinforcing ethically indefensible assumptions about the relative value of children and the justifiability of excluding some children from schools or school systems that should be serving all.

One value of the case will be to promote conversations about the beliefs still dominant in schools and districts. The power of the threat of exit discussed in the case lies as much in the persistence of those beliefs as it does in any rational consequences of exit. Again, in looking at a choice in isolation, the case ignores the real granularity of implementation and the broader moral and political contexts in which decisions are made.

CHOICE, SCHOOL ASSIGNMENT, AND SOCIAL CAPITAL

Finally, and in the same vein, we must consider the practical impact of school choice on the fabric of schools' relationships with their communities, and what this conveys morally about social capital, especially in poor communities. If we believe that social capital matters, it can't be limited to social capital in the middle class, which is what the case study and the Home-Based Plan implicitly do.

When I was a deputy chancellor in New York City, and later CEO in Baltimore, I found that some community organizers deeply opposed school choice—and the school closures and openings that often accompany choice—because they felt their collective social capital and efficacy were threatened. They believed they were stronger working together on behalf of communal neighborhood schools than they would be with students dispersed all around the city. They also mistrusted the choices. For these parents and community organizers, and for many teachers in neighborhood schools, the growth of charters and new types of schools, and the closing of neighborhood schools that served as the hub of a web of community relationships, had numerous ill effects. Local schools lost resources and attention, "good students" and "great parents" chose new schools, "challenging" children and families became concentrated in lower-priority schools, and different types of schools developed toxic relationships.

Another reason to take the larger social fabric into account is that deficient *schools* signal deficient *systems* more broadly. The claim that integration will automatically improve poor children's educational outcomes rests on the fallacious assumption that schools determine learning to the exclusion of everything else in children's lives. Communities, in my experience, know differently. A democratic approach to developing ethical and just education policy will take these more situated understandings into account. If they truly want to improve education, leaders will engage disadvantaged communities in a meaningful dialogue so as to learn from their insights, convictions, and aspirations, and will not just impose policy decisions from the outside.

In sum, ethical analysis of education policy must address the political and organizational elements at play in school district decisions, seek new insights into the nature of school improvement, recognize the status of diverse and especially vulnerable children, and encompass the interactions among decisions about schools and the larger context of communities. It must also be more nuanced in its discussion of how research assumptions actually play out in the differentiated contexts of actual settings, or it will risk asking the wrong questions. This case represents an important beginning. It is not where we should end.

Andres A. Alonso is currently professor of practice at the Harvard Graduate School of Education, having served as chief of staff and deputy chancellor for teaching and learning in New York City, and chief executive officer of Baltimore City Public Schools. He taught English language learners and classified emotionally disturbed adolescents in Newark, New Jersey, public schools for twelve years.

Means and Ends

Practical Considerations for Equitable School Reform

JAMES E. RYAN

The Boston Public Schools' (BPS') school assignment plan raises a perplexing set of questions, including the fundamental question regarding the lengths to which district leaders should go to ensure that middle-income White families choose to remain in the school system. I do not have a precise answer to that question, and I am not exactly of a philosophical bent. In this brief commentary, therefore, I would like to frame what I see as the practical choices that need to be made and offer some initial thoughts regarding those choices.

As a starting point, I am generally in favor of efforts to ensure that middle-income families with options choose to remain within the BPS system. For reasons detailed clearly in the case study, and expanded upon below, I am convinced that urban school systems will not succeed if they remain hypersegregated and predominantly poor. Middle-income families are crucial to the health and success of schools and the system.

The question then becomes, obviously, how to attract and retain middle-income families and at what cost to poorer families and their children. The case study poses this question in terms of "pandering," which I believe is both a slightly loaded and somewhat inaccurate term. Pandering is typically defined as indulging or gratifying an immoral or distasteful desire, which in turn implies that the desire of parents to ensure their children are in good schools is somehow immoral or distasteful. It surely is not. All but the most neglectful parents share this desire. The real dilemma is whether to favor one set of parents over others in the hope that doing so will, over time, work to the benefit of all.

This is a genuine ethical dilemma. On the one hand, the idea of favoring those who are already relatively advantaged over those who are relatively disadvantaged seems outrageous. On the other hand, if doing so will ultimately work to the benefit of the disadvantaged, it might be exactly the right thing to do. Like most dilemmas, especially those that involve the general question of whether the ends justify the means, this one has no easy or clear solutions, but instead requires considering several related trade-offs.

SCHOOL IMPROVEMENT VERSUS SYSTEM IMPROVEMENT

First, it is important to consider the trade-off between the school system as a whole and the schools themselves. The BPS assignment plan rests on the implicit assumption that one way to attract and retain middle-income families is to offer them opportunities to enroll their children in a high-quality school. If that assumption is correct, as I believe it is, the key question then becomes: will the school system itself be better in the long run even if the schools remain (at least in the short run) unequal because middle-income families are clustered in higher-quality schools?

This is a vexing question to answer, though it is ultimately an empirical question. One could imagine that the system would be better over time, and that poorer families would share in the benefits of a healthier system as schools throughout the system improve. If middle-income families are successful, for example, in bringing more resources to the school system through legislative lobbying, and those resources are distributed equally throughout the system, then over time all schools could improve (if the resources are used wisely). Similarly, if middle-income families are more effective at monitoring the performance of systemwide leaders—the superintendent, school board, chief officers, and the like—we might expect overall improvement in all schools.

Conversely, one could imagine that middle-income families would "work the system" in countless ways to ensure that their schools—but only their schools—benefit, which would simply exacerbate the existing inequalities and not lead to overall improvement. If middle-income parents resist efforts to diversify their schools, for example, or if they work to channel discretionary district resources to their schools, short-term inequalities could become entrenched features of the system.

TAKING THE LONG VIEW

The second, related trade-off concerns the time frame one should use to assess the assignment plan. Is it advisable to accept some inequalities among schools in the short run if one believes that those inequalities will lead to overall improvement over the longer term? There is a tendency among some to oppose education policies that will not lead to equity or improvement for all in the short run. (A good example is the argument that we should not experiment with charter schools because they will benefit only a small portion of students and do nothing for, or perhaps even harm, other students.) This short-term perspective is understandable, both because legislators and policy makers often have short time horizons and because parents, for very good reasons, are concerned about what happens to their children today.

This tendency to focus on short-term results, however, can often make it politically impossible to introduce changes that would have long-term benefits that ultimately outweigh any short-term costs. In the case of the BPS assignment plan, it is impossible to know how much short-term inequity it might be necessary to endure to achieve longer-term gains. That will depend, to a certain extent, on the first trade-off and whether short-term inequalities will lead, over time, to overall improvement and an increase in high-quality schools for all students.

One could imagine, to pose an extreme example, a short-term effort to do everything possible to attract a critical mass of middle-income families into the system, even if this effort does nothing at all to help poorer families—or even if it makes some of them worse off. Once that critical mass is achieved, one might expect to see overall improvements across the system, and one could even imagine efforts at that point to make the system more equitable in terms of school assignments, teacher and principal placement, and resource distribution.

Consider the example of Montgomery County School District in Maryland. In some respects, Montgomery County started from the opposite point from Boston, as Montgomery County is the most populous and affluent county in the state. Despite its wealth, however, in the 1990s there were growing pockets of poverty concentrated in urban areas composed of mostly racial and ethnic minorities and immigrant families. Student outcomes there were far behind those in the more affluent areas.

Superintendent Jerry Weast, appointed in 1999, took a deliberate approach to improving student performance in the struggling areas. He strategically implemented a plan to differentiate resources based on school need—meaning struggling schools would receive more funds, more staff, and more support—all while he and others worked to maintain the high quality of the schools in the middle- to high-income areas. Weast repeatedly used the word "equity" to refer to equitable opportunities instead of simply equal funding, setting the stage for a cultural shift in how residents viewed the need for a differential distribution of resources.

To convince parents of the more affluent students that they would not be shortchanged, he used several tactics, including introducing the theory that investing in schools in impoverished areas throughout the district would raise property values for everyone. He was also able to concretely demonstrate that, despite differences in resource distribution, the affluent students continued to excel while the poorer students' schools began to catch up. Even during a time when poverty rates were rising in the county, Weast's strategy resulted in large gains for poor and minority students, including in kindergarten reading, eighth-grade math, and enrollment in Advanced Placement (AP) courses.[36] Montgomery County, as mentioned, started in a very different place than Boston, but the example suggests that it is not implausible to imagine a school system with a large number of middle-income families that offers equitable access to a high-quality education across schools. The short-term inequities designed to draw and retain middle-income families, in other words, could lead to a more equitable system over time.

THE IMPORTANCE OF UNCERTAINTY

The final, related trade-off concerns the right balance between chance and certainty. The question here is whether BPS may be doing too little, rather than too much, to attract middle-income families. I start from the premise that all parents, all else equal, would prefer their children to be in the best school possible. For all sorts of reasons, not all parents are able (for financial reasons or limited job opportunities) or willing (because of competing considerations about where to live) to place their children in the best school possible. But most parents with options can be counted on to ensure, at the very least, that their children will attend what is referred to in the case as a "decent" school—one that the parents believe will adequately educate their children.

If these assumptions are correct, parents are necessarily going to favor the *certainty* of their children attending a high-quality school over the *chance* that their children will attend a high-quality school. It follows that parents will favor a guaranteed placement over a choice system when they know that the guaranteed placement will be in a high-quality school. Parents with the financial means to send their children to private school or to live in a town with high-quality schools can guarantee that their children are placed in good schools. They can, in other words, control where their children attend school. It also follows, therefore, that, as between a guaranteed placement and a choice plan with no guarantee, most parents with financial means would prefer (and will choose) the former.

All of which is to say that the current means chosen by BPS to attract middle-income families may lead, at least in the short run, to only marginal increases in the number of middle-income students in the BPS system. There appears to me to be sufficient uncertainty in the system that many risk-averse parents will avoid it entirely. Whether this particular approach, which seeks to balance equity with some favoritism toward middle-income families, will be sufficient to induce systemwide improvements in BPS remains anyone's guess. But it seems to me fairly clear that if BPS wishes to attract and retain a larger number of middle-income families, more certainty will have to be either built into the system or developed over time—as perhaps it will, if the number of high-quality schools increases. BPS could build more certainty into the system now by guaranteeing placement in neighborhood schools, while also allowing choice beyond those schools. Whether to do so, however, leads right back to the two earlier trade-offs and the questions they present.

James E. Ryan is the Charles William Eliot Professor of Education and dean of the Harvard Graduate School of Education.

From Principles to Practice and the Problem of Unintended Consequences

CHRISTOPHER WINSHIP

The case study of Boston's school assignment plan is clearly framed by a value trade-off between equal access to quality schools and the overall quality of the school system. Yet, I propose that the ethical dimensions of this trade-off can be (relatively) easily resolved by applying John Rawls's difference principle. The greater challenge for school officials flows from the false assumption that once they identify the appropriate ethical principle(s), specific policy directives follow. My aim here is to show just how complex and difficult this second problem can be.

THE DIFFERENCE PRINCIPLE

As I understand it, the trade-off presented by the school assignment policy is a classic case of the "difference principle," perhaps one of the most recognizable features of John Rawls's seminal work, *A Theory of Justice*. In brief, the difference principle proposes that deviations from an equal distribution of basic "goods" that people need to lead meaningful lives are justified only if the resulting inequality benefits the least advantaged members of a society.[37] By favoring advantaged (middle-income White) Bostonians, Boston's Home-Based Plan sacrifices equal access to quality schools in order to improve the overall quality of the school system. Less advantaged (lower-income communities of color) Bostonians should, in theory, benefit from such a proposal even though they do not have the same chances of attending a quality school as their more advantaged peers. As the quality of the system improves, the baseline educational experiences of the least advantaged improve as well. Thus, they would be better off than if the district allocated school access equally to all and if, as a result, families with means left Boston public schools for the suburbs or private schools.

Admittedly, the actual case may not be as strong as it seems in theory. Some less advantaged children will be sent to schools that do not reap the benefits of socioeconomically diverse student bodies. As such, these children will be no better off than if advantaged families had exited the system. Thus, some less advantaged students and families would bear the burden of unequal access to quality schools without experiencing any benefit. Because such instances would likely exist under Boston's assignment plan, we might consider this case a weak version of the difference principle. Nonetheless, if the assignment plan improves the chances for at least some of the least advantaged Bostonians, the difference principle would recommend the policy.

UNINTENDED CONSEQUENCES

This case truly becomes difficult once we consider what policies should follow from employing the difference principle to resolve the value trade-off. It is simply not true that an ethical principle automatically determines specific policies that officials should put in place. Indeed, it may seem clear that a narrowly tailored school assignment policy may benefit the least advantaged. However, if we consider the likely effects of this policy in a broader context, how it actually benefits the least advantaged becomes murky.

For example, consider the unintended consequences of improving the quality of the school system on housing prices. If Boston's public schools improve considerably, Boston's already extremely high housing prices may climb even higher. One effect of such an increase may be that more of Boston's poor families will be forced to leave the city. Over the years there has been much talk about the need in Boston for more affordable housing, but only very modest progress has been made. Given its slow progress up to this point, it would be overly optimistic to think that in future Boston will provide anything like the amount of affordable housing that would be needed to counteract widespread increases in real estate value.[38]

Another unintended consequence might be that less advantaged families *voluntarily* leave Boston because they find the new assignment policy to be disrespectful, particularly as they are asked to shoulder the burden of school-assignment policy without experiencing any benefit. Though this case focuses on the exit options of more advantaged families, poorer families in Boston also have exit options, via what are known as satellite or gateway cities: Brockton, Everett, Lawrence, Lynn, Lowell, Malden, Revere, and others. Most are old manufacturing cities where housing is considerably cheaper than in Boston. Most have unimpressive school systems, though Brockton has recently received national attention for the improvements that it has made in it schools.[39] Although these school systems may be no better (and possibly worse) than Boston's in terms of the quality of instruction and learning, lower-income families might well prefer them to Boston. At least they would not have to bear the disrespect of their children attending weaker Boston schools while children from advantaged families fill the seats in the city's quality schools.

In both examples, the school assignment plan plausibly generates disadvantage in other domains. It may even result in lower-income families leaving the city, either by choice or by necessity. The possibility of such an exodus raises the question, whom should Boston be for? The obvious related question is whom should Boston's public schools be for? An answer to either question based on Rawls's difference principle, at least in its weak form, would be that Bostonians should work for a city and school system that do the best job possible to serve the least well-off given the political and social constraints that any such efforts face. Yet, what I have tried to show thus far is that this goal is difficult to achieve with any single policy. Policies designed to mitigate disadvantage in one domain may end up generating or exacerbating disadvantage in another.

ALTERNATIVE POLICY APPROACHES

It may be the case that the best way to approach serving the interests of the least well-off is to avoid policies that divisively pit the interests of the less advantaged families against those of more advantaged families. Here I briefly examine two such possibilities: a broadly tailored, compensatory policy of resource distribution and a more fundamental shift toward inclusive "win-win" policies.

The current case treats the school assignment system as the sole focus of inquiry. Is it possible that by considering a series of related policies some of the negative effects of an assignment system that privileges well-off families could be counterbalanced? Brookline High School, just over the border from Boston, has a very interesting policy: the higher the academic level of a class, the larger it is. Thus, AP classes are the largest, and the standard, nonhonors classes are the smallest. What if the Boston school system was structured analogously? Classes in weaker schools would have lower student-to-teacher ratios, and better schools, higher ratios. Hopefully, this would improve weaker schools, as teachers would have fewer children to teach in any one classroom. Such a policy might also mean that stronger teachers would be more interested in teaching in schools that served children from lower-income families.

The point of the Brookline High example is to suggest that by narrowly focusing on the desirability of school assignment policies, we make the mistake of precluding consideration of a broad set of policy options that involve a mix of assignment systems with other program options that would involve more teaching and other resources for children in weaker schools. Pursuing such a strategy could have four consequences: the quality of education would be improved in weaker schools; as a result, children from lower-income families would be compensated, at least in part, for having to attend weaker schools; middle-income families might be far more willing to send their children to weaker schools, especially if those schools had resources their children needed (e.g., special education programs); and a far greater number of middle-income families might send their children to Boston Public Schools, thus improving overall school quality. In short, we may be able to approach the ethical aims underscored in the difference principle by widening the scope of issues and policies that are simultaneously considered. Evaluating the assignment policy in isolation is almost certainly a mistake.

Another option would be to focus on policies that enable "win-win" solutions. In *The Political Construction of Business Interests: Coordination, Growth, and Equality,* Cathie Jo Martin and Duane Swank analyze the development of the political economy of Scandinavia, with a particular focus on Denmark. They argue that the comparatively high levels of equality and equity in these Scandinavian societies were not the result of a deep commitment to these values, but rather to the pursuit of win-win solutions that were good both for business and workers of all types. It was the resulting system of cooperativism and inclusiveness that produced the egalitarian societies that the American Left so often praises.[40] Perhaps prioritizing the interests of the least advantaged—or of any one group, for that matter—is not the most effective strategy for achieving the aims of justice. Focusing narrowly on the injustice or unethical nature of process may be divisive, creating an "us versus them" situation. In the present case, this means pitting the interests of lower-income families against the interests of middle-income families. This divisiveness may then make political progress difficult, if not impossible. Framing the issue as a matter of inclusiveness and a search for win-win solutions may in fact be more productive.

Christopher Winship is the Diker-Tishman Professor of Sociology and a member of the Harvard Kennedy School's senior faculty. He has a broad range of research interests, including counterfactual causal models, youth violence, pragmatism, and the ethics of public policies.

CHAPTER SIX

How, If at All, Should Charters Be Compared to Local Districts?

MEIRA LEVINSON

Academy of the Pacific Rim (APR) is a charter school in Boston that serves roughly five hundred students in grades 5–12.[1] Its mission is "to empower urban students of all racial and ethnic backgrounds to achieve their full intellectual and social potential by combining the best of the East—high standards, discipline and character education—with the best of the West—a commitment to individualism, creativity and diversity." Having opened as a middle school back in 1997, APR has expanded both forward into high school and backward into late elementary school. APR takes pride in its diverse student body, "reflect[ing] the demographics and diversity of our city." But APR also makes clear that its "ambitious goals for academic and personal development" may not be for everyone. "As a charter public school we do not choose our students. We do, however, choose and create our own culture," which they describe as a mix of "best practices from Pacific Rim and Western cultures."

Like many charter schools—and an increasing number of district schools, too—APR's requirements for students go beyond the minimum district and state standards. Students take Mandarin Chinese every year starting in seventh grade. Both the school day and the school year are significantly extended. Seventh and eighth graders are required to complete ten hours of community service each year in order to be promoted to high school. Every summer in high school, students are required to complete the Pacific Rim Enrichment Program (PREP) by spending at least seventy-five hours "performing community service, exploring career possibilities through internships, or broadening their academic horizons through college prep summer programs." These hours are required for graduation from APR.

Academy of the Pacific Rim credits these requirements—along with its other rigorous expectations for academics and character, strong school and professional culture, tutoring program, family partnerships, data-driven instruction, and opportunities for students to earn rewards—for its outstanding statewide standardized test (known as MCAS) and college placement results. It touts its 100 percent MCAS pass rate among its tenth graders, and its 100 percent acceptance rate for graduates into two- and four-year colleges, with the vast majority (over 80 percent) matriculating into four-year institutions.[2] By comparison, Massachusetts Department of Education data indicate that only 50 percent of Boston Public Schools' (BPS) graduates in 2014 even aspired to attend a four-year college, with another 16 percent of BPS graduates aspiring to attend a two-year college. A full 27 percent of BPS graduates had "unknown" plans.[3] APR seniors also trounce BPS seniors on the SAT, usually surpassing their average scores by 100 points or more.[4] It achieves these goals with a student body that is over 80 percent students of color and two-thirds identified as "high needs." In particular, over half of students are low-income, and one-fifth have identified disabilities.[5]

On the flip side, APR's achievements are potentially less impressive when they are placed in context of both who is left by senior year and Boston's overall public school demographics. The APR class of 2014 dropped by 60 percent from sixth grade to twelfth grade, starting at eighty-four students in sixth grade, shrinking to fifty ninth graders, and ending at thirty-four seniors, of whom twenty-nine graduated. These attrition patterns are virtually identical year-after-year.[6] To trumpet APR's near or full "100 percent" college acceptance and attendance rate among graduates, therefore, is misleading if the implication is that (close to) 100 percent of all APR students end up going to college; instead, these data apply only to the minority of APR students who remain through graduation rather than transferring out somewhere along the way. This attrition rate is far worse than Boston Public Schools', as is evidenced in table 6.1, showing attrition rates at each grade level. Furthermore, APR serves a much smaller high-needs population than BPS does from the start, and APR's retention of high-needs students is far worse than BPS', as both table 6.1 and table 6.2, "Special populations," show.

Yet on the other hand, these metrics are arguably not fully comparable in judging a whole district (like Boston) against a single school (like APR), regardless of the fact that charters are considered to be separate districts for legal and accountability purposes. Any student who wants to switch out of APR for any reason is counted

TABLE 6.1   2013–2014 Attrition report

District	Percent attrition by grade							
	5	6	7	8	9	10	11	All
Academy of the Pacific Rim (all students)	6.7	18.9	11.1	21	16.7	7.8	10.5	13.9
Boston (all students)	15.2	6.3	4.9	15.4	6.6	5.3	6	9.3
APR (high-needs students)	5.6	18	11.7	23.1	20.8	8.8	16.7	14.9
Boston (high-needs students)	15.1	5.9	5.3	15.6	6.9	5.7	6.6	9.5
APR (students with disabilities)	11.8	21.4	20	25	26.3	5.9	28.6	19.3
Boston (students with disabilities)	12.2	4.6	4.9	16	6.9	5.8	5.8	8.4

Source: Massachusetts: 2014–15 Attrition Report (DISTRICT), All Students (Malden, MA: Massachusetts Department of Elementary and Secondary Education, 2015), http://profiles.doe.mass.edu/state_report/attrition.aspx.

against APR's attrition rate, for example, since there's no other APR "district" school for APR students to attend. Students in Boston, however, may change schools multiple times within Boston and it will not count against the district attrition rate since there are over one hundred schools—and dozens of high schools—within Boston Public Schools. This difference explains some of the disparities evident in the attrition table, particularly in sixth grade, when a number of APR students may have been admitted to one of Boston's three selective-entry "exam schools" for their initial seventh-grade entry point. Taking a place at an exam school is not "attrition" for a BPS student, since they are part of the district, but it is for an APR student. APR's high attrition rate at eighth grade may also reflect ninth-grade entry into Boston exam schools and other well-respected BPS high schools, of which there are many.

A different way of understanding APR's attrition rate, therefore, may be to compare it to average attrition from each school in Boston, rather than from the district as a whole. When we pose these numbers against each other, a very different picture emerges, as illustrated in table 6.3.

TABLE 6.2   Special populations (2013–2014)

	% of APR	% of BPS
First language not English	7.4	46.3
English language learner	0	29.9
Low-income	54.6	77.7
Students with disabilities	20.5	19.5
Free lunch	44.8	74.6
Reduced-price lunch	9.8	3.1
High needs	65.9	85.2

It turns out that students switch out of schools within the Boston Public Schools at slightly *higher* rates than do students from APR; this is true not only for all students in BPS, but also specifically for high-needs students. So on a school-to-school comparison, it no longer seems that APR loses high-needs students at unusually high rates. This isn't to say that table 6.1 is irrelevant or even misleading; after all, most students who leave one school in BPS simply move to another BPS school, so they are remaining within the system, unlike APR students. BPS schools also gain new students—often also with high needs—who fill the places of the students who were lost. That is not true at APR after eighth grade. Furthermore, the high BPS attrition rates at fifth, sixth, and eighth grades seem to be due substantially (but not solely) to students' entering specially designated Advanced Work Classes at certain schools in sixth grade, and the exam schools in seventh and ninth grades. So despite the high attrition rates in BPS schools, the students generally remain part of the district, as table 6.1 demonstrates.

This means that Boston's and APR's test score and graduation rates are similarly incomparable—especially when students who find it hard to succeed at APR likely end up reentering the Boston Public Schools. APR's near-perfect graduation rates merely indicate that students who leave before graduation transfer to another school rather than dropping out directly from APR. Students in Boston, by contrast, tend not to have this option before dropping out. They would have to transfer to a private school or to another district—either by moving or by gaining admission to a charter school, and these are not required to take students in their upper grades—in order not to bring down BPS' graduation rate. Similarly, the Academy of the Pacific Rim's MCAS and SAT scores represent the achievement solely of stu-

TABLE 6.3   2013–2014 Attrition report comparing APR to average of BPS schools

District	Percent attrition by grade							
	5	6	7	8	9	10	11	All
Academy of the Pacific Rim (all students)	6.7	18.9	11.1	21	16.7	7.8	10.5	13.9
Average among Boston schools (all students)	15.4	27.5	10.4	28.7	13.5	11.6	10.6	15.8
APR (high-needs students)	5.6	18	11.7	23.1	20.8	8.8	16.7	14.9
Average Boston schools (high-needs students)	15.8	20.9	11.2	23.8	12.9	11.5	10.5	14.9
APR (students with disabilities)	11.8	21.4	20	25	26.3	5.9	28.6	19.3
Average Boston schools (students with disabilities)	15.3	10.9	10.7	33.3	12.3	8.9	6.8	12.3

Source: Boston school averages were calculated by the author using state data for every school in Boston.

dents who stick with APR from tenth through twelfth grade, who, the attrition report makes clear, are disproportionately non-high needs. The rest of APR's student body—in general, the more high-needs fraction—are most likely entering BPS and contributing their presumably lower MCAS and SAT scores to BPS' average.

Consider, for example, if Boston were judged merely by the achievements of the top 50 percent of its students—and in particular, the top 50 percent of its students who were in BPS from ninth through twelfth grade (what the state calls its "adjusted cohort"). Since its four-year adjusted cohort graduation rate in 2014 was 70.8 percent, meaning well over half of its students graduated on time, BPS would feature a 100 percent on-time graduation rate. Furthermore, students in virtually every subcategory—ELLs, low income, high needs, Latino, etc.—would also achieve 100 percent on-time graduation rates. The only exception is students with disabilities, who would have about a 93 percent graduation rate (since, overall, 42.5 percent of the adjusted cohort of students with disabilities graduate in four years in BPS). MCAS results would look similarly strong. These calculations are, of course, absurd and tendentious—but they do highlight the challenge of comparing the achievements of the unusual few dozen students who have stayed in a single charter school for years with those of thousands of students across an entire district.

This suggests that comparative statistics may miss the point altogether: Academy of the Pacific Rim and Boston are simply two very different "districts" serving increasingly different populations in quite different ways. Perhaps APR couldn't achieve the results it does without Boston's availability to take up the slack with students who chafe at APR's expectations. If so, then expecting APR to serve a more diverse and representative population that mirrors BPS' student population would set APR up for failure, which may serve no student well. And after all, it's not that APR successfully serves only an elite group who would necessarily succeed anywhere, since the vast majority of APR's graduates every year are low-income students of color.

Perhaps, alternatively, APR would retain and serve *more* students if BPS were not available as an "escape valve." As the head of a New York charter school network expressed in frustration, "We've had a bunch of kids go and enroll in a regular school" when they realize that the district requirements were less burdensome than the charter's. "You [therefore] have to get rid of the easy-out option for kids and families . . . You have to raise the bar for everyone in equal ways, because as soon as you create this lower bar, somebody is going to jump out and say, 'That's easier, I'll take that path.'" APR itself noted in frustration that a large number of ninth graders who were due to be retained chose instead to leave the school in 2014, and it sets stemming the tide of attrition as a school priority.[7] Under this perspective, APR isn't given the opportunity to show it can attract, retain, and serve as diverse an array of students as Boston, because students who feel unduly challenged by APR leave rather than learn that they could persist and succeed.

Or perhaps this battle of numbers and speculations simply isn't informative in any respect. Maybe comparisons just can't be made. But then policy makers, educators, and parents alike are in a bind, since so many decisions depend on comparisons: funding, school approvals and closures, instruction, governance, where to send one's children.

In spring 2014, for instance, the Massachusetts House of Representatives passed a bill specifying that charters that wished to expand (e.g., by opening up new campuses) would be given preference if their average attrition rate (calculated as a moving three-year average) was equal to or less than the average three-year attrition rate of schools in the sending district.[8] A charter that had a higher attrition rate would be asked to "include in its application for expansion a plan to reduce its attrition rates" (line 400). Preference would also be given to charters that chose to serve a geographic area that had an "equal or higher percentage of low-income students" as compared to the sending school district. In considering the bill that summer, some Massachusetts state senators proposed amending the bill to toughen these requirements. Charters could expand *only if* they demonstrated attrition rates *and* stability rates—which measure how many students remain in a school throughout the school year (rather than being pushed out before standardized testing, for example)—that are equal to or lower than the attrition and stability rates of schools in the sending district.

In light of the data and analysis presented above about the Academy of the Pacific Rim and Boston Public Schools, would you support legislation that restricts charter school expansion to schools whose demographics and attrition rates are comparable to those of sending districts? Why or why not? How might your views change depending on your role (as a BPS or APR teacher, a low-income parent of a three-year-old child in Boston, a charter school leader, a school board member, or a state senator from a struggling school district)?

The Trouble with Universality

FREDERICK M. HESS

I do not think it is a good idea to allow only those charter schools that have demographics or attrition rates similar to those in the local district to expand. The issue, at least for me, turns less on how one thinks about the role of charter schools than on what one thinks it takes to create terrific schools.

Great schools require a coherent culture, a shared set of demanding expectations, faculty members committed to the school's mission, and students and families that want to be there. These traits are not sufficient to spell success, but they are essential preconditions. The promise of charter schooling is largely about increasing the possibility that schools can create these conditions. The leeway to establish rigorous expectations, serve only those students and families who choose to buy into the program, and to unapologetically maintain a culture is crucial to what makes successful charters successful. I think this applies twice over when it comes to educating low-income children in communities where circumstances can make success especially tough and where academic excellence is an unusual thing.

ATTRITION IS NOT NECESSARILY SKIMMING

Now, if a charter school is actively or explicitly skimming, that is a problem. While it may facilitate the creation of a great school, the cost of such behavior is generally too high a price to pay. However, charter laws already constrain (or prohibit) such activity, and there are mechanisms for addressing efforts to selectively recruit students. After all, charter schools—unlike some magnet schools—are prohibited from using entrance criteria and are required to admit students by lottery. Special education statute and case law already fully applies to charter schools. If those norms prove insufficient to rein in bad actors or to stop inappropriate practices, they should be strengthened.

That kind of unsavory skimming is not what we're dealing with in this case, however. Here, we are dealing with a high performing school whose student body is mostly low income and that actually has a slightly larger share of students with special needs than does the typical Boston district school. Here the issue is that the students who choose to enroll and then remain in the Academy of the Pacific Rim are not wholly reflectively of the Boston student population. To that, my reaction is, "So what?"

EXCELLENCE IS RARELY UNIVERSAL

This brings us back to how one understands what is required for schools to be successful—including the need for shared expectations that are demanding. APR expects middle schoolers to complete ten hours of community service each year, high schoolers to spend at least seventy-five hours each summer in an enrichment program, all students in grades 7 through 12 to study Mandarin, and more. That is not for everyone; many students may be unwilling (or unable—for a variety of reasons) to do what the school asks.

In such circumstances, one can either accept the distinctiveness of APR or demand that it modify its expectations, norms, and routines until it attracts and keeps a more "representative" sample of students. After all, the students who opt out—whether because BPS is easier, or because they are more resistant to the "college-for-all" message of a school like APR, or for any other reason—are (almost by definition) going to be different than the students who opt in. Is it okay to construct a vision of excellence that isn't going to be for everybody? I think it clearly is. In fact, I will put it more strongly—I have never seen a vision of excellence that *is* for everybody.

That's the crux of the matter. The universal is, almost by definition, not excellent. Now, various patchwork strategies are certainly worth trying if they can help expand the pool of students that APR is educating (these might include making an extra effort to enroll certain populations or to better support those students in the school). Given its mission and orientation, I suspect the school is already attempting to do this. But, in any event, efforts to do more of all this and to do it better are welcome, so long as they do not compromise the qualities that make APR successful. We should not imagine, though, that such tactics will ever "solve" the central tension here between universalism and excellence; at best, I suspect, they'll alleviate it.

TWO PITFALLS OF DEMOCRATIC UNIVERSALISM

The issue here really lies with two frustrating characteristics of educational universality in a democratic system. One is the temptation to focus on the lowest common denominator. The second is that standardizing educational provision requires applying the crude tools of policy to complex, intensely human organizations.

First, there is the question of the lowest common denominator. When goals are defined universally, systems are inevitably managed and measured with uniform metrics (whether those relate to inputs or outcomes). So the focus is on making sure every student completes Algebra II, is proficient in reading, or what have you. Many students clear this bar. Some will not.

When expectations are universal, the charge is to focus on those students who have not cleared the bar. When universal provision is taken seriously, it discourages the embrace of exceptional demands—because they ensure that struggling students will have more difficulty clearing the bar. Creating smaller communities that set their own, more particular expectations is a way to combat this gravitational pull. (Historical note: It is no coincidence that what is expected of a generic high school graduate or a college student has tended to decline over the past century as expectations for each have become more universal.)

Second, universal provision entails standardizing practices around things like assessment, standards, curricula, staffing, and so on in order to ensure that students are universally served. The problem: schools are complex, intensely personal organizations. This means that excellence is typically the product of intensely human qualities, like impassioned leadership, engaged teaching, strong cultures, and involved parents. Policies can help facilitate these things, but they cannot mandate them. That's a challenge for universality, given the desire for comparable levels of success everywhere.

Pursuing that goal means either using policy levers and mandates to force these good things to happen or seeking to engineer success through the proper combination of course requirements, supports, and such. Unfortunately, it turns out to be enormously difficult to do either of these things. Meanwhile, the search for these "solutions" tends to result in churning policy—disrupting schools and frequently undermining key components in those schools where things are working.

THE TRICKY THING ABOUT EXTENDING EXCELLENCE

No one really knows how to make other schools as successful as APR or how to replicate APR's success. So, at least to me, it seems the decision is either to embrace its benefits, encourage APR to grow, and spur the emergence of more imitators, or to forthrightly conclude that we don't want to help APR's five hundred students unless and until we can serve their BPS peers equally well. For reasons already discussed, I think option two is a nonstarter.

APR can insist on expectations for students that the district as a whole would never embrace, or that it would embrace and then lack the stomach to enforce. In almost any event, the need to satisfy tens of thousands of families yields mushy, compromise-laden norms that enjoy little widespread backing and that are only loosely upheld. The result is mediocrity.

Many observers appreciate APR's results, want to see them delivered more universally and to a student body that more precisely reflects the local district, and imagine that the right rules will produce that happy result. Thus the well-intentioned push for these new charter regulations. I am suggesting, however unwelcome the message may be, that the very dynamics that make APR successful may be compromised by the proposed strictures. Indeed, I'll go further—it is precisely because APR *does not* embrace the universal that it is positioned to achieve excellence.

Now, in all this, there are at least three provisos worth noting. The first is that we are talking about a continuum. It is not that schools either *do* or *do not* have the ability to create terrific communities of learning, but that circumstances can make it easier or harder to do so. Those circumstances are a question partly of policy and partly of community norms, familial expectations, instructional coherence, and the rest.

A second is that many people have a heartfelt desire to want to deny the existence of any such trade-offs. (Less commendable is the tendency of some to depict those who see trade-offs as mean-spirited, covert racists, or other unsavory things.) However understandable this impulse, keep in mind that denying a tension does not make it go away.

Third, when it comes to parents, school board members, legislators, and so forth, even if they believe that such trade-offs exist, they may reasonably decide they are more concerned with universality than with what it takes to enable schools like APR to best serve their students. That kind of disagreement is healthy, and that is why having these issues in the political arena is an important part of finding stable compromises that reflect our competing views.

Ultimately, for what it is worth, I am more concerned about the ability of the educators at APR to keep educating their students than about the hypothetical utopias proposed by professional second guessers in their well-appointed offices. This leaves me leery of well-meaning proposals that seem likely to hinder the vision, focus, and work that characterizes schools like APR.

Frederick M. Hess is director of education policy studies at the American Enterprise Institute in Washington, DC. An author, political scientist, and educator, his books include The Cage-Busting Teacher *(2015),* Education Unbound *(2010),* Common Sense School Reform *(2006), and* School Choice in the Real World *(2001).*

Compromising Charter Schools' Efforts to Serve Disadvantaged Youth

Harry Brighouse

The primary purpose of certain kinds of charter schools is to benefit students from low-income urban backgrounds, especially Black and Latino students. This proposal appears to ensure that charter schools serve a broader, more representative selection of a school district's population, thus extending their benefits to a broader swath of a community's population. Yet, will forcing charter schools to serve a more representative disadvantaged population compromise their ability to serve the disadvantaged well? This proposal actually makes it less likely that charter schools will serve the interests of those who need charters most. In fact, it will likely increase the incentives for charters to favor the more advantaged among the least advantaged students.[9]

CHARTER SCHOOLS AND EDUCATING DISADVANTAGED STUDENTS

For me, the single most urgent imperative for school policy in the United States is to prioritize benefit to the least advantaged members of our society. Scholars conceive of disadvantage in various ways, but here, for simplicity's sake, I refer to the bottom roughly 30 percent of the income distribution. Such individuals typically have the least rewarding and least secure jobs and inhabit the neighborhoods least well served by various amenities, including public safety and clean air. Their children typically have the worst access to good education.[10]

Charter schools have emerged as one potential way to address the last worry. In urban communities across the country, charter schools have become alternatives to traditional public schools or, in some cases, have replaced traditional public schools. The best empirical evidence suggests that, on average, charter schools make little difference to the educational outcomes of the students who attend them, and that the effectiveness of charters varies greatly both between and within states. But evidence suggests that those charters that *do* improve educational outcomes are disproportionately schools that serve low-income Black and Latino students.[11]

One type of charter in particular—high-commitment charter schools (HCCs)—seem to make a significant difference for those students. From students, HCCs demand commitment to excellent behavior and to large amounts of time devoted to schoolwork and the culture of the school. From parents, they demand commitment to support students. From teachers, they demand long hours, far exceeding the normal hours public school teachers are required to work given their contracts, as well as evidence of success in the form of test score gains. HCCs often expect teachers to visit students' homes and monitor their individual progress.

The best-studied example is the Knowledge Is Power Program (KIPP) franchise. High-quality studies of KIPP schools found that they produce "positive, statistically significant, and educationally substantial" achievement gains in reading, math, science, and social studies among students who attend them.[12] Research finds that, by the third year after enrollment, the average KIPP middle school student has realized gains in achievement equivalent to approximately 40 percent of the local Black-White test score gap in math, 26 percent of the gap in reading, and 33 percent of the gaps in science and social studies. Of course, test score gains are a highly imperfect proxy for meaningful educational growth, but I do not think it is unreasonable to conjecture that significant growth at the low end of the spectrum in math and reading scores is evidence (if inconclusive evidence) of real academic gains.

One common complaint against HCCs is that children are regimented and disciplined in ways that are stressful and that we would never accept in the treatment of adults. I have seen qualitative evidence that children are regimented and disciplined in some schools in ways that I would not accept for my own children, or for the children in question if I were their parent. But some of the urban schools with which these charter schools compete are also stressful to inhabit, though in different ways. For some students, regimentation may be a better choice than the other options. I do not mean to downplay this issue, but we should compare the actual alternatives with each other rather than with some ideal.

COMPROMISING THE MISSION OF CHARTER SCHOOLS

The current climate makes it difficult even for HCCs to successfully serve the interests of the most disadvantaged. For one thing, the mechanism by which charter schools admit students favors active, engaged parents. Charter schools must use lotteries to determine admissions. Students whose parents are neglectful or disconnected or simply overstressed—the least advantaged *of all*, in other words—will likely not even enter the lottery. For another, there is a significant amount of risk in attempting to educate the worst-off because of increasing demand for accountability. Both the public and policy makers judge underperforming schools serving these populations more harshly than schools serving more advantaged populations. Indeed, schools in advantaged communities can be mediocre without being penalized: their mediocrity often does not show up in test scores or other kinds of outcomes because educated or affluent parents compensate with their own inputs. Schools in disadvantaged communities, however, do not have such protections. To avoid harsh scrutiny, charter schools likely favor the more advantaged families within disadvantaged populations.

Holding charter schools to the demographic composition and attrition standards of BPS, given that movement *within* BPS does not count as attrition, would further skew the preference for serving the more advantaged members of disadvantaged populations. Disadvantage is typically measured crudely: school districts typically use the free or reduced-price lunch (FRPL) designation as the sole formal measure. But even in income terms FRPL is quite heterogeneous: the income threshold for reduced-price lunch is 185 percent of the poverty rate (in 2013, $43,568 for a child from a household of four people), considerably higher than for free lunch, which is 130 percent of the poverty rate (in 2013, $30,615 for a child from a household of four). Within the free lunch category, a $10,000 difference in income is far more consequential than for a family living even near the median income level. The point is that schools can skim more advantaged students within the FRPL category without violating the requirement to mimic district demographics.

The demographic and attrition requirements also encourage charter schools to cherry-pick students. Charter schools, although constrained by lotteries, are not powerless about whom they enroll. First, they can skew the applicant pool through targeted marketing; that is, they can market specifically to students who will be least likely to leave the school. For example, they might appeal to parents with unionized (and thus more secure) jobs, or target churches with stable congregations, or market to families in newer housing developments, which enable families who would otherwise move around to remain settled. Thus, charters can enroll a more stable—because they are more advantaged—population while complying with the requirement that the population resemble that of the other local schools or of the district.

The policy may even compel charter schools to reduce attrition rates by refraining from exercising their power to expel students for disciplinary infractions. BPS has a duty to educate all students, regardless of what they have done, but no charter school has that duty. Given that, BPS intrinsically faces problems that charter schools do not, one of the many factors that make it difficult to make fair comparisons. And it is possible that charter schools expel students for disciplinary infractions for which they should be disciplined in some other way (in APR's case, we are not given data about this, so it is hard to be confident). But the capacity of schools to deliver a coherent instructional program and an acceptable daily-lived experience for children is severely compromised by inhibitions on expulsion. Students who persistently disrupt instruction in the classroom prevent other students from learning, deter teachers who have less stressful employment options from continuing in the profession, and distract school leaders from promoting instructional improvement.[13] Such an outcome seems to favor the interests of no one.

If school leadership knows that it will be penalized for higher-than-normal attrition rates, it will have increased incentives to avoid taking a chance on the kinds of students who are more likely to leave of their own accord and the kinds of students who might need to be expelled. They might also feel compelled not to expel students once they are in the school and behaving in ways that compromise the learning opportunities of other students.

CONCLUSION

For these reasons, I am generally opposed to proposals that force charter schools to mimic the demographics of district schools. It is the case that we ask charter schools to perform tasks for which our traditional public schools are not well suited. Yet, even if I thought, as some do, that charter schools are sufficiently bad for the school system (for any number of reasons), I would still be unenthused about the proposed legislation. If charter schools serving disadvantaged communities are positively harmful, more stringent regulations are, at best, second-best to legislation that would prohibit charter schools or that would, at least, halt their expansion. This legislation will not halt their expansion. Rather, it will just make charter schools less likely to contribute optimally to the urgent public purpose of benefiting the least advantaged populations.

Harry Brighouse is Carol Dickson-Bascom Professor of the Humanities, professor of philosophy, affiliate professor of educational policy studies, and director of the Center for Ethics and Education at University of Wisconsin–Madison. He is author (with Adam Swift) of Family Values: The Ethics of Parent-Child Relationships *(Princeton University Press, 2014) and editor (with Michael McPherson) of* The Aims of Higher Education: Problems of Morality and Justice *(University of Chicago Press, 2015).*

The Need for Equity-Based Policy

PEDRO NOGUERA

The debate over the expansion of charter schools has become increasingly acrimonious, and as the polarization has increased, it has become more difficult to objectively determine what impact charter schools are having and what role they should play in public education. The question posed in this case study—whether legislation should restrict or enable charter school expansion because of attrition and demographic data—is thus politically fraught. But that does not mean that every answer must be merely political or necessarily ideological. Rather, I suggest that we can best answer this question by fully examining the impact that charter school education policy has on *equity* in public education.

By equity, I mean the educational opportunities available to students who have historically experienced the greatest disadvantages and been most likely to be assigned to the lowest performing schools, including students with learning disabilities, English language learners (ELLs), homeless children, and low-income African American and Latino children. When we examine charters' systemic impact on the educational options available to our most disadvantaged students, we can see that in many cases they increase *inequity* by hypersegregating historically disadvantaged students in the public system, making it nearly impossible for those remaining public schools to succeed. Ideally, policy makers should put into place policies that mandate that every charter and regular public school serve a representative share of disadvantaged students. In addition, charters should be required to work in partnership with public schools to share innovative practices as laboratories of reform, be held accountable for student attrition, and be mandated to be transparent about their finances and their roles as selective rather than fully accessible educational institutions. Under these circumstances, charter schools *might* be justified in expanding, because they would serve educational equity—or at least, not exacerbate inequity quite so badly.

THE ROLE OF CHARTER SCHOOLS

In most cities across the country, there is a dual system of education in place: a private system for the affluent and a public system for the rest. Within the public system, too, there are frequently dual tracks, with magnet schools and schools for the gifted screening out the most disadvantaged students. This leaves the remainder of urban public schools composed of the most disadvantaged students and characterized by "hypersegregation," where low-income students of color are concentrated.[14] The case study shows such patterns at work in Boston, where 85 percent of children in BPS are categorized as "high needs," 87 percent are students of color, and nearly a third are English language learners. Furthermore, many of BPS' nonpoor, White, and Asian students attend the tracked Advanced Work Classes and selective-entry "exam schools."

In the nineteenth and twentieth centuries, some low-income and working-class children also escaped the public system by attending parochial schools. (This system was especially pervasive in Northeastern cities such as Boston, New York, and Philadelphia.) These children had parents who were willing to pay private school tuition, often at considerable sacrifice, in order to avoid public schools that were perceived as of lower quality.[15] For a variety of reasons, large numbers of parochial schools have closed over the last twenty years.[16] Increasingly, charter schools have filled the void previously occupied by parochial schools in many cities. Although some charters have been created to serve a specific disadvantaged group (e.g., recent immigrants, formerly incarcerated youth, etc.), most urban charter schools serve minority and low-income students. However, as was true for many parochial schools, the parents of these students are often better informed and more assertive in seeking access to what are regarded as high-quality schools.[17] The students are also less high needs, as the Academy of the Pacific Rim data clearly demonstrate.

I do not think that the parents of these children should be penalized for choosing schools they regard as superior to the public schools. However, policy makers have a responsibility to address an educational landscape that is becoming increasingly inequitable as a result of policies that enable such choices. There is a dire need for an equity-based education policy that provides additional resources to public schools serving the most disadvantaged students.

THE IMPACT OF CHARTER SCHOOLS IN NEW YORK CITY

The experiences of Latino high school students in New York City during the twelve years that Michael Bloomberg served as mayor may prove useful to those considering the implications of charter school expansion for equity. From 2001 to 2013, 136 charter schools were opened in New York City. This was part of a deliberate effort undertaken by the Bloomberg administration

to use choice and competition as a means to force improvements in public schools. Throughout much of this period, critics of Bloomberg's policies
pointed out that charter schools were underenrolling Latino and ELL students. In particular, Latino students—who disproportionately remained in
the public system—became increasingly segregated, especially by class; by
2013, almost a third of Latino students were in schools where over 90 percent of students qualified for free or reduced-price lunch, and only 16 percent
attended schools in which the majority of the student body was not poor.[18]

At the same time that Bloomberg was opening charter schools, he was
closing traditional public high schools that were regarded as "failing."
Bloomberg sold this as an equity-driven policy on the grounds that students
should all be attending high-achieving schools. However, in many cases the
schools these students were assigned to were no better than the schools that
had been closed.

Existing research suggests that the most effective way to elevate the performance of students of low socioeconomic status is to provide them with access to schools with greater socioeconomic diversity.[19] This is the opposite of
what happened in NYC high schools—with predictable results. An in-depth
study by the Parthenon Group found that *none* of the secondary schools in
New York City serving "high-needs" populations were "beating the odds"
and achieving academic success.[20] Both Parthenon and a 2011 study by the
Urban Youth Collaborative found that failing schools were larger, had higher concentrations of "level 1" students in reading and math, served higher
concentrations of ELLs and low-income students, and served disproportionate numbers of Latino students than more successful schools.[21]

New York City's Latino students, then, were caught in a double bind. On
the one hand, the schools they attended did not serve them well according to
most academic metrics. On the other hand, very few Latino students—and
even fewer ELLs—found their way into the charter schools that the district
claimed would replace many of the struggling traditional schools. They thus
not only failed to benefit from high performing charter schools, but also found
themselves stuck in schools that were getting worse precisely because of the
charter school expansion. The APR case suggests similar patterns might be
at work in BPS, as ELLs, students with disabilities, and low-income students
seem to be disproportionately represented in BPS as opposed to APR.

ENSURING EQUITY

In deciding whether to permit charter school expansion, policy makers
must address the inequities created by the growing number of schools—

charter and traditional public (magnet, gifted, etc.)—that screen out disadvantaged children. In particular, they must ensure that charter schools do not exacerbate existing race-class segregation within schools. Rather than merely limiting the number of charter schools, it might be more effective to require all charters and traditional public schools to take a percentage of the most disadvantaged students. While such a policy would be controversial, challenging to implement, and undoubtedly resisted by some, the consequence of allowing current patterns to persist is clear: most schools serving our neediest children will continue to fail.

In the meantime, three further initiatives are crucial to promoting equity. First, we should refocus on the original purpose of charter schools—that they serve as laboratories of innovation to improve public schools.[22] Rather than promoting competition between charters and traditional public schools, policy makers should actively incentivize collaboration and cooperation. Understood in this light, the case study might ideally focus not on comparing Boston Public Schools and Academy of the Pacific Rim to determine which is "better," but instead on the question of what each system could learn from the other.

Second, charter schools should also be held accountable if they lose large numbers of disadvantaged students, since such losses diminish charters' relevance as laboratories of innovation and also overtax an already-burdened public system. We see this at work in the APR case, as well. Third, based on a more accurate accounting of enrollment patterns, the state should require truth in advertising. A school like APR should honestly state what it is: a selective school for high-achieving, low-income children. If the state is to authorize schools like this, it should do so with a clear recognition that it will result in the most disadvantaged students being concentrated in a smaller number of traditional public schools, and acknowledge that these schools will undoubtedly experience greater difficulty in successfully meeting their academic needs. While in many respects public schools in urban areas have been headed in this direction for some time, the role of public policy should be to acknowledge, and compensate for, the inequity created by these practices.

Pedro Noguera is the Peter L. Agnew Professor of Education at New York University and the executive director of the Metropolitan Center for Equity and the Transformation of Schools.

Not Perfect for All, But Perfect for Some

AYO MAGWOOD

In the world in which policy makers and school board administrators operate, data rules. Test results, graduation and attrition rates, demographics, and other quantifiable dimensions of schools often determine decisions about school approvals, closures, and funding, among other things. So it is understandable that the question posed by this case study is whether or not data support a policy decision. However, the conversation about comparing demographics and attrition rates misses a more fundamental point: decisions about schools should reflect the needs of different students, parents, and teachers. Policy makers and school board administrators should thus favor the protection of student and parent choice in determining whether to expand Academy of the Pacific Rim, if only because not all students or student preferences are the same, and it is entirely difficult for policy makers to know what particular families and students want and need from their schools.

SAFETY AND BELONGING

In my personal experience as both a teacher and a parent, I have found that parents' and students' decisions about schools are rarely based on the measurable performance criteria that policy makers and administrators tend to swear by. I taught for eight years at a charter school in Washington, DC. I was attracted to it for its particular curriculum focus, but I stayed for the relative freedom I enjoyed to innovate my curriculum (I did not teach a tested subject), for the collaboration with a team of dedicated, passionate, creative, and highly educated teaching faculty, for the small-school community feeling, and for the zealous "can-do" spirit. About 85 percent of the approximately four hundred students were African American, about 15 percent were Latino; two-thirds were eligible for free or reduced-price lunch, and a small number were English language learners. In a recent year, the attrition rate from ninth grade to twelfth grade was, as at APR, about 60 percent. The big jump in attrition typically occurs between tenth and eleventh grade, with only marginal losses between ninth and tenth grade and between eleventh and twelfth grade. Students typically leave in large numbers after the tenth grade, when it is determined that they do not have enough credits to graduate on time. Many hope that by transferring to DC public schools, where social promotion is more common, they will be able to graduate on time. But this is simply the primary reason why students leave the school.

The reasons that my students cited for attending my school were rarely on the radar of school board bean counters. When I first started working there, I naively assumed that most students were attracted to the school because of either the school's mission or the school's claims of superior academic rigor—just as I was. However, I found that most students I asked cited physical safety as their family's principal reason for choosing to attend our school. Some of the larger public schools in our city can be physically unsafe at times for those who don't belong to the neighborhood "crews," or who are perceived as social misfits. For example, over the years, I noticed that our student body appeared to have a disproportionate number of "out" (LGBT) students, "nerds," "geeks," and students who would otherwise have a difficult time at a typical large urban school.

The small size, sense of community, attentive faculty members, open-minded culture, and strict security at some of the charter schools in Washington, DC—but in particular at ours—protected these students and encouraged the student body to embrace, or at the very least to tolerate, these students. For example, at least one gay or lesbian student couple attended the senior prom almost every year I worked there, and nobody batted an eye. Similarly, I never saw an academic-minded student being accused of "acting White" or having to play down his or her academic interest or competence in order to be popular. And while the handful of students fascinated with Japanese anime, rock music, or skateboarding did tend to prefer each other's company, the student body was generally tolerant of them and their interests.

I suspect that similar factors might also have been what attracted and retained many of our students with learning or emotional disabilities. While many criticize charter schools for having slightly lower numbers of students who receive special education services, I think we might alternatively consider admiring the number of students with special needs that many charters are able to retain despite the high level of academic rigor and demanding behavioral standards.

Again, I think that the safe environment and sense of belonging our school was able to provide was crucial to such students. In my last year as the senior thesis teacher, I worked closely with a student with learning disabilities who struggled to read and write. Her senior thesis on marriage equality analyzed and applied the due process clause, the equal protection clause, the full faith and credit clause, the Tenth Amendment, and the establishment clause. She won first prize for her senior thesis presentation. At graduation, she confided to me that if it were not for the pull of the gratifying work on her thesis, she would not have shown up to school each day. Admittedly our school was not appropriate for all students with disabilities, or perhaps not even for a majority of them, but some students with disabilities found exactly what they were looking for and, perhaps, exactly what they needed at our school.

BASING POLICY ON CHOICE

The question, then, is how policy makers factor the dimensions of schools that students and their families value into decisions about whether to expand a charter school or not. I submit that this is not an easy task. For many students like those I taught, the trade-off of spending an extra year in school in exchange for more one-on-one attention might be worth it. But how do we know this, and how should this factor into broad policy decisions? If the examples I reference in the previous section are any guide, these decisions typically vary from student to student and family to family. Individual students and families value different aspects of schools. The processes by which they arrive at their decisions may also be different, involving, for example, differential access to resources to explore school options.

Thus, rather than try to model how individual decisions are made, or even predict what students and families will want, I propose that it is enough for school boards to ensure that schools meet adequate fiscal, management, and academic standards, and then let students and parents choose for themselves. In this way, choice functions as a proxy for all the inner workings of schools that cannot be adequately captured in brain-numbing reports about various performance and climate indicators. By protecting choice, policy makers indirectly protect not only the different reasons students and parents favor some schools over others, but also students' and parents' ability to make decisions about what education they value for themselves.

PERFECT FOR SOME

In advocating for choice, I am suggesting that education policy should not focus on creating schools that are perfect for each and every child. Rather, we should aim for schools that are perfect for some, but not necessarily for all. Such schools may not be superior to others according to commonly measured indicators or standard performance criteria. They may not be right for all students, or even for the majority of students. But they may be the best choice—or at least *a* choice—for the students that choose them.

These students and families know that a school is more than a set of indicators or performance criteria. A school like APR may have poor retention statistics, and that may indicate that it is not perfect for a large minority or even a majority of students. Still, it may be perfect for other groups of students. The same school may excel at challenging and supporting gifted minority students. It may engage students in long-term, problem-based group projects that develop real, meaningful knowledge. It may inspire students by preparing them to compete in academic competitions. Or it may build confidence in students by supporting them through challenging individual projects.

A school does not have to be perfect in order to be perfect for a particular student, or even to inspire the sense of commitment and belonging that make schools safe and welcoming. Moreover, students and their families are in the position to know what is best for them far more intimately than any single performance or demographic measure can demonstrate. When we focus on these broader measures of performance, we lose track of the choices that students and their families ought to be able to make about the course of their education.

Ayo Magwood is a high school history educator who has taught for eight years in urban charter schools and two years at an independent school. She lives with her husband and son in Washington, DC.

Charter Schools, Education Markets, and Democracy

LAWRENCE BLUM

The Massachusetts legislature recognizes that the public school system as a whole has responsibilities to all its students, that it must be especially vigilant in serving the state's neediest students, and that requirements for charter schools positioned as public schools must be guided by that responsibility. This responsibility is discharged and assessed in part by comparing the performance of a given charter school or group of charter schools with traditional district schools, but also by examining the impact of proposed charter schools on other schools in the system. Public schools have civic responsibilities and democratic purposes that are not discharged purely through students' academic performance, and these must also be factored into the overall decision.

COMPARING CHARTER AND DISTRICT SCHOOLS

The case write-up makes clear that Academy of the Pacific Rim (representing similar charter schools that would be permitted under the proposed legislation) is currently serving a distinctly less disadvantaged student body than BPS as a whole. This fact is somewhat masked by the familiar categories used to measure disadvantage in educational contexts. Take "low-income," for example, conventionally taken to encompass students eligible for "free and reduced-price lunch." The upper limit of "free lunch" is 130 percent of the family poverty line, which was $23,850 in 2013. "Reduced-price lunch" is 130–185 percent of the poverty line (185 percent was $43,568). While no child in the larger category can be regarded as advantaged, there is quite a significant difference between $43,000 and, say, $8,000.[23]

On average, APR students come from much higher income families than BPS students. Only 44.8 percent of APR's students qualify for free lunch, compared to 74.6 percent of BPS students, and we cannot be sure that the "free lunch" students served by APR are as disadvantaged as those in the BPS. To have a fully accurate picture of the difference would require a more refined set of categories.

A second category of disadvantage, "English language learner" (ELL) finds APR with no students and BPS with 29.9 percent—again, a very large difference.

A third category of disadvantage, "students with disabilities," is virtually equivalent in APR and BPS—20.5 percent and 19.5 percent, respectively. However, there are very different kinds of disabilities—physical, behavioral, emotional, cognitive impairment, among others—and each comes in widely varying degrees. We cannot say that the two systems are serving comparably disabled students unless they are serving roughly equal percentages along the mild/severe spectrum, as well as similar types.

It is both more costly monetarily and more challenging pedagogically to educate poorer, ELL, and significantly disabled students compared to students who are not poor (or who are less poor), speak English fluently (whatever their first language), and have no disabilities.[24] The cost is compounded by peer and concentration effects, in that a critical mass of disabled students in the absence of adequate personnel support in a classroom, for example, threatens the teacher's ability to meet the educational needs of the whole class.

So, if a school garners better results, according to whatever measure, with a significantly lower proportion of challenging students, as APR appears to do, we do not know what combination of the student demographics and the school's approach to education is producing those results. Some studies have attempted to isolate the demographic and the school components of student test scores by comparing students in charter schools with those who applied to the charter lottery but were not selected. For various reasons, this methodology does not adequately do the trick.[25] In short, such research suggests that APR's educational accomplishment, in comparison with BPS or particular schools within BPS, is impossible to assess.

However, we can assess the impact of schools like APR on the district as a whole. Shifting a higher percentage of relatively advantaged students to APR-like charters increases the proportion of more challenging students in traditional district schools. This shift increases educational inequality, weakening the educational environment for the most challenged and intensifying whatever differences already exist between these groups. Lifting a cap on such schools would further exacerbate that inequality.

WHAT KIND OF CHARTER SCHOOL IS THE LEGISLATURE LOOKING FOR?

Presumably the legislature's interest in attrition rates is primarily in its impact on the demographic issue, since the legislature's main concern is how well the proposed schools are serving a representative slice of the district. The author makes a good case that neither a single school in BPS (or average of single schools) nor BPS as a whole provides an appropriate standard for comparing and assessing APR with respect to attrition. But her point that "APR's retention of high-needs students is far worse than BPS'" is the crucial one here.

The proposed legislation appears to assume that schools like APR could be forced to serve the district in an egalitarian and democratic way through imposing demographic and attrition standards. But such schools cannot be remade in a democratic, inclusive mold without becoming a completely different kind of school, losing their current character entirely. They look for students and families able and willing to sign on to a particular behavioral and academic regimen. That group of students is almost certain to be among the more advantaged segment of the BPS district population.[26]

In essence, the legislation pulls for a different kind of charter school than an APR-like one—one that is entirely nonselective and sees itself as serving the same types of students as in the regular Boston public schools, and that regards itself as allied with the district in having a duty to educate all children. Such charter schools exist—they are inclusive and often neighborhood based. "Innovation schools," created in the 2010 Massachusetts school reform law (and mentioned in Pat Jehlen's commentary), have essentially this character, although they are not charter schools.[27]

THE MARKET APPROACH TO EDUCATION

By contrast, the APR-like sector is governed by a marketlike approach, which is defined by several features. Schools have a responsibility only to their own "consumers" (students and their families). Finding an appropriate school for each child is a parental responsibility rather than a function of the school district. Inequality in parental capital is taken as a given, though generally not acknowledged as such. Charter schools compete with traditional district schools for resources to support their own vision(s). Finally, at least implicitly, such logic no longer expects that a school system can and should try to provide something like an equal education to all its students.

Another way to put the last point is that APR-like charter schools are closer to private schools than public schools in important respects. They are not required to accept students who come into the system in the middle of a school year; they can set behavioral, academic, and "cultural" standards that are a basis for excluding students, in fact and partly in law and policy;

they have no responsibility to a larger school district to take students who leave another school in that or another system.[28] The force of this proposed legislation is that the type of charter school it implicitly seeks to fashion would have none of these private-like characteristics.

UNDERMINING DEMOCRATIC AIMS

In considering the role of charter schools in a public school system, the legislature must also take into account the larger effects of signing on to this market-based approach to public schooling. This approach weakens the sense of schooling as a public good from which the society as a whole benefits and has (therefore) a public responsibility to provide. Thus, it may also diminish public support for the use of tax money for public schools over time.[29]

The market approach also generates no entity tasked with ensuring that education will aim to prepare students to be knowledgeable and engaged citizens. It is not grounded in the democratic purposes of public education that require forging a sense of shared fate and mutual respect among students from different backgrounds.[30] Rather, the market approach detracts attention from (and some features of it actively oppose) trying to rectify the intensified general inequality of recent decades that has multifarious ill effects on democratic education.

Finally, the market approach diverts attention from school reforms that, in contrast to charters, have proven records in enhancing achievement, integration, or civic purposes in education, such as regional/metropolitan districting, racial- and class-integrative initiatives (such as magnet schools), heterogeneous classes, and wrap-around in-school services to buffer some of the ill effects of extreme poverty.

The legislature should have all these considerations in mind in deciding which segments of the charter sector it will permit to expand.

Lawrence Blum is Distinguished Professor of Liberal Arts and Education, and professor of philosophy at the University of Massachusetts Boston. He is the author of High Schools, Race, and America's Future: What Students Can Teach Us About Morality, Diversity, and Community *(Harvard Education Press, 2012).*

The author extends many thanks to Christopher Lewis for his excellent feedback and comments on a previous draft.

Schools for All Our Children

PATRICIA D. JEHLEN

In 1993, I was among the legislators who voted for the Education Reform Act, which established charter schools in Massachusetts. At the time, we expected charter schools to be innovation labs that would give teachers and others the chance to try out new educational ideas.[31] Successful innovations would then spread to district schools and reach more children.

By 2014, many legislators believed that the initial promise of charter schools had not been fulfilled, that charters were not serving students with the greatest needs, and that their expansion threatened opportunities for other children. So, roughly twenty years after initially supporting charters, I was among the three-quarters of the Massachusetts State Senate that voted against a bill to raise the cap on charter school tuition in the "lowest performing" 10 percent of districts in the state, where it is already twice as high as in other districts. Now, instead of asking how charters can serve as laboratories for innovation, policy makers like me ask: What is the end game? Is it two parallel school systems?

THE CHANGING ROLE OF CHARTERS

In the first years after the Education Reform Act, charters opened in urban, suburban, and rural school districts. Many different groups submitted charter applications for new schools—some based on the arts.

But things changed. New legislation in 2010 doubled the percentage of the funding "low performing" districts could budget to charters. The Board of Elementary and Secondary Education defined "low performing" to mean low scores on state tests.[32] This measure, though modified in 2014, continues to correlate highly with family income. Since then, Massachusetts has granted fifteen new charters: eight have gone to existing charter operators; all are in urban districts; all but one are in one of the twenty-nine districts that serve the highest percentage of low-income students, that have the lowest test scores, and where the district has doubled the charter tuition cap. The Pioneer Institute reports that "all of the schools authorized under the *Smart Cap* in underperforming districts are replications of existing charter schools or schools operated by proven providers who have merely made tweaks to the programming they have traditionally offered."[33]

The 2010 law required the state to authorize only schools or contractors with successful track records to open or expand charter schools in districts where the cap had been raised. This provision was intended to act as a quality control measure. However, the law implicitly changed—or at least confirmed—a different role for charter schools. Charters became a way for children to escape "failing" district schools. New charters are now rarely innovative schools. They do not experiment with new methods and approaches that could be passed on to district schools. Instead, their methods can only be replicated in additional charters.

SEPARATE, NOT EQUAL

Charter schools now commonly employ three innovations that range from challenging to impossible for districts to implement: extended learning time, limited admission points, and inflexible behavioral and academic standards.

First, most districts that would consider extended school days find it hard to increase learning time dramatically because of severe budget constraints. Charter schools avoid the funding problem and provide longer learning time partly by raising outside funds and partly by paying lower teacher salaries so they can hire more staff. For example, the Academy of the Pacific Rim (APR) pays over $20,000 less in average teacher salary than BPS.[34]

Second, charter schools use limited admission points to create a stable school culture. Charters are not required to admit students midyear or after the first few grades. This helps to explain why a charter school like APR graduates fewer than thirty students a year when more than one hundred enter in fifth grade. Such a policy is just not an option for regular public school districts. Granted, a few selective-admission schools like Boston Latin also restrict admission to particular years, but most public schools must welcome students at any point in the year and at any grade level, regardless of when or why they arrive.

Third, charter schools are able to set inflexible disciplinary and academic standards to build or enforce school culture. "No excuses" schools like APR require students to meet demanding academic and behavioral standards. For example, APR's out-of-school suspension rate is almost three times higher than Boston's, and its in-school suspension rate is almost *twenty times* higher. In 2013–2014, more than 26 percent of all students at APR were suspended at least once during the year.[35] Many of the suspended students chose to return to Boston district schools.

A recent blog post by Steven Thomas, a 2015 graduate of New Mission High School in Boston, describes his year at APR. Despite his having an Individualized Education Program (IEP) and struggling to overcome learning disabilities, APR gave Steven demerits and detentions every day for behaviors like slouching in class. He learned to hate school and even started to think, "Maybe I'm a bad kid." Fortunately, after returning to Boston public schools, Steven made honor roll, took Advanced Placement classes, and was accepted to seven colleges.[36]

By contrast, public school districts are obligated to teach any child (of age) who walks through their doors. They generally cannot set behavioral or academic standards that exclude students from their schools—nor should they. District schools are making great efforts to *avoid* suspending students and to *help* students succeed academically; increasing suspensions and academic retentions is not a practice they will or should emulate.

A TALE OF TWO SYSTEMS?

When some schools can avoid or shed students who have more challenges, all the students not in those selective schools are harmed. In addition to charters' capacities to exclude students with academic or behavioral difficulties, charter schools also tend to enroll almost no English language learners (ELLs). Only one ELL student attends APR. By contrast, nearly 30 percent of the students in Boston Public Schools are ELLs.[37] Similarly, most charter schools—though not APR—enroll fewer students with special needs, and even fewer enroll students with severe disabilities.

As more students are able to access exclusive charter schools, more students with challenges that charter schools do not serve will be concentrated in district schools. Currently the limit on students in charters is 18 percent in Boston and other "low performing" districts. Another 10 percent of Boston students are in selective-entry exam schools—which similarly serve low numbers of ELL students and student with disabilities. Expanding charter schools could mean that up to a third of Boston students—many of those with the highest scores—would likely leave district schools, and would likely further concentrate students with high needs in nonselective district schools. Thus, the creation of two parallel school systems is a distinct possibility.

The reliance on test scores to measure school quality accelerates this separation. As students with more challenges—for example, homeless students and those who move frequently, new immigrants, students with disabilities—are concentrated in BPS district schools, test scores for the district fall and it appears that the schools are "failing." Parents with options leave for charter, private, or suburban schools with fewer problems and higher scores. With fewer students and less money, the district closes schools. Some of the remaining district schools are labeled "low performing" because of the test scores; their principal and teachers are displaced, programs are dismantled, or the schools are closed. All of these disruptions occur predominantly in poorer neighborhoods and drive more families to leave the increasingly unstable district.

PROMOTING QUALITY AND INNOVATION FOR ALL CHILDREN

The reliance on test scores to measure school quality has reduced innovation in both charter and district schools. As Ludlow Superintendent Todd Gazda writes: "Our current system rewards compliance rather than creativity. It inhibits creative professionals from taking appropriate risks with their lessons and practice because failure comes with severe consequences for both the individual and the school."[38]

The Board of Elementary and Secondary Education, which in Massachusetts ultimately decides whether to authorize a charter application or not, says that it does not—and cannot—consider the effect of a new charter school on the rest of the students in the district. Other policy makers, like many in the state senate, believe that our responsibility is to all of the students in our districts. School policy should not just build lifeboats; it should fix the ship!

But what would that require? For a start, adequate funding of *all* schools is necessary. Escalating costs of health care and special education make it challenging for most communities just to fund adequate regular education staff, technology requirements, and professional development. And this does not include the challenge of finding stable funding for improvements such as expanded learning time. The poorest districts, of course, are struggling the most to find adequate funding even for core operations.[39]

Improving education for all children will also require innovations in assessing educational success. This case study underscores the complexity of judgments about school quality. Any simple list of criteria will inevitably distort decisions, and will thus likely cause unanticipated problems. The focus on English language arts and math scores, for example, has driven out instructional time for history, music, art, physical education, and even recess. By contrast, broader measures, such as performance assessment, would reflect the real needs of students, as well as the expectations of parents and future employers.

To be successful in school or in life, children need a lot more than the ability to take standardized tests. They need to learn self-control, the ability to work with other people, and perseverance. Schools need to pay attention to social and emotional skills and attitudes. It's not just about instruction, it's about how adults and children treat each other, how the classroom is organized, whether there's room for creativity, collaboration, and independent exploration. When we only measure students and schools on test scores, children lose the chance to grow in important ways. Recognizing that children have different learning styles and interests would allow a return to the initial vision of charter schools, trying diverse models that might benefit diverse learners and better prepare students for college, career, and life. In some places, efforts are already underway. New Hampshire is working to develop this kind of assessment, and New York Performance Standards Consortium schools already have a solid track record.[40] In Massachusetts, the same 2010 law mentioned earlier created an innovation school model that allows school autonomy and more local control. Fifty-four schools in geographically diverse districts have chosen this option in just five years with some promising results.

The charter school movement has moved far from the vision of experimentation we hoped for in 1993. At this point, I don't believe that expanding the charter school sector is in the interests of all children—even with requirements like matching demographics and attrition rates of charters to district schools. Instead, we should focus on efforts that will improve all schools and benefit all students.

Massachusetts State Senator Patricia D. Jehlen is senate vice-chair of the Joint Committee on Education and chair of the Special Senate Committee on Innovative and Alternative Education. She has experience as a mother and grandmother of public school students, as a teacher, as a school committee member, as a founder of an alternative public elementary school program, and as a state representative.

CHAPTER SEVEN

Engaging with Dilemmas

**JACOB FAY AND MEIRA LEVINSON,
WITH ELISABETH FIELDSTONE KANNER**

Akin to Jal Mehta's reaction to reading the "Promotion or Retention?" case, you may feel, in reading this book, as if we have spun you back and forth, twirled you around, and left you with more questions than answers. The cases themselves cover substantial ground, from discipline to grading to state charter policy. The commentaries for each case are similarly diverse. Taken together, they rarely present one course of action. Often they present six, some of which clearly conflict with others. We assure you, however, such spinning and twirling is intentional.

Our aim in this book is to provide a starting point for collective phronetic inquiry into the dilemmas that comprise some of the most pressing yet quotidian concerns in the world of education. In short, this book eschews definitive answers. We understand the cases in this volume as provocations to explore the ethical dimensions of education practice and policy; likewise, the commentaries provide models for doing so in a way that iterates among theory, research, and practice. Together, the cases and commentaries are an invitation to think along with us about dilemmas of educational ethics.

Thus, it is our sincere hope that these cases and commentaries find their way into spaces that have an affinity for asking questions. In faculty meetings, principal and school board training sessions, teacher education classes, leadership team meetings, professional development settings, and Critical Friends groups, educators, school leaders, and policy makers can use normative case studies to promote reflective practice or develop expertise, elements of successful practice that Elisabeth Kanner, Diana Hess, and Joshua Wakeham's commentaries on "Rocky Choices" all emphasize. In philosophy classrooms, normative case studies can provide tools for thinking about perennial topics like justice, responsibility, and equality, diverse conceptions of which thread among commentaries across many of the cases. In sociology classrooms, we hope normative case studies can shed new light on familiar phenomena such as the social relationships that define schools as both professional organizations and communities of citizens, as in David Knight's and Mary Pattillo's "Stolen Trust" commentaries. Preservice teachers, veteran educators, and policy makers may find that our cases and commentaries provide a useful means to view the challenges they face (or expect to face) in their work from other perspectives.

In turning these cases over to inquiry-minded people, we intend this final chapter to serve as a usage guide of sorts. We offer some tools that we have found to be effective in facilitating discussions about normative case studies. Like the cases and commentaries themselves, we do not mean the content of this chapter to be viewed as a definitive "how to talk about normative case studies" manual. It is a starting point rather than an ending point.

SELECTING DISCUSSION MATERIAL

Simply put, there is a lot of material in this book. This observation prompts the first challenge to any potential case discussion: What should we discuss? Should we just read one case study? Which one? Should we read one commentary, two, or all of them? The audience, goals for discussion, amount of time participants will have to prepare and then discuss, and desired sort of interaction between participants all contribute to answers to these questions. Table 7.1 provides a range of content options.

TABLE 7.1   Reading and discussion options

Option	Works well if...
Read and discuss one case.	• Groups have limited time. • Goal is to draw from the group's expertise and experience.
Read and discuss a case and all of the commentaries.	• Groups have enough time for this amount of reading. • Goal is to thoroughly expand the group's ideas.

Option	Works well if . . .
Read and discuss a case and one or more of the commentaries.	• Groups have some time, but not enough to read all of the commentaries. • Goal is to begin to expand the group's expertise.
Read and discuss a case and two or three sharply contrasting commentaries.	• Groups have some time, but not enough to read all of the commentaries. • Goal is to gain depth by comparing and contrasting a particular way of approaching the problem or thinking about an issue.
Read a case and assign participants different commentaries to read. Participants informally represent or formally present the ideas in their commentary to the group.	• Groups have some time, but not enough for everyone to read several commentaries. • Goal is to expand the group's ideas. • You can count on participants to accurately present ideas of a text to the larger group. • Participants will be comfortable presenting to each other.
Read a case and then have participants write their own commentary. Do not share commentaries.	• Groups have enough time for reading and writing, but less time for discussion. • Goal is to deepen participants' thinking and take a stand on an issue.
Read a case and then have participants write their own commentary. Share commentaries.	• Groups have enough time for reading and writing. • Goal is to deepen participants' thinking and take a stand on an issue. • Participants feel comfortable sharing ideas with each other.
Read more than one case study and discuss.	• Groups have enough time for the amount of reading (at once or over time). • Goal is to compare how similar values, phenomena, or challenges surface in different situations. • Goal is to learn about the case study approach and possibly how to write your own cases.

In his comment in chapter 1, "The Pedagogical Implications of Case Study Structure," Brendan Randall cautions that the narrative structure of a case can influence what questions preoccupy the reader. A similar counsel is applicable to the structure of this book, insofar as the way we have organized the cases and commentaries suggests reading individual cases grouped with corresponding commentaries. However, as we reread, edited, and refined the cases and commentaries, we became attuned to commonalities across cases. For example, commenters recognize the importance of voice in both "Stolen Trust" and "Promotion or Retention?" Concern for social phenomena like stratification surfaces in "Inflated Expectations" and in "Is Pandering Ethical Policy?" Commenters call attention to race in "Stolen Trust" and "How, If at All, Should Charters Be Compared to Districts?" and to dimensions of teacher integrity in "Rocky Choices," "Promotion or Retention?," and "Inflated Expectations." How to address structural inequality is front and center in the two policy cases, but many commenters make it clear that structural inequality is also a relevant concern in each of the other cases. Thus, as the final option in table 7.1 suggests, we think there is fertile ground to examine these cases and commentaries in different combinations than we provide here, and we encourage groups to explore different arrangements.

DISCUSSION STRUCTURE

Each case and commentary in this book is adaptable to different discussion formats. Consider the purpose for your discussion and the size of the group when deciding which structure to use. With all discussions, we suggest that participants are given an opportunity to prepare before the discussion begins and that a facilitator is assigned to guide the discussion. Table 7.2 details some possible discussion structures.

TABLE 7.2   Discussion structures

Option	Description
Whole group	• Typically one facilitator guides the conversation of the whole group.
	• This is an appropriate format for groups that have fewer than fifteen participants.
	• For larger groups, you can involve more participants by having several partner talks during the whole-group discussion.

Option	Description

Small group	• This is a way to break up larger groups into discussion-sized sections.
	• Form smaller groups of four to eight, each with its own facilitator.
	• Ideas between small groups are shared. Ways to do this include:
	  – Reconvene to the larger group and have a group presenter share a key idea from the group—perhaps the group's response to the question at the end of the case.
	  – Reconfigure, or "jigsaw," the groups so that each new group includes at least one member from the original groups.
	  – End with a final whole-group discussion.

Fishbowl	• This is ideal for medium to large groups. • This option encourages careful, active listening. • Some participants begin as speakers while others are assigned the role of listeners. Often a group of chairs is placed in the center of the room for the speakers, and the listeners sit outside this circle. • Sometimes listeners may be asked to comment on the discussion: who is participating, what kinds of arguments are being presented, or where points of agreement versus disagreement are arising. • About halfway through, participants switch roles. • Sometimes facilitators allow a final round of discussion where everyone can participate. • Fishbowl participants may speak for themselves or as representatives of a particular author or perspective.
Town hall	• This is ideal for larger groups. • This offers a great way to get ideas from multiple perspectives onto the table, including roles or perspectives that members of the group might not represent on their own. • Participants speak from a particular role or perspective. Facilitators begin by having participants introduce themselves, identify their roles, and then speak briefly (1–2 minutes) on the case. • Facilitators can assign participants to speak from the perspective of someone in the case (e.g., a parent, a teacher, a student, an administrator), to represent the viewpoint of one of the commentary authors, or to speak from their real-life role. • If there is enough time, the facilitator can assign participants different roles during different rounds of discussion. • Often facilitators allow participants to break out of their assigned perspective in the final round of discussion.

continued

TABLE 7.2   *continued*

Option	Description
Online/digital	• This option can work for groups of any size.
	• Different programs and apps will determine the structure of the discussion.
	• Popular formats include threaded online discussions, video conferencing, digital collaborative spaces such as wikis and shared docs, and social media.
	• This can be a good way to document and preserve case discussions.

In addition to structure, it is important to consider the end goal of the discussion. That is to say, identify what you hope to accomplish by the end of the discussion and how the discussion structure can encourage that result. For example, if the end goal is for the group to reach a decision, discussion of the case could end with a vote. If the end goal is for participants to deepen their own understanding, the discussion could end with a writing assignment. Or, if the end goal is team building, participants could conclude by sharing what they have learned about the values embraced by their community.

DISCUSSING THE CASES AND COMMENTARIES

Normative case discussions do not have to follow a prescribed path. The composition of the group, the aims and structure of the discussion, and participants' experience with normative case studies will all influence the flow of the discussion. Even so, it is helpful to know what to expect from case discussions. Here we suggest some general guidelines for discussing normative case studies. The questions in exhibit 7.1, which emerged from our own work piloting and refining the cases in this book, comprise a possible discussion protocol. The questions we suggest reflect three general aims for case discussions. The first four questions guide discussion participants to identify and analyze what is at stake in the case or commentary. The fifth question creates space for participants to synthesize and apply insights gained from the cases, commentaries, and ensuing discussion. The final two questions ask participants to reflect on the process and address next steps.

EXHIBIT 7.1 Case discussion protocol

Sample questions

1. What is the dilemma in this case? For whom is it a dilemma?
2. Why is this a dilemma?
   - What values or principles are at stake? Is there disagreement about these values? Do they compete in some way?
   - What practical and/or policy considerations are at stake? Is there disagreement about these? Do they compete in some way?
3. What choices are available, and to whom?
   - How does each of these choices frame and address the issues at stake?
   - For each choice, what is gained? What is lost?
4. Who should take action? What should they do? Why?
5. What have you learned from talking about this case that might apply elsewhere?
   - What principles or values are you thinking about for the first time, or thinking about in a new way? Why?
   - What policies or practices are you thinking about for the first time or in a new way? Why?
   - How, if at all, do you think you will draw on these ideas in your own work?
6. What value is there, if any, to talking through a case like this with others?
   - What did you learn about yourself?
   - What did you learn about others?
   - What did you learn about your setting or context?
   - What did you learn about the process itself?
7. Is there anything else you want to bring up or discuss? What issues, concerns, or questions should we address in the future?

USING VARIATIONS OF THE CASES

In some circumstances, it may be helpful to change a case to pursue further discussion. In fact, we encourage readers to do so, with one caveat that we will soon address. After all, the fundamental goal of these cases is to encourage careful thinking about familiar problems. In service of that goal, altering some aspects of a case study can challenge the assumptions—unspoken or otherwise—undergirding people's initial reactions to the cases.

Variations to the cases can emphasize particular dimensions of the dilemma. For example, consider changing the setting of "Inflated Expectations" to a public high school, located first in an upper- or middle-income suburb, then in a mixed-income urban school, and finally in a low-income rural school. In placing the case in a public school, this variation lessens the influence of the "education as a purchased commodity" that has more strength at a private school like Hamaskil than at typical public schools. Second, changing the location and economic background of the school community can help surface some of the concerns that Peter Demerath raises in his commentary about the broader context in which grade inflation is situated.

Another possible variation involves altering the characters within each case study. We could, for example, make Kate a high school student rather than a third grader in "Rocky Choices." Or, we could stipulate that Ms. Brown is a first-year teacher rather than a veteran with experience teaching special-needs students. How would such changes shift our thinking about the case? Would we expect Kate to have more control over her behavior because she is older? Why? What would our expectations for Ms. Brown be, given her lack of experience? The commentaries to the case raise different values that should guide Ms. Brown's decision making. Is there a shift in the relative importance of those values, given the different age and experience of the characters?

We might also alter some of the general context of the case. For example, in "Is Pandering Ethical Policy?" we could specify that a well-organized community group is advocating for the expansion of an Academy of the Pacific Rim–like charter school into their neighborhood. Such an addition changes the nature of the question at the end of the case. Rather than focus on a general rule about attrition, demographics, and graduation rates as constraints on charter schools, the case now shifts to whether those numbers matter at all in the face of popular will—a point similar to one Ayo Magwood raises in her commentary.

Now, the caveat. As much as we encourage such creative adaptations of the cases, there are some alterations that we caution against. For example, consider changing the options the teachers face in "Promotion or Retention?" such that the alternative school is known to serve students well. In contrast to the previous variations, replacing the presumptively broken alternative school with a self-evidently working one likely fails to promote further thinking, because it undermines the dilemma at the heart of the "Promotion or Retention?" case. In the original case, the teachers are faced with no good options, yet they must act. By providing the teachers one reasonable option, this variation would make the case relatively easy to respond to; it would enable an "escape" from the dilemma. This sort of variation should typically be avoided.

ABBREVIATED CASES

We want the normative case study approach to be practical for any audience, even those that face severe time constraints. For example, given the demands of their jobs, it might not be possible for some practitioners to read the cases and commentaries in advance. In other instances, the facilitator might want to present the case and commentaries immediately before the discussion. In either circumstance, using an abbreviated format for the cases and commentaries might be appropriate. By reducing the case study scenarios and commentaries to a brief description, this structure allows participants to move through the material quickly and still have ample time for discussion.

While using an abbreviated case may be time efficient for the participants of a case discussion, the work of condensing the case likely will fall on the facilitator. Below, we provide one example of an abbreviated case, derived from "Stolen Trust." Our abbreviated case has two components. First, we summarize the case in three paragraphs, focusing on details that are absolutely essential to the dilemma. In this case, such details include those necessary to establish the setting of the school, the characters of Ms. Smith and Wesley, the relationship between Ms. Smith and Wesley, and the incident of interest: the stolen cell phone. Second, we briefly summarize the commentaries in order to create six potential "Options for Action." Each option emphasizes a possible course of action drawn from one of the six commentaries accompanying the case. However, some commentaries do not recommend a course of action; rather, they consider a particular value that pertains to the case. In such instances, we address the questions for action that such a value raises. We also number them for ease of reference during the discussion.

Sample Abbreviated Case: "Stolen Trust"

THE CASE

Ms. Smith is a young, White teacher at North High School (NHS), one of two high schools in a low-income suburb of St. Louis. In 2003, NHS adopted a "zero tolerance" code of conduct for student discipline as a way to create and maintain a safe learning environment at the school. The policy mandates specific consequences for defined violations and requires teachers to report theft, violence, "horseplay," and the presence of prohibited substances to the main office. Teachers themselves are subject to zero-tolerance consequences for diverging from the discipline code, including poor reports in their personnel file, suspension without pay, or even termination of employment.

Ms. Smith is in her third year at NHS. She is well liked and respected by NHS students. Though she rarely finds herself in power struggles with students, Wesley, a junior in her history class, has been testing her. Wesley had been suspended so much in ninth and tenth grade that the principal was on the verge of expelling him, and his troubles had involved the police at times. Ms. Smith similarly struggled to find common ground with him, and the first quarter ended with Wesley receiving an F. The next quarter, Ms. Smith had Wesley stay after school for tutoring. Things improved by leaps and bounds. By the end of the semester, there was a degree of trust between them, and Wesley had earned a B.

On the last day before winter break, however, Ms. Smith leaves Wesley alone in her classroom with her purse while she talks with another teacher in the hallway; as she leaves school, she discovers that her cell phone is missing. She realizes that Wesley has stolen her phone. Feeling trapped, Ms. Smith tells her story to Ms. Hampton, a veteran teacher in the next room. Ms. Hampton is sympathetic, but she tells Ms. Smith, "Look, I know you're more sympathetic than most, but you can't be naive. We all love these kids, but we also need our jobs, and the administration doesn't give us a choice on these cases. We have to report everything. That means major consequences—an automatic suspension and a police report." Ms. Smith has a difficult decision to make: should she report Wesley to the principal?

OPTIONS FOR ACTION

(1) Ms. Smith should consider how much self-sacrifice it is reasonable for her to make to protect Wesley's interests. As a citizen in an unjust society, Ms. Smith has a duty to promote a more just society. But this does not mean that she should do whatever she can without regard for her own well-being. While a reprimand or docked pay may be a small price to pay for potentially saving a child's life, sacrificing her job or her livelihood may be too great a cost to justify protecting Wesley. Indeed, it may make it impossible for Ms. Smith to continue to help other students like Wesley, as well. [Adapted from Tommie Shelby]

(2) Ms. Smith should call Wesley, let him know that she has misplaced her phone, and ask him if he has seen it. This response accomplishes a few things. First, it breaks out of the binary option of reporting or not reporting, and it gives Wesley a chance to make things right. Second, Ms. Smith lets Wesley know that he has betrayed her trust. Third, by giving him a chance to make things right, Ms. Smith also demonstrates the possibility of her continued faith in him. Granted, Ms. Smith may still be breaking

the rules, but there are certainly circumstances where smaller wrongs may prevent larger ones. [Adapted from Jeffrey Smith]

(3) As a teacher at NHS, Ms. Smith should not violate school policy because she thinks doing so would lead to a better result. While there are certainly aspects of NHS's zero-tolerance policy that are unjust, Ms. Smith has an obligation as a teacher at NHS to follow the policy. That said, as a person and a citizen, Ms. Smith also has a duty to oppose injustice. Thus, she may take some steps within the policy to advocate for Wesley. For example, she may advocate to the principal not to involve the police, or she may refuse to cooperate with the police or testify in court. But, in general, there are limits to what teachers can and may do to protect individual students from the unjust consequences of their rash conduct. [Adapted from Elizabeth Anderson]

(4) Ms. Smith should not report her cell phone missing if doing so places Wesley at undue risk. Teachers have agency to create or promote social justice in schools, even under highly constrained circumstances such as at NHS. One important aspect of such agency is how teachers see, understand, and imagine their students and their students' possibilities. Though Ms. Smith has a record of using her agency as a teacher to promote justice—for example, treating her students with respect, reaching out to Wesley, and the like—here she is quick to assume Wesley stole her cell phone. In other words, while Ms. Smith may see the best in Wesley as a learner, she still does not see the best in him as a citizen. If she did, she would likely treat him differently from the outset—asking him if he saw the phone, reporting the phone as missing rather than stolen, or, given the realities of zero tolerance, not reporting anything at all. [Adapted from David Knight]

(5) Ms. Smith should focus on making sure Wesley learns that actions have consequences. Part of Ms. Smith's conflict over reporting Wesley may stem from the different dimensions of her relationship with Wesley—teacher to student, citizen to citizen, and person to person. Each dimension may seem to suggest a different course of action. However, emphasizing any one role over the others also fails to provide a clear answer as to whether she should report Wesley or not. For example, as a teacher, she has an obligation to nurture and develop young children into caring adults, as well as an obligation to teach them that their actions have consequences. Given the lack of certainty about the circumstances, Ms. Smith should report Wesley while still showing him that she continues to support and care for him. [Adapted from Howard Gardner]

(6) Ms. Smith should explain her relationship with Wesley to Ms. Hampton and ask for her discretion in the matter of the missing cell phone.

Given the culture of surveillance and suspicion that emerges from zero-tolerance policies, however, this is potentially an overly idealistic ending. It is clear from the case that NHS's zero-tolerance policy makes it difficult for adults to trust each other, as they are required to report violations and may be sanctioned if they do not. Indeed, these factors may contribute to Ms. Smith's quick assumption that Wesley stole her phone in the first place. [Adapted from Mary Pattillo]

FACILITATING DISCUSSION ABOUT ABBREVIATED CASES

Because abbreviated cases and commentaries lack the detail and depth of full-length examples, the ensuing discussion may also take a slightly different form. In exhibit 7.2, we have outlined one possible way to facilitate a discussion based on abbreviated cases and commentaries.

EXHIBIT 7.2   Discussion format for abbreviated cases

- Pass out the case study, but not the "Options for Action." After allowing some time for reading, ask participants to explain what they see as the central dilemma of the case. What makes the decision difficult? Invite participants to suggest values and other considerations that might be at stake in this situation.

- Pass out the "Options for Action." Have the participants read them.

- Give participants some time to think about what choice they would make, encouraging them to come up with their own responses if they are not satisfied with the ones listed in the comments.

- Invite participants to share any new options. Write them up on a board and give each a letter or number so they can be easily identified. Recognize that participants may change their minds as a result of new options.

- Before opening up the discussion to the whole group, have participants turn and talk with a partner about the choice they would make and why.

- You might begin the whole-group discussion by polling participants about their top option(s) and then asking them to share their reasoning. Encourage participants to ask each other questions to better understand one another's thinking. The goal of such discussion is understanding rather than persuasion.

- You may refer to the questions in exhibit 7.1 (or provide a copy of the protocol to participants) in order to broaden and deepen the conversation.

CONSTRUCTING NORMATIVE CASE STUDIES

In some instances, however, neither altering nor abbreviating a case will do. Perhaps a school or team of teachers is wrestling with a particular dilemma not covered in this book. Similarly, perhaps key questions of a course syllabus could be effectively explored through normative case studies, but the examples we offer are not a perfect fit. Or, consider a philosopher or social scientist who wants to develop a normative case study as part of her own research. In each case, it would be necessary to write new normative case studies to attend to these particular needs (and others like them).

Our invitation to join us in thinking about dilemmas of educational ethics extends to the construction of new normative case studies. Though we certainly thought long and hard about which cases to include in this book, there are many more dilemmas to ponder, and just as many more cases to be written. Indeed, we hope that the examples we provide prompt other scholars, practitioners, and students to look and listen carefully to the educational spaces they live in, work in, or study. And we hope that they then take up their pens, settle in at their keyboards, find collaborators, and write new normative case studies and commentaries.

We encourage aspiring case writers to pay attention to several aspects of the cases and commentaries in this book as they construct their own. First, these cases emerge from common dilemmas. When we started to generate cases, we drew from our experiences in the classroom and also listened to educators and policy makers talk about the problems they wrestled with on a daily basis. While visiting one middle school, for example, we had only to explain what a normative case study was and our interest in dilemmas before the school principal offered up a laundry list of potential topics, from allocating special services to students without identified special needs, to whether to continue their tradition of honor roll breakfasts in light of concerns about meritocracy and developmental appropriateness. What he wanted help understanding were everyday events, not unique, unfamiliar problems.

Second, finding the right balance of generality and detail matters. When we first wrote and discussed "Stolen Trust," for example, we assumed the exchange between Ms. Smith and Ms. Hampton was a minor event in the case. However, when Mary Pattillo honed in on this detail in her commentary, she revealed another dimension to the case we had not even considered: the implications of the zero-tolerance context for the relationships among the adults in the school. What had once been a case we viewed through the lens of an individual decision maker was now refracted through the web of relationships that make up a school community.

Third, and closely related to the previous point, the normative case studies in this book were researched, and often written and refined, in collaboration with others. Sharing cases with others reveals insights that a single educator, theorist, or scientist might not see. Mary Pattillo's commentary demonstrates precisely this point. Yet, just as collaboration may emerge from people speaking *about* the case—through commentaries, for example—collaboration may also emerge from people *within* the case. Interviews, ethnographic research, and other forms of data collection can frame the dilemma in accessible language, as well as shape the design and focus of the case study.

Fourth, it is sometimes useful to fictionalize parts of a case study. Normative case studies should always start from problems of practice, and should always aim to be realistic rather than fanciful. However, in order to enhance the narrative flow of the case study or strengthen the tension among the choices facing the protagonist(s), authors may find it helpful to add constraints, to create new or composite characters, or to introduce divergent perspectives more strongly than in the real case. "Rocky Choices," "Stolen Trust," and "Inflated Expectations" all began as fully empirical cases, but as we tested them with colleagues, we tweaked (or even overhauled) the narratives to emphasize and clarify the central dilemmas. Moreover, "Promotion or Retention?" is made from whole cloth, though it draws on Levinson's eight years of experience as a middle school teacher struggling through such decisions with her colleagues every spring.

Finally, a major reason why the case studies in this book are challenging is because none has a self-evident right course of action. Some individuals may argue for one course of action above others in their commentaries, but taken together the commentaries often disagree more than they agree. The normative uncertainty such disagreement reveals is at the heart of this project. Thus, the design of normative case studies should prioritize those problems where the answer is not yet known.

It is in response to such uncertainty we urge our readers to turn their collective insight and wisdom. As you read this final chapter, understand that it is a beginning, not an end. Even if you exhaust these case studies of all possible avenues of inquiry, or talk them through so many times that they become old friends, we hope you realize that more generative work lies ahead.

Notes

INTRODUCTION

1. Doris Santoro discusses such challenges in her commentary in this volume, "Protect Teacher Integrity"; see also Meira Levinson, "Moral Injury and the Ethics of Educational Injustice," *Harvard Educational Review* 85, no. 2 (2015): 203–228.

2. Arne Duncan, "Statement by U.S. Secretary of Education Arne Duncan on the 50th Anniversary of the Civil Rights Act of 1964" (speech, July 2, 2014), http://www .ed.gov/news/press-releases/statement-us-secretary-education-arne-duncan-50th -anniversary-civil-rights-act-1964; see, for example, the Masters of Arts in Teaching: Urban Education and Social Justice degree offered at the University of San Francisco School of Education, https://www.usfca.edu/education/programs/masters-credential -programs/teaching-urban-education-social-justice; see, for example, "About KIPP," KIPP Schools, http://www.kipp.org/about-KIPP; U.S. Department of Education, "Executive Summary: No Child Left Behind Act," (January 2001), http://www2 .ed.gov/nclb/overview/intro/execsumm.html.

3. Our use of the term "normative case study" is inspired by David Thatcher, "The Normative Case Study," *American Journal of Sociology* 111, no. 6 (2006): 1631– 1676. We define the term differently, however, from how Thatcher uses it in his article.

4. Aristotle, "Nicomachean Ethics," Book VI.

5. See Bent Flyvbjerg, *Making Social Science Matter: Why Social Inquiry Fails and How It Can Succeed Again* (New York: Cambridge University Press, 2001); Bent Flyvbjerg, Todd Landman, and Sanford Schram, eds., *Real Social Science: Applied Phronesis* (Cambridge: Cambridge University Press, 2012); Hans Georg Gadamer, *Truth and Method*, trans. Joel Weinsheimer and Donald G. Marshall, 2nd ed. (New York: Continuum, 2004).

6. In response to such disconnects between theory and practice, in fact, Eric Mazur and the Harvard physics department have revamped how students are taught, with much greater emphasis on frequent application of concepts to complex, novel problems.

CHAPTER 1

1. This case is a work of fiction.
2. Sarah Almy and Christina Theokas, "Not Prepared for Class: High Poverty Schools Continue to Have Fewer In-Field Teachers," *The Education Trust*, November 18, 2010, http://www.edtrust.org/dc/publication/not-prepared-for-class-high-poverty -schools-continue-to-have-fewer-in-field-teachers.
3. Maryann Mraz and Timothy Rasinski, "Summer Reading Loss," *International Reading Association* (2007): 784–789, http://www.readingrockets.org/article /summer-reading-loss.
4. Bradford Holmes, "Hone the Top 5 Soft Skills Every College Student Needs," *U.S. News & World Report*, May 12, 2014, http://www.usnews.com/education/blogs /college-admissions-playbook/2014/05/12/hone-the-top-5-soft-skills-every-college -student-needs.
5. "School Transit Subsidy Program," District Department of Transportation, http:// ddot.dc.gov/page/school-transit-subsidy-program.
6. "Key Concepts: Toxic Stress," Center on the Developing Child, Harvard University, http://developingchild.harvard.edu/index.php/key_concepts/toxic_stress_response/.
7. Michael Karpman, "Kids Living in Combat Zones . . . in U.S. Cities," National League of Cities, http://citiesspeak.org/2012/05/04/kids-living-in-combat-zones in-u-s-cities/.
8. Annie Murphy Paul, "School of Hard Knocks," review of *How Children Succeed*, by Paul Tough, *New York Times*, August 23, 2012, Sunday Book Review, http:// www.nytimes.com/2012/08/26/books/review/how-children-succeed-by-paul-tough .html.
9. "Defining the Medical Home," Patient-Centered Primary Care Collaborative, http:// www.pcpcc.org/about/medical-home.
10. Christina Samuels, "Response to Intervention Policy and Practice Inconsistent Across States," *Education Week*, April 4, 2013, http://blogs.edweek.org/edweek /speced/2013/04/response_to_intervention_polic.html?utm_source=feedburner& amp;utm_medium=email&utm_campaign=Feed%3A%2BOnSpecialEducation %2B(Education%2BWeek%2BBlog%3A%2BOn%2BSpecial%2BEducation.
11. "Building the Legacy: IDEA 2004," U.S. Department of Education, http://idea .ed.gov.
12. For an account of different theories of justice, see Adam Swift, *Political Philosophy: A Beginner's Guide for Students and Politicians*, 3rd ed. (Malden, MA: Polity Press, 2014).
13. Mark Moore, *Creating Public Value: Strategic Management in Government* (Cambridge, MA: Harvard University Press, 1995); Michael Lipsky, *Street-Level Bureaucracy: Dilemmas of the Individual in Public Service* (New York: Russell Sage, 1980).
14. See the recent report by Leila Morsy and Richard Rothstein, "Five Social Disad- vantages That Depress Student Performance," *Economic Policy Institute*, June 10, 2015, http://s2.epi.org/files/2015/Morsey-Rothstein-07-06-2015.pdf.
15. "Convention on the Rights of the Child," United Nations, Treaty Series, vol. 1577, November 20, 1989, 45, https://treaties.un.org/doc/Publication/UNTS/Volume%20 1577/v1577.pdf.

16. Ibid., 46.
17. David A. Garvin, "Making the Case: Professional Education for the World of Practice," *Harvard Magazine* 106, no. 1 (2003), http://harvardmagazine.com/2003/09/making-the-case-html.
18. Ibid., 59.
19. Ibid., 60.

CHAPTER 2

1. This case is a work of fiction, inspired by a real case researched by Sigal Ben-Porath.
2. Barry Schwartz and Kenneth Sharpe, *Practical Wisdom: The Right Way to Do the Right Thing* (New York: Riverhead Books, 2010); Aristotle, *Nichomachean Ethics*, trans. Terence Irwin, 2nd ed. (Indianapolis: Hackett Publishing Company, 1999); Joseph Dunne, *Back to the Rough Ground: "Phronesis" and "Techne" in Modern Philosophy and in Aristotle* (Notre Dame, IN: The University of Notre Dame Press, 1993).
3. Ting Zhang, Francesco Gino, and Joshua Margolis, "Does 'Could' Lead to Good? A Theory of Moral Insight" (working paper, Harvard Business School, Harvard University, Cambridge, MA, June 2, 2014), http://www.hbs.edu/faculty/Publication%20Files/14-118_8214f29c-c4dc-4e35-ae77-95034e9b94db.pdf.
4. Of course, it would be inappropriate to simply *use* children with disabilities to secure these educational benefits for nondisabled students. To do so would be to treat students with disabilities disrespectfully, and in order to be justifiable, inclusion must be consistent with treating each student with respect.
5. Some argue that students are entitled to *adequate* or *sufficient* educational opportunities, and others argue that they are entitled to *equal* educational opportunities. Under conditions of resource constraints, and in an inclusive classroom filled with diverse students, it is more practical to aim for adequacy. I do not mean to suggest, however, that we should not aim for more equal opportunity for all under better circumstances. For philosophical expressions of the entitlement to adequacy, see: Amy Gutmann, *Democratic Education* (Princeton, NJ: Princeton University Press, 1987); Elizabeth Anderson, "Fair Opportunity in Education: A Democratic Equality Perspective," *Ethics* 117, no. 4 (2007): 595–622; Debra Satz, "Equality, Adequacy, and Education for Citizenship," *Ethics* 117, no. 4 (2007): 623–648. For a philosophical argument for equality of educational opportunity, see Harry Brighouse and Adam Swift, "Putting Educational Equality in Its Place," *Education Finance and Policy* 3, no.4 (2008): 444–466.
6. John Rawls gives an argument that social justice involves prioritizing the well-being of the least advantaged citizens, once certain other conditions are met (including that all citizens have secure freedoms of various sorts as well as fair equality of opportunity). See John Rawls, *Justice as Fairness: A Restatement* (Cambridge, MA: Harvard University Press, 2001).
7. Placating the principal and parents is not itself a moral priority, though it is a precondition of Ms. Brown meeting her obligations to her students. If she is fired because she cannot garner enough support from parents and school administrators, then Ms. Brown is also in a position in which she cannot serve her students appropriately. Satisfying parents and administrators is thus of central importance, and

sets a boundary against what Ms. Brown can do in circumstances like this one. Of course, a longer-term strategy might involve more and better communication with frustrated parents about the value of inclusion and Ms. Brown's methods.

8. My limited claim here is that, in inclusive classrooms, teachers should be guided by principles like these. I have provided only an account of the general value of inclusion, and have not argued that all classrooms should be inclusive or that all student should be mainstreamed. There may well be cases in which separate learning environments achieve the best outcomes for students with disabilities, or better meet the basic educational interests of all students involved.

9. For more information, see the National Center on Universal Design for Learning's website, http://www.udlcenter.org/.

10. In fact, one of the items on the BTR performance-assessment rubric for novice teachers is "Resident anticipates ideas, challenges, and misconceptions that students might have as they work on the task/activity. Resident plans multiple teaching moves that demonstrate knowledge of his/her students."

CHAPTER 3

1. This case is a work of fiction, inspired by a true case researched by Kailey Burger.

2. See, for example, Tommie Shelby, "Liberalism, Self-Respect, and Troubling Cultural Patterns in Ghettos," in *The Cultural Matrix: Understanding Black Youth*, ed. Orlando Patterson and Ethan Fosse (Cambridge, MA: Harvard University Press, 2015), 498–532; Tommie Shelby, "Justice, Work, and the Ghetto Poor," *Law & Ethics of Human Rights* 6 (2012): 70–96; and Tommie Shelby, "Justice, Deviance, and the Dark Ghetto," *Philosophy & Public Affairs* 35 (Spring 2007): 126–160.

3. See, for example, David Cole, *No Equal Justice: Race and Class in the American Criminal Justice System* (New York: The New Press, 2000); Bruce Western, *Punishment and Inequality in America* (New York: Russell Sage Foundation, 2006); Deval Pager, *Marked: Race, Crime, and Finding Work in an Era of Mass Incarceration* (Chicago: University of Chicago Press, 2008); Loïc Wacquant, *Punishing the Poor: The Neoliberal Government of Social Insecurity* (Durham, NC: Duke University Press, 2009); Paul Butler, *Let's Get Free: A Hip-Hop Theory of Justice* (New York: The New Press, 2010); and Michelle Alexander, *The New Jim Crow: Mass Incarceration in the Age of Colorblindness* (New York: The New Press, 2010).

4. See Alexander, *The New Jim Crow*; Glenn C. Loury, *Race, Incarceration, and American Values* (Cambridge, MA: MIT Press, 2008); Bruce Western, *Punishment and Inequality in America*.

5. For further study of how social scientists have theorized agency as a concept, see Sherry B. Ortner, *Anthropology and Social Theory: Culture, Power, and the Acting Subject* (Durham, NC: Duke University Press, 2006).

6. See Ray C. Rist, "Student Social Class and Teacher Expectations: The Self-Fulfilling Prophecy in Ghetto Education," *Harvard Educational Review* 70, no. 3 (Fall 1970): 257–301; and Marvin Lynn et al., "Examining Teachers' Beliefs About African American Male Students in a Low-Performing High School in an African American School District," *Teachers College Record* 112, no. 1 (January 2010): 289–330.

7. Albert O. Hirschman, *Exit, Voice, and Loyalty* (Cambridge, MA: Harvard University Press, 1970).

8. Howard Gardner, Mihaly Csikszentmihalyi, and William Damon, *Good Work: When Excellence and Ethics Meet* (New York: Basic Books, 2002); Howard Gardner, ed., *GoodWork: Theory and Practice* (Cambridge, MA: GoodWork Project, 2010), http://www.thegoodproject.org/pdf/GoodWork-Theory_and_Practice-with_covers.pdf; Daniel Mucinskas and Howard Gardner, "Educating for Good Work: From Research to Practice," *British Journal of Educational Studies* 61, no. 4 (December 2013): 453–470; see also www.thegoodproject.org.
9. Oscar Wilde, *An Ideal Husband* (London: Methuen & Co, 1912).
10. Anthony S. Bryk and Barbara Schneider, *Trust in Schools: A Core Resource for Improvement* (New York: Russell Sage Foundation, 2002); Patrick B. Forsyth, Curt M. Adams, and William K. Hoy, *Collective Trust: Why Schools Can't Improve Without It* (New York: Teachers College Press, 2011).
11. Anthony S. Bryk et al., *Organizing Schools for Improvement: Lessons from Chicago* (Chicago: University of Chicago Press, 2010); Roger D. Goddard, Wayne K. Hoy, and Anita Woolfolk Hoy, "Collective Teacher Efficacy: Its Meaning, Measure, and Impact on Student Achievement," *American Educational Research Journal* 37, no. 2 (2000): 479–507.
12. Kevin Gaines, *Uplifting the Race: Black Leadership, Politics, and Culture in the Twentieth Century* (Chapel Hill, NC: University of North Carolina Press, 1996).
13. Evelyn Brooks Higginbotham, *Righteous Discontent: The Women's Movement in the Black Baptist Church, 1880–1920* (Cambridge, MA: Harvard University Press, 1993), 15.
14. Higginbotham, *Righteous Discontent*, 14.
15. Mary Pattillo, *Black on the Block: The Politics of Race and Class in the City* (Chicago: University of Chicago Press, 2007).
16. Phillip Atiba Goff et al., "The Essence of Innocence: Consequences of Dehumanizing Black Children," *Journal of Personality and Social Psychology* 106 (2014): 526–545.
17. Devah Pager, *Marked: Race, Crime, and Finding Work in an Era of Mass Incarceration* (Chicago: University of Chicago Press, 2007).

CHAPTER 4

1. This case is a work of fiction, inspired by research conducted by Ilana Finefter-Rosenbluh about ethical dilemmas at a Jewish day school in the northeastern United States. Some of the teachers' comments are drawn verbatim from those interviews. As noted below, all quotations about Princeton are also drawn verbatim from its internal Ad Hoc Committee report. But all of the characters in the case, and many of the quotations from the teachers and parents, are fictionalized.
2. All quotations and claims in this and the next paragraph are taken from *Report from the Ad Hoc Committee to Review Policies Regarding Assessment and Grading*, Ad Hoc Committee (Princeton University, Princeton, NJ, August 5, 2014), https://www.princeton.edu/main/news/archive/S40/73/33192/PU_Grading_Policy_Report_2014_Aug.pdf. Quotations are from p. 2 ("provide common grading standards . . ."), p. 12 ("shark tanks"), p. 13 ("pressure cooker"), and p. 6 ("Grade compression").

3. National Association of Independent Schools, "Board of Trustees: Principles of Good Practice," *National Association of Independent Schools*, 2003, http://www.nais.org/Series/Pages/Board-of-Trustees.aspx.

4. Daniel Cutler, "The Private-School Stigma," *The Atlantic*, January 21, 2015, http://www.theatlantic.com/education/archive/2015/01/bridging-private-and-public-schools/384673/.

5. Peter Gow, *The Intentional Teacher: Forging a Great Career in the Independent School Classroom* (Gilsum, NH: Avocus, 2009), 72.

6. Theodore R. Sizer and Nancy Faust Sizer, *The Students Are Watching: Schools and the Moral Contract* (Boston: Beacon Press, 1999), 18.

7. Grant P. Wiggins and Jay McTighe, *Schooling by Design: Mission, Action, and Achievement* (Alexandria, VA: Association for Supervision and Curriculum Development, 2007).

8. Ibid., 48.

9. Ibid., 47.

10. Gow, *The Intentional Teacher*, 60.

11. Thomas R. Guskey and Lee Ann Jung, "Four Steps in Grading Reform," *Principal Leadership* 13 no. 4 (2012): 23–28, http://www.nassp.org/Content/158/pl_dec12_guskey.pdf.

12. Mancur Olson, *The Logic of Collective Action* (Cambridge, MA: Harvard University Press, 1965), 9–10.

13. Ibid., 3.

14. Gunnar Trumbull, *Strength in Numbers: The Political Power of Weak Interests* (Cambridge, MA: Harvard University Press, 2012).

15. David Harvey, *A Brief History of Neoliberalism* (Oxford: Oxford University Press, 2005), 3.

16. Nikolas Rose, "Governing the Enterprising Self," in *The Values of the Enterprise Culture: The Moral Debate*, ed. Paul Heelas and Paul Morris (New York: Routledge, 1992), 149.

17. Annette Lareau, *Unequal Childhoods: Class, Race, and Family Life* (Berkeley: University of California Press, 2003); Thomas Friedman, *The World Is Flat: A Brief History of the Twenty-First Century* (New York: Farrar, Straus and Giroux, 2005).

18. Katherine Newman, *Falling from Grace: Downward Mobility in the Age of Affluence* (Berkeley: University of California Press, 1988); Barbara Ehrenreich, *Fear of Falling: The Inner Life of the Middle Class* (New York: Pantheon, 1989).

19. Ken Zeichner, "Competition, Economic Rationalization, Increased Surveillance, and Attacks on Diversity: Neo-liberalism and the Transformation of Teacher Education in the U.S.," *Teaching and Teacher Education* 26, no. 8 (2010): 1544–1552.

20. Peter Demerath, "Practicing Responsibilisation: The Unwritten Curriculum for Achievement in an American Suburb," in *The Social Life of Achievement*, ed. Nick Long and Henrietta Moore, 182–205 (London: Berghahn, 2014).

21. Peter Demerath, *Producing Success: The Culture of Personal Advancement in an American High School* (Chicago: University of Chicago Press, 2009).

22. Peter Demerath, Jill Lynch, and Mario Davidson, "Dimensions of Psychological Capital in a U.S. Suburb: Identities for Neoliberal Times," *Anthropology & Education Quarterly* 39 (2008): 270–292.

23. Aaron Cicourel and John Kitsuse, *The Educational Decision-Makers* (Indianapolis: Bobbs-Merrill, 1963).

24. Jay MacLeod, *Ain't No Makin' It: Aspirations and Attainment in a Low-Income Neighborhood* (Boulder, CO: Westview, 1987).

25. Douglas Foley, *Learning Capitalist Culture: Deep in the Heart of Tejas* (Philadelphia: University of Pennsylvania Press, 1990); Bradley Levinson, "Social Difference and Schooled Identity at a Mexican Secundaria," in *The Cultural Production of the Educated Person*, ed. Bradley Levinson, Douglas Foley, and Dorothy Holland, 211–238 (Albany: State University of New York Press, 1996); Signithia Fordham, *Blacked Out: Dilemmas of Race, Identity, and Success at Capital High* (Chicago: University of Chicago Press, 1996).

26. Lisa Delpit, *Other Peoples' Children: Cultural Conflict in the Classroom* (New York: The New Press, 2006), 104.

27. Carol Dweck, *Mindset: The New Psychology of Success* (New York: Ballantine, 2007).

28. Camille A. Farrington et al., *Teaching Adolescents to Become Learners: The Role of Noncognitive Factors in Shaping School Performance* (Chicago: The University of Chicago Consortium on Chicago School Research, 2012).

29. Adam Gamoran, "American Schooling and Educational Inequality: A Forecast for the 21st Century" *Sociology of Education Extra Issue* (2001): 143.

30. Jack Schneider and Ethan Hutt, "Making the Grade: A History of the A–F Marking Scheme," *Journal of Curriculum Studies* 46, no. 2 (2014): 201–224.

31. Alfie Kohn, "The Case Against Grades," *Educational Leadership* 69, no. 3 (2011): 28–33.

32. Caroline Pulfrey, Fabrizio Butera, and Céline Buchs, "Why Grades Engender Performance-Avoidance Goals: The Mediating Role of Autonomous Motivation," *Journal of Educational Psychology* 103, no. 3 (2011): 683–700; Ruth Butler, "Enhancing and Undermining Intrinsic Motivation: The Effects of Task-Involving and Ego-Involving Evaluation on Interest and Performance," *British Journal of Educational Psychology* 58 (1988): 1–14.

33. Dan Ariely et al., "Large Stakes and Big Mistakes," *The Review of Economic Studies* 76, no. 2 (2009): 451–469.

34. Alfie Kohn, *Punished by Rewards* (Boston: Houghton Mifflin Company, 1993), 35.

35. Richard M. Ryan and Edward L. Deci, "Intrinsic and Extrinsic Motivations: Classic Definitions and New Directions," *Contemporary Educational Psychology* 25 (2000): 54–67.

36. Dorothy De Zouche, "The Wound Is Mortal: Marks, Honors, Unsound Activities," *The Clearing House* 19, no. 6 (1945): 341.

37. "FAQs," The International Montessori Index, http://www.montessori.edu/FAQ.html.

38. "Frequently Asked Questions," Youth Initiative High School, http://www.yihs.net/frequently-asked-questions1.html.

39. David B. Marshall et al., "Understanding Student Learning Outcomes Through Narrative Transcript Analysis: Assessing General Education in an Institution Without Grades or Required Courses," *Assessment Update* 17, no. 5 (2005): 4–5.

40. Jonathan Nash, "Hampshire College President: Grades Are Not Enough," *Education Week* 34, no. 7 (2014): 24.

41. Richard Shaull, foreword to *Pedagogy of the Oppressed, 30th Anniversary Edition*, by Paulo Freire (New York: The Continuum International Publishing Group, 2005), 34.

42. Susan M. Brookhart, "Starting the Conversation About Grading," *Educational Leadership* 69, no. 3 (November 2011): 10; Kohn, "The Case Against Grades," 28; Robert J. Marzano and Tammy Heflebower, "Grades That Show What Students Know," *Educational Leadership* 69, no. 3 (November 2011): 34; Matt Townsley, "Redesigning Grading Districtwide," *Educational Leadership* 71, no. 4 (December 2013): 68.

43. Doris A. Santoro, "'I Was Becoming Increasingly Uneasy About the Profession and What Was Being Asked of Me': Preserving Integrity in Teaching," *Curriculum Inquiry* 43, no. 5 (2013): 563–587. The author acknowledges *Curriculum Inquiry*, the Ontario Institute for Studies in Education and Blackwell Publishing for the use of figure 4.1.

44. Ibid., 564.

45. Thomas F. Green, *Voices: The Educational Formation of Conscience* (Notre Dame, IN: University of Notre Dame Press, 1999), 76.

46. Doris A. Santoro, "Good Teaching in Difficult Times: Demoralization in the Pursuit of Good Work," *American Journal of Education* 118, no. 1 (2011): 1–23.

47. Howard Gardner, Mihaly Csikszentmihalyi, and William Damon, *Good Work: When Excellence and Ethics Meet* (New York: Basic Books, 2001), 163–164.

48. Santoro, "Good Teaching in Difficult Times."

49. Doris A. Santoro and Lisa Morehouse, "Teaching's Conscientious Objectors: Principled Leavers of High-Poverty Schools," *Teachers College Record* 113, no. 12 (2011): 2671–2705.

CHAPTER 5

1. This is a true case.

2. The plan works somewhat differently for English language learners (ELLs) and children with identified special needs. I do not address those school assignment policies in this case study.

3. Tiers were initially determined by ranking schools according to their Massachusetts Comprehensive Assessment System (MCAS) average, calculated as a combination of absolute performance (counting for two-thirds) and growth scores (counting for one-third). Tier I schools, therefore, were those with a weighted MCAS average in the top 25% of the city. Everyone agrees that standardized test scores are a very poor proxy for quality, and also that dividing schools into rank-ordered quartiles impedes the district from demonstrating overall increases or decreases in quality. In September 2014, therefore, the Boston School Committee adopted a new School Quality Framework that includes a wider array of measures, although it still gave 75% weight to "student performance" as measured by MCAS scores. The new framework also reversed the amount of weight given to growth versus performance in calculating each school's MCAS ranking. See School Quality Working Group, *Recommendations of School Quality Working Group* (Boston: Boston Public Schools report, September 3, 2014), http://www.bostonpublicschools.org/cms/lib07/MA01906464/Centricity/Domain/162/SchoolQualityFrameworkFull.pdf.

4. This is assuming that all families prefer higher-tier to lower-tier schools. Evidence from the first year of implementation shows that this formal assumption may be mistaken. Available data by race (which closely tracks income in Boston) show that barely half of Black and Latino families selected a Tier I or II school as a top choice for their kindergartner, as compared to about 85% of White and Asian families. It is impossible to know at this stage whether these disparities were due to differences in parents' knowledge about schools, their assessments of relative school quality, geographic proximity to higher-tier schools, preexisting patterns of sibling attendance, or other factors. As a result, Black and Latino families were assigned one of their top three choices at higher rates than White families were—but they ended up on average at much worse schools. See "Update on Home Based Assignment System, Boston Public Schools, October 15, 2014.

5. This research is well summarized in Richard D. Kahlenberg, "Turnaround Schools and Charter Schools That Work," in *The Future of School Integration*, ed. Richard D. Kahlenberg (New York: The Century Foundation Press, 2012), 283–308. See also Ann Mantil, Anne G. Perkins, and Stephanie Aberger, "The Challenge of High Poverty Schools: How Feasible Is Socioeconomic School Integration?" in the same volume.

6. Douglas N. Harris, "High Flying Schools, Student Disadvantage and the Logic of NCLB," *American Journal of Education* 113, no. 3 (2007): 367–394. The article gives the number of schools in each demographic category and the percentage of each category that are high achieving. I used this data to calculate the number of high-achieving schools within each demographic. It is also worth noting that "low-income schools" are defined as having a student body that is over 50% low-income. If truly hypersegregated schools were studied—that is, schools with 80% or more low-income students and/or students of color—the results would look even worse.

7. Calculated using 2013–2014 school profile data from the Massachusetts Department of Education.

8. Gary Orfield, Genevieve Siegel-Hawley, and John Kucsera, *Sorting Out Deepening Confusion on Segregation Trends* (Los Angeles: UCLA, Civil Rights Project/Proyecto Derechos Civiles, 2014); Kahlenberg, ed., *The Future of School Integration*; Gary Orfield and Erica Frankenberg, *Educational Delusions? Why Choice Can Deepen Inequality and How to Make Schools Fair* (Los Angeles: University of California Press, 2013).

9. Tim Reardon, *Comparative Analysis of Boston Public School Proposed Assignment Plans* (Boston: Metropolitan Area Planning Council, 2012), http://www.mapc.org /sites/default/files/MAPC_BPS_AssignmentMemo_10_12_12.pdf.

10. This was calculated using the Census Bureau's Census Flows Mapper. Migration flows into Boston from surrounding counties among very low income households, but switches direction out among higher-income households, and rises inexorably by income.

11. I am assuming that high-quality schools are the schools that better promote pupils' opportunities for x.

12. It is worth noting that a prioritarian stance of this kind may be recommended by more than just the principle of equality of opportunity for x. For instance, if the better-off children's position of advantage is the result of past and/or present

injustices against the least advantaged, then considerations stemming from "reparatory justice" would also suggest a balance in favor of the least advantaged. It is also important to note that other reasons could be put forward to promote equality of opportunity to access a high-quality school—e.g., reasons that may be rooted in the value of procedural justice or equity. However, I doubt that considerations of the latter kind are sufficient to trump considerations for equality of opportunity for x.

13. See Jennifer Morton's commentary on this case for a more detailed view regarding how we should understand the parental attitudes in this instance.

14. Of course, if parents have a fundamental right to try to ensure that their own children receive a high-quality education, then this argument does not hold. However, I doubt (as does Levinson) that this view is correct.

15. Matthew DiCarlo of the Shanker Institute does an excellent job explaining why proficiency rates are poor measures of school quality in this collection of posts: "Resources on Testing and School Accountability," Albert Shanker Institute, http://www.shankerinstitute.org/resource/resources-testing-and-school-accountability.

16. "Colorado Growth Model FAQs (General)," Colorado Department of Education, http://www.schoolview.org/GMFAQ.asp#Q29.

17. School Quality Working Group, *Recommendations*.

18. Meg Cotter Mazzola, "Study Finds Bay State Charter Schools Remain Positive and Boston Charter Schools Standout" (The Center for Research on Education Outcomes (CREDO), Stanford University, Stanford, California, February 28, 2013), http://credo.stanford.edu/documents/Mass2013PressReleaseFINAL2_000.pdf.

19. Michael J. Petrilli, "3 Thoughts About the Future of School Integration," *Flypaper*, March 12, 2012, http://edexcellence.net/commentary/education-gadfly-daily/flypaper/2012/3-thoughts-about-the-future-of-school-integration.html.

20. Heather Schwartz, *Housing Policy Is School Policy: Economically Integrative Housing Promotes Academic Success in Montgomery County, Maryland* (New York: The Century Foundation, 2010), https://tcf.org/assets/downloads/tcf-Schwartz.pdf.

21. "Urban Charter School Study Report on 41 Regions" (The Center for Research on Education Outcomes (CREDO), Stanford University, Stanford, California, 2015), http://urbancharters.stanford.edu/download/Urban%20Charter%20School%20Study%20Report%20on%2041%20Regions.pdf.

22. Debra Vaughan, *K–12 Public Education Through the Public Eye: Parents' Perceptions of School Choice* (New Orleans: Cowen Institute for Public Education, 2012), http://www.coweninstitute.com/our-work/applied-research/2011poll.

23. Laura Moser, "How Not to Get Your Kid into Kindergarten: Playing the DC Public Schools Lottery Is a Crazy, Soul-Crushing Pursuit," *The Washingtonian*, March 24, 2014, http://www.washingtonian.com/articles/work-education/education/how-not-to-get-your-kid-into-kindergarten.

24. "Urban Charter School Study Report on 41 Regions."

25. Editorial Board, "An Improving Record for D.C. Public Schools," *The Washington Post*, October 21, 2013, http://www.washingtonpost.com/opinions/an-improving-record-for-dc-public-schools/2013/10/21/21d2265c-3a92-11e3-b7ba-503fb5822c3e_story.html.

26. "Guest Blog: Worst Case Scenario Turns into the Happy Ending," *Braving the BPS Lottery Blog: A Mother's Journey Through the Public School Selection Process in*

Boston (blog), October 18, 2010, http://bravingthelottery.blogspot.com/2010/10/guest-blog-worst-case-scenario-turns.html.

27. See Harry Brighouse and Adam Swift, "Legitimate Parental Partiality," *Philosophy & Public Affairs* 37, no. 1 (2009): 43–80.

28. "Guest Blog: Now Nearing the BPS Lottery Starting Line . . .," *Braving the BPS Lottery Blog: A Mother's Journey Through the Public School Selection Process in Boston* (blog), November 30, 2010, http://bravingthelottery.blogspot.com/2010/11/guest-blog-now-nearing-bps-lottery.html.

29. Meira Levinson, from "Justice in Schools Workshop Description," personal communication, May 4, 2013.

30. Jal Mehta, *The Allure of Order* (New York: Oxford University Press, 2013).

31. The data in the Harris research involved the years 1997 to 2001, and Harris recommended a nuanced interaction of school and social interventions ("High Flying Schools," 2007). The Kahlenberg summary makes the case far more forcefully, but ignores every study or argument that points in a different direction (Kahlenberg, "Turnaround Schools," 2012).

32. In the fourth-grade mathematics NAEP, for example, all nine districts that participated between 2003 and 2013 made gains, eight of them with significance. While the nation improved by 7 scale score points, eight of the ten participating districts improved by 9 to 24 points. The overall story (most participating districts improved with significance, most of them outpacing national results by large amounts, some more than doubling the rate of improvement) remained consistent across disciplines and levels (see "The Nation's Report Card: A First Look: 2013 Mathematics and Reading Trial Urban District Assessment: NAEP at Grades 4 and 8," NCES, 2014-466).

33. The types of district changes and interventions in the TUDA districts are hard to categorize, simply because the nature of school improvement in many districts contains so many interdependent elements that are difficult to isolate in their impact, and that often happened in the context of multiple administrations bringing different approaches. Those approaches ranged from a focus on instructional coherence in Atlanta to a focus on teacher evaluation in Washington, DC. We should be looking carefully at the nature of those local changes in order to learn from them. Some of the district contexts, like Washington, DC, and New York City, included strong elements of choice, but that came about through the expansion of charters and middle and high school selection processes, not through a strategy to increase integration.

34. The persistence of academic tracking in American schools, and its correlation with class and race, makes that abundantly clear.

35. Hartford, Connecticut, currently has the most robust interdistrict integration program—notable especially because many students voluntarily come into the city from the suburbs, and children from the city select schools outside district lines. See Jacqueline Rabe Thomas, "Nearly Half the Students from Hartford Now Attend Integrated Schools," *The Connecticut Mirror*, November 26, 2013, http://ctmirror.org/2013/11/26/nearly-half-students-hartford-now-attend-integrated-schools/; and Gerald Grant, *Hope and Despair in the American City: Why There Are No Bad Schools in Raleigh* (Cambridge, MA: Harvard University Press, 2009).

36. Stacey Childress, Denis Doyle, and David Thomas, *Leading for Equity: The Pursuit of Excellence in the Montgomery County Public Schools* (Cambridge: Harvard Education Press, 2009).

37. John Rawls, *A Theory of Justice* (Cambridge: Harvard University Press, 1971), 5–6.

38. Katie Johnston, "Demand Soars for Affordable Housing in Boston Area," *Boston Globe*, November 28, 2014, https://www.bostonglobe.com/business/2014/11/28/demand-for-affordable-housing-soars/hCb4RSkLTbpqdMJR1eCYTI/story.html.

39. James Vaznis, "Turnaround at Brockton High," *Boston Globe*, October 12, 2009, http://www.boston.com/news/education/k_12/mcas/articles/2009/10/12/turnaround_at_brockton_high/.

40. Cathie Jo Martin and Duane Swank, *The Political Construction of Business Interests: Coordination, Growth, and Equality* (New York: Cambridge University Press, 2012).

CHAPTER 6

1. Information and quotations in this case study come from the Academy of the Pacific Rim's website, http://www.pacrim.org/, unless otherwise cited.

2. These results have been consistent over the past four years. See *Academy of the Pacific Rim Charter School: 2011–12 Graduates Attending Institutions of Higher Education, All Colleges and Universities* (Malden, MA: Massachusetts Department of Elementary and Secondary Education, 2012), http://profiles.doe.mass.edu/nsc/gradsattendingcollege_dist.aspx?orgcode=04120530&fycode=2012&orgtypecode=6&.

3. *Boston: Plans of High School Graduates (2013–14)* (Malden, MA: Massachusetts Department of Elementary and Secondary Education, 2014), http://profiles.doe.mass.edu/profiles/student.aspx?orgcode=00350000&orgtypecode=5&leftNavId=307&.

4. *Massachusetts: 2013–14 SAT Performance Report (DISTRICT), All Students* (Malden, MA: Massachusetts Department of Elementary and Secondary Education, 2014), http://profiles.doe.mass.edu/state_report/sat_perf.aspx.

5. *Academy of the Pacific Rim Charter Public School: Selected Populations (2014–15)* (Malden, MA: Massachusetts Department of Elementary and Secondary Education, 2015), http://profiles.doe.mass.edu/profiles/student.aspx?orgcode=04120530&orgtypecode=6&leftNavId=305&.

6. *Academy of the Pacific Rim Charter Public School: Enrollment Data* (Malden, MA: Massachusetts Department of Elementary and Secondary Education, 2015), http://profiles.doe.mass.edu/profiles/student.aspx?orgcode=04120530&orgtypecode=6&leftNavId=300&.

7. Academy of the Pacific Rim, *Annual Report 2013–2014*, http://www.pacrim.org/ourpages/auto/2012/11/5/52910360/Academy%20of%20the%20Pacific%20Rim%20CPS%20Annual%20Report%202014.pdf.

8. Massachusetts H4108, § 35 (May 21, 2014), https://malegislature.gov/Document/Bill/188/House/H4108.pdf.

9. The following draws on the analysis developed in Harry Brighouse and Gina Schouten, "To Charter or Not to Charter: What Questions Should We Ask, and What Will the Answers Tell Us?" *Harvard Educational Review* 84, no. 3 (2014): 341–364.

10. See Gina Schouten, "Fair Educational Opportunity and the Distribution of Natural Ability: Toward a Prioritarian Principle of Educational Justice," *Journal of Philosophy of Education* 46, no. 3 (2014): 472–491.

11. "Multiple Choice: Charter School Performance in 16 States" (The Center for Research on Education Outcomes (CREDO), Stanford University, Stanford, California, June 3, 2009), http://credo.stanford.edu/reports/MULTIPLE_CHOICE_CREDO .pdf.; "National Charter School Study 2013" (CREDO, Stanford University, Stanford, California, 2013, http://credo.stanford.edu/documents/NCSS%202013%20 Final%20Draft.pdf.

12. Phillip Gleason et al., "The Evaluation of Charter School Impacts: Final Report," *Mathematica Policy Research*, 2010, http://www.mathematica-mpr.com/~/media /publications/PDFs/education/charter_school_impacts.pdf.; Christina Clark Tuttle, Phillip Gleason, and Melissa Clark, "Using Lotteries to Evaluate Schools of Choice: Evidence from a National Study of Charter Schools," *Economics of Education Review* 31, no. 2 (2012): 237–253.

13. It is important to bear in mind that the students whose learning is disrupted and whose daily lived experience is undermined by disciplinary infractions are *other disadvantaged students.*

14. Gary Orfield et al., *Brown at 60: Great Progress, a Long Retreat and an Uncertain Future* (Los Angeles: UCLA, Civil Rights Project/Proyecto Derechos Civiles, May 15, 2014), http://civilrightsproject.ucla.edu/research/k-12-education/integration-and -diversity/brown-at-60-great-progress-a-long-retreat-and-an-uncertain-future/Brown -at-60-051814.pdf.

15. Derek Neal, "The Effects of Catholic Secondary Schooling on Educational Attainment," *Journal of Labor Economics* 15 (1997): 98–123.

16. See Peter Meyer, "Can Catholic Schools Be Saved?" *Education Next* 7, no. 2 (2007), http://educationnext.org/can-catholic-schools-be-saved/.

17. Erica Frankenberg, Genevieve Seigel-Hawley, and Jia Wang, "Choice Without Equity: Charter School Segregation," *Education Policy Archives Analysis* 19, no. 1 (2011): 1–96.

18. Schott Foundation for Public Education, *A Rotting Apple: Education Redlining in New York City* (Cambridge, MA, 2012), http://www.otlcampaign.org/sites/default/ files/resources/redlining-full-report.pdf.

19. New York City Department of Education, *NYC Secondary Reform Selected Analysis* (Boston: Parthenon Group, 2006), http://www.parthenon.com/GetFile.aspx?u= %2FLists%2FIndustries%2FAttachments%2F9%2FNYC%2520DOE%2520 Secondary%2520Reform_Select%2520Analyses%25202006.pdf.

20. Ibid.

21. Ibid; Urban Youth Collaborative, *No Closer to College: NYC High School Students Call for Real School Transformation, Not School Closings* (New York: Urban Youth Collaborative, 2011), http://www.urbanyouthcollaborative.org/wp-content /uploads/2011/05/No-Closer-to-College-Report.pdf.

22. Richard Kahlenberg and Halley Potter, "The Original Purpose of Charter Schools," *New York Times*, August 30, 2014, http://www.nytimes.com/2014/08/31/opinion /sunday/albert-shanker-the-original-charter-school-visionary.html?_r=0.

23. The June 22, 2015, edition of the *Boston Globe* reports that the Massachusetts Department of Elementary and Secondary Education has revised its methodology for

identifying "low income" and "poor" students, scrapping the "free or reduced-price lunch" criterion, in part because BPS now provides free meals to all students. See James Vaznis, "State Revises Count of Impoverished Students," *Boston Globe*, June 22, 2015, 1, 7.

24. One study estimates that it costs twice as much to educate a poor, ELL student than a nonpoor, non-ELL student. See Bruce D. Baker and Richard Ferris, *Adding Up the Spending: Fiscal Disparities and Philanthropy Among New York Charter Schools* (Boulder, CO: National Education Policy Center, 2011), 10.

25. See Sean Reardon, *How New York City's Charter Schools Affect Achievement* (Boulder, CO: Education and the Public Interest Center & Education Policy Research Unit, 2011); and Lawrence Blum, "Race and Class Categories and Subcategories in Educational Thought and Research," *Theory and Research in Education* 13, no. 1 (2015): 94–97. APR also has a longer school day and year than BPS schools. I leave aside this complex issue in my discussion for reasons of space, but see Pat Jehlen's excellent discussion in her commentary.

26. Nothing I have said assumes or implies that the students unwilling or unable to sign on to an APR-like regimen have less intellectual potential than those who do sign on (students with certain cognitive disabilities being a possible exception). The disadvantages of low family socioeconomic status, less fluency in English, and various disabilities are distinct from intellectual potential, though they may be related to how outside observers assess that intellectual potential.

27. "An Innovation School shall be a public school, operating within a public school district, that is established for the purpose of improving school performance and student achievement through increased autonomy and flexibility," M.G.L. Ch. 71, §92, https://malegislature.gov/Laws/GeneralLaws/PartI/TitleXII/Chapter71/Section92.

28. On state judiciaries' attempts to sort out the public and the private characteristics of charter schools, see Preston C. Green III, Bruce D. Baker, and Joseph Oluwole, "The Legal Status of Charter Schools in State Statutory Law," *University of Massachusetts Law Review* 10, no. 2 (2015): 240–276.

29. We are already starting to see a reduction in funding for public schools; while other aspects of the economy have rebounded from the 2008 recession, public school funding has not. See Education Law Center, *Is School Funding Fair? A National Report Card*, 4th ed. (New Brunswick, NJ: Rutgers Graduate School of Education, Spring 2015).

30. See Amy Gutmann, *Democratic Education*, rev. ed. (Princeton, NJ: Princeton University Press, 1999); David Tyack, *Seeking Common Ground: Public Schools in a Diverse Society* (Cambridge, MA: Harvard University Press, 2007).

31. In this commentary, "charters" refers to Commonwealth charter schools. Commonwealth charter schools are distinct from Horace Mann charter schools because they function entirely independently of the local school district.

32. To measure school and district performance, Massachusetts now combines standardized test scores with growth scores, giving raw scores three times the weight of growth scores. Growth scores measure the change in individual students' scores compared to the scores of similar students. This comparison is similar to the measure used by Stanford's CREDO and other groups that do studies that compare

charter schools with district schools. If growth were the measure of performance, Boston schools would not be in the lowest 10 percent.

33. Cara Stillings Candal, *Innovation Interrupted: How the Achievement Gap Act of 2010 has Redefined Charter Public Schooling in Massachusetts* (Pioneer Institute, White Paper No. 126, December 2014), 5.

34. *Academy of the Pacific Rim Charter Public: Teacher Salaries (2012–13)* (Malden, MA: Massachusetts Department of Elementary and Secondary Education, 2013), http://profiles.doe.mass.edu/profiles/teacher.aspx?orgcode=04120000&orgtypecode=5&leftNavId=815&.

35. *Academy of the Pacific Rim Charter Public: 2013–14 Student Discipline Data Report, All Offenses* (Malden, MA: Massachusetts Department of Elementary and Secondary Education, 2014), http://profiles.doe.mass.edu/ssdr/default.aspx?orgcode=04120000&orgtypecode=5&=00350000&.

36. Steven Thomas, "Maybe I'm a Bad Kid," *EduShyster* (blog), May 20, 2015, http://edushyster.com/maybe-im-a-bad-kid/.

37. *Academy of the Pacific Rim Charter Public: Selected Populations (2014–15)* (Malden, MA: Massachusetts Department of Elementary and Secondary Education, 2015), http://profiles.doe.mass.edu/profiles/student.aspx?orgcode=04120000&orgtypecode=5&leftNavId=305&.

38. Todd Gazda, "No Matter How Far You've Gone Down the Wrong Road . . .," *Todd Gazda, Superintendent, Ludlow Public Schools* (blog), June, 9, 2015, http://superintendentlps.blogspot.com/2015/06/no-matter-how-far-youve-gone-down-wrong.html.

39. See Luc Schuster, *Cutting Class: Underfunding the Foundation Budget's Core Education Program* (Boston: Massachusetts Budget and Policy Center, 2011), http://www.massbudget.org/report_window.php?loc=Cutting_Class.html; and *Foundation Budget Review Commission Report* (Boston: Massachusetts Department of Education, 2015), http://www.doe.mass.edu/finance/chapter70/FBRC-Report.pdf.

40. "NH Performance Assessment Network," New Hampshire Department of Education, http://www.education.nh.gov/assessment-systems/; "Home Page," New York Performance Standards Consortium, http://performanceassessment.org/.

Acknowledgments

We are grateful for support from numerous sources for helping this book come to fruition. An early seed grant from the Milton Fund at Harvard University enabled us to start researching and testing normative case studies as a method for phronetic inquiry and theory development. The Radcliffe Institute for Advanced Study Academic Ventures program provided crucial funding, space, and logistical support for a two-day workshop on "Justice in Schools" in June 2014. Fifteen participants came together from multiple disciplines and professional worlds to attend this workshop on three of the cases, sharing initial written commentaries and reflecting about how best to share this thinking with others. This book grew directly out of that workshop. We are especially glad that all of the Radcliffe participants remained invested in the project and were willing to revise their commentaries for publication. We are also grateful to the many commentators who subsequently accepted our invitations to write about one of the three additional cases. Meira benefited from a 2014–2015 Guggenheim Fellowship that enabled her to further develop the theoretical foundations for phronetic inquiry and normative case study research. Finally, a major grant from the Spencer Foundation provided essential funding for commissioning commentaries and for our editorial time. We hope that the Spencer Foundation continues to support philosophy of education research for many years to come!

In "Is Pandering Ethical Policy? Power, Privilege, and School Assignment," we also gratefully acknowledge permission from SAGE to create an abridged and modified version of Meira Levinson's "The Ethics of Pandering in Boston Public Schools' Home-Based School Assignment Plan," *Theory and Research in Education* 13, no. 1 (2015): 38–55.

About the Editors

Meira Levinson is professor of education at the Harvard Graduate School of Education, following eight years as a middle school teacher in the Atlanta and Boston public schools. Her most recent books include *Making Civics Count*, which she coedited with David Campbell and Frederick Hess, and *No Citizen Left Behind*, which won awards in political science, philosophy, social studies, and education. A Chinese translation is forthcoming. Meira's recent work on educational ethics has been supported by a Guggenheim Fellowship, the Radcliffe Institute for Advanced Study, and the Spencer Foundation. She earned a BA in philosophy from Yale University and a DPhil in political theory from Nuffield College, Oxford. Meira lives in Boston with her husband and two school-age daughters.

Jacob Fay is a doctoral student and member of the Early Career Scholar Program at the Harvard Graduate School of Education. His research focuses on the ethics of education policy and practice, as well as contemporary theories of injustice. He has served as the cochair of the board of the *Harvard Educational Review* and was a member of the Spencer Foundation's Philosophy of Education Institute. Prior to his doctoral studies, he taught eighth-grade history at the Dwight-Englewood School in New Jersey. He holds an AB in history from Princeton University, an MA in American history from Brandeis University, an EdM from the Harvard Graduate School of Education, and is a proud graduate of the Shady Hill Teacher Training Course. Jacob lives in Cambridge with his wonderful wife, Sarah.

About the Case Study Contributors

Sigal Ben-Porath is professor of education and (by courtesy) political science at the University of Pennsylvania. Her research focuses on normative aspects of education policies, citizenship education, and postconflict education. She is the author of *Citizenship Under Fire: Democratic Education in Times of Conflict* (2006) and *Tough Choices: Structured Paternalism and the Landscape of Choice* (2010), both from Princeton University Press; and the editor, with Rogers Smith, of *Varieties of Sovereignty and Citizenship* (University of Pennsylvania Press, 2013). She is a former classroom teacher and currently serves as the academic director of Teach for America's Philadelphia region. Her current research focuses on school choice and on the opportunities to develop civic capacities that are available to students in different types of schools.

Kailey Burger is the deputy director of systems analysis and improvement at the New York City Administration for Children's Services, where she is focused on developing community-based preventive policies and services for child-welfare-involved families. Prior to this, she served as the assistant corporation counsel in the Bronx County Family Court juvenile delinquency unit. Burger is a member of the New York State Bar Association and holds a master's in education policy and management from the Harvard Graduate School of Education, where she was a Zuckerman Fellow at the Center for Public Leadership. As a law student, Burger cofounded a chapter of the Marshall-Brennan Constitutional Literacy Project and taught constitutional law in an underserved St. Louis public high school. Burger graduated with her JD from Washington University School of Law in St. Louis and completed her undergraduate studies in political science at Truman State University.

Ilana Finefter-Rosenbluh is a postdoctoral fellow at the Harvard Graduate School of Education. She holds a BA in education and sociology and an MA in school counseling from the Hebrew University of Jerusalem, as well as a PhD in education from the Bar-Ilan University. Her research interests include teaching and learning, educational ethics, and social perspective taking. Finefter-Rosenbluh is a former high school guidance counselor who taught and continues to teach in American-Jewish schools. Her doctoral research focused on the teaching and learning processes in an American-Jewish high school that is built upon concepts of pluralism and community—two values that to some extent contradict one another. She discussed the Jewish school's major challenges in bridging this gap while maintaining high academic standards and striving for the development of high intellectual abilities among students. She is currently writing a book on the complexities of the American-Jewish pluralistic school.

Elisabeth Fieldstone Kanner has been passionate about teaching and education ever since she took Ted Sizer's ED 100 class as a freshman at Brown University. She was a founding teacher at the Francis W. Parker Charter Essential School, teaching arts and humanities to middle and high school students. In 2000, she began the doctoral program at the Harvard Graduate School of Education (HGSE), where her research focused on how teachers prepare students for participatory and social justice–oriented citizenship. During this time she also worked in the teacher education programs at Tufts University and HGSE. Inspired by a commitment to civic education, Dr. Kanner worked as a curriculum writer at Facing History and Ourselves, where she developed workshops, study guides, and curriculum units for secondary school history and social studies teachers. In 2011, she joined the Boston Teacher Residency (BTR) program as a clinical teacher educator for history. She currently works at BTR supporting graduates in their first years of teaching in the Boston Public Schools.

Index

abbreviated cases, 219–222

academic engagement, 58–61

academic programs, in summer, 14, 36

academic standards, 22–25, 28, 36, 113–114, 117–118

Academy of the Pacific Rim (APR)
  attrition rate, 180–185, 203–204
  disadvantaged students and, 202–203
  factors in success of, 188–189
  requirements for students at, 179–180, 187
  teacher salaries at, 207

accountability, 29, 192, 197

administrative ethics, 18–20

administrators
  authority of, 62, 65, 89–90
  instrumentalization of education and, 127–128
  leadership by, 103
  professional development for, 57

admission restrictions, in charter schools, 207

advocacy, 29

affordable housing, 176

African American students, 89, 103–104. *See also* minority students

age-appropriate education, 16

agency, 93–94

alternative schools, 35, 36

Aristotle, 4, 19, 44, 48

Asian students, 195

attrition rates
  at charter schools, 180–185, 186, 192–193, 203–204
  at public schools, 181–185, 192

authority, 62, 65, 89–90

autonomy, 25

behavior management, 58–61. *See also* discipline

belonging, 198–200

bias, 94–95

binary choices, 83–84

Black politics, 103

Bloomberg, Michael, 195–196

Boston Public Schools
  attrition rates, 181–185, 192, 204
  charter schools compared with, 179–185
  disadvantaged students and, 202–203, 208–209